Finding Lost Words

Australian College of Theology Monograph Series

SERIES EDITOR GRAEME R. CHATFIELD

The ACT Monograph Series, generously supported by the Board of Directors of the Australian College of Theology, provides a forum for publishing quality research theses and studies by its graduates and affiliated college staff in the broad fields of Biblical Studies, Christian Thought and History, and Practical Theology with Wipf and Stock Publishers of Eugene, Oregon. The ACT selects the best of its doctoral and research masters theses as well as monographs that offer the academic community, scholars, church leaders and the wider community uniquely Australian and New Zealand perspectives on significant research topics and topics of current debate. The ACT also provides opportunity for contributors beyond its graduates and affiliated college staff to publish monographs which support the mission and values of the ACT.

Rev Dr Graeme Chatfield
Series Editor and Associate Dean

Finding Lost Words

The Church's Right to Lament

Edited by
G. GEOFFREY HARPER
& KIT BARKER

Foreword by
DAVID G. FIRTH

WIPF & STOCK · Eugene, Oregon

FINDING LOST WORDS
The Church's Right to Lament

Copyright © 2017 Wipf and Stock Publishers. All rights reserved. Except for brief quotations in critical publications or reviews, no part of this book may be reproduced in any manner without prior written permission from the publisher. Write: Permissions, Wipf and Stock Publishers, 199 W. 8th Ave., Suite 3, Eugene, OR 97401.

Wipf & Stock
An Imprint of Wipf and Stock Publishers
199 W. 8th Ave., Suite 3
Eugene, OR 97401

www.wipfandstock.com

PAPERBACK ISBN: 978-1-5326-1747-8
HARDCOVER ISBN: 978-1-4982-4217-2
EBOOK ISBN: 978-1-4982-4216-5

Manufactured in the U.S.A. 03/13/17

Scripture quotations marked "ESV" are from the ESV® Bible (The Holy Bible, English Standard Version®), copyright © 2001 by Crossway, a publishing ministry of Good News Publishers. Used by permission. All rights reserved.

Scripture quotations marked "NIV" are taken from the Holy Bible, New International Version®, NIV®. Copyright © 1973, 1978, 1984, 2011 by Biblica, Inc.™ Used by permission of Zondervan. All rights reserved worldwide. www.zondervan.com The "NIV" and "New International Version" are trademarks registered in the United States Patent and Trademark Office by Biblica, Inc.™

Scripture quotations marked "NLT" are taken from the Holy Bible, New Living Translation, copyright ©1996, 2004, 2007, 2013, 2015 by Tyndale House Foundation. Used by permission of Tyndale House Publishers, Inc., Carol Stream, Illinois 60188. All rights reserved.

Scripture quotations marked "NASB" are from the New Revised Standard Version Bible, copyright 1989, Division of Christian Education of the National Council of the Churches of Christ in the United States of America. Used by permission. All rights reserved.

לְעָנִי ("for one afflicted")
(Ps 102:1)

Contents

Tables and Figures | xi

Contributors | xiii

Foreword | xvii

Preface | xix

Abbreviations | xxi

Introduction:
"Weeping May Endure for a Night": The Need to Find Lost Words | 1
—G. Geoffrey Harper and Kit Barker

Part I: The History of Lament

1. Lament Psalms in the Church: A History of Recent Neglect | 9
—Rachel Ciano

2. A Song Once Known: The Use of Psalm 77 by Calvin, Henry, Wesley, and Simeon | 24
—Ian J. Maddock

3. "Consolation for the Despairing": C. H. Spurgeon's Endorsement of Lament Psalms in Public Worship | 37
—Alan J. Thompson

Part II: The Theology of Lament

4. Lament as Divine Discourse: God's Voice in Our Cry | 55
—Kit Barker

5. "Why O Lord?" Lament as a Window to the Human Experience of Distress | 66
—David J. Cohen

6 Lament and the Sovereignty of God: Theological Reflections
   on Psalm 88 | 80
   —G. Geoffrey Harper

7 Finding Our Words in His: Christology and Lament | 94
   —Kit Barker

8 The Shape and Function of New Testament Lament | 108
   —Donald West

9 Man of Sorrows, What a Name! The Place of Lament
   in the New Testament | 116
   —David K. Burge

Part III: The Exegesis of Lament

10 The Role of Lament in the Shape of the Psalter | 133
   —Dan Wu

11 Silence of the Lambs: A Lost Cry of Lament in Psalm 8 | 148
   —G. Geoffrey Harper

12 Weeping with the Afflicted: The Self-Involving Language
   of the Laments | 162
   —Andrew Sloane

13 Baking the Bread of Tears: A Recipe for Translating Psalm 80 | 175
   —Andrew G. Shead

Part IV: The Practice of Lament

14 Preaching Lament | 191
   —Peter J. Davis

15 Singing Lament | 204
   —Robert S. Smith

16 Praying Lament | 223
   —Malcolm J. Gill

17 Lament and Pastoral Care | 237
   —Kirk R. Patston

Part V: The Demonstration of Lament

18 "A Strengthening Song for the Sad Soul": A Sermon
   on Psalm 13 | 251
   —Malcolm J. Gill

19　"My Only Friend—Darkness": A Sermon on Psalm 88 | 260
　　—G. Geoffrey Harper

20　"How Could We Sing?": A Sermon on Psalm 137 | 268
　　—Kit Barker

21　"You Are the God Who Saves Me": Singing Psalm 88 | 276
　　—Nick Freestone (with reflections from Kit Barker
　　and G. Geoffrey Harper)

22　If Jesus Wept, You Can Too | 283
　　—Sharon Wood

Tables and Figures

Tables

10.1 Lament psalms in canonical order | 143
13.1 Exegetical workings (Ps 80:1) | 179
17.1 An individual lament | 245
17.2 A corporate lament | 247

Figures

10.1 Overview of the five Books of the Psalter | 142
10.2 Overview of the theological message of the Psalter | 143
21.1 You Are the God Who Saves Me: Lead Sheet | 280

Contributors

Kit Barker is Lecturer in Old Testament at Sydney Missionary and Bible College. He serves as an elder at Narrabeen Baptist Church and regularly preaches and teaches on the Psalms. He is the author of a monograph on theological interpretation and the Psalms, entitled *Imprecation as Divine Discourse: Speech Act Theory, Dual Authorship and Theological Interpretation* (JTISup 16; Winona Lake: Eisenbrauns, 2016).

David Burge lectures in Theology and New Testament at Sydney Missionary and Bible College. Prior to this, he lectured at the Union Bible Theological College in Ulaanbaatar, Mongolia, and has served as a Presbyterian minister in Australia. He is author of *First-Century Guides to Life and Death* (Milton Keynes: Paternoster, 2017).

Rachel Ciano lectures in Church History at Sydney Missionary and Bible College. Rachel is part of the Anglican Church in Sydney; she and her husband planted a church in a multi-cultural, inner-city area several years ago. She is particularly interested in the English Reformation, and her thesis, "Cranmer's Doctrine of the Monarchy and Eucharist," appears in *Lucas: An Evangelical History Review* 2:3 (2011).

David Cohen is head of Biblical Studies and lectures in Hebrew Bible and Language at Vose Seminary. David is an ordained Churches of Christ minister and previously spent fifteen years pastoring in various parishes. His doctoral research focused on the efficacy of praying lament psalms as a pathway to engaging with personal distress and he is author of *Why O Lord?* (Carlisle: Paternoster, 2013) and *Praying Lament Psalms* (Carlisle: Paternoster, 2016). David currently fellowships at Perth Central Baptist.

Peter Davis is Academic Director at Excelsia College Sydney. Prior to that, Peter worked as minister at Pittwater Uniting Church NSW from 1990 to 2005. He was President of the Australasian Academy of Homiletics from 2000 to 2015. With degrees in theology and higher education, his research interests include preaching, missiology, and the leadership of higher education.

Nick Freestone is husband to Sam, father to Judson and Isla, and loves Jesus. He is Corporate Worship Pastor at St Paul's Anglican Church in Chatswood, Sydney. His passion is to see churches authentically express faith, declare devotion, and proclaim the truth of the gospel in song. His songs aim to communicate and celebrate the gospel with memorable melodies, approachable accompaniments, and unashamedly Jesus-centered lyrics.

Malcolm Gill lectures in New Testament, Greek, and Preaching at Sydney Missionary and Bible College. He has traveled widely and has ministered in the Americas, Europe, Asia, the Middle East, and the Pacific. An ordained minister, he has served as a pastor at two churches. He is the author of *Knowing Who You Are: Eight Surprising Images of Christian Identity* (Wipf & Stock, 2015). Malcolm attends St. Barnabas Anglican Church, Sydney.

Geoff Harper is Lecturer in Old Testament at Sydney Missionary and Bible College where he teaches Hebrew, Psalms, and Pentateuch. Geoff has completed theological studies in Ireland, England, and Australia. His doctoral work examined the use of allusion to Genesis 1–3 in the book of Leviticus and he has published a number of articles on intertextuality in the Old Testament. Geoff currently serves as an elder at Petersham Baptist Church, Sydney.

Ian Maddock is Senior Lecturer in Theology at Sydney Missionary and Bible College and a Research Fellow at the Jonathan Edwards Center, South Africa. Ian completed theological studies in Australia, the United States, and Scotland, and served as a pastor at Trinity Baptist Church in New Haven, Connecticut. He is author of *Men of One Book: A Comparison of Two Methodist Preachers, John Wesley and George Whitefield* (Eugene, OR: Pickwick, 2011), and editor of *Wesley and Whitefield? Wesley Versus Whitefield?* (Eugene, OR: Pickwick, forthcoming).

Kirk Patston lectures in Old Testament at Sydney Missionary and Bible College. He has worked as a Presbyterian minister in Sydney's Western Suburbs and Lake Macquarie and is currently the part-time pastor of a congregation in the Blue Mountains. He is the author of *Surprising Salvation: Reading Isaiah Today* (Sydney South: Aquila, 2010) and a number of articles addressing disability from experiential and theological perspectives.

Andrew Shead is head of the Old Testament department at Moore Theological College. His research interests include Hebrew poetry, the Septuagint, and Jeremiah, on which he is writing his third (and hopefully final) book.

He is a member of the NIV Committee for Bible Translation. An ordained Anglican minister, Andrew has served in a number of churches around Sydney.

Andrew Sloane is Senior Lecturer in Old Testament and Christian Thought and Director of Postgraduate Studies at Morling Theological College. He is a member of Northside Baptist Church and was formerly a Baptist pastor. His research interests include Old Testament hermeneutics, ethics, and philosophical theology. His most recent book is *Vulnerability and Care: Christian Reflections on Philosophy of Medicine* (London: Bloomsbury T. & T. Clark, 2016).

Rob Smith is lecturer in Theology, Ethics, and Music Ministry at Sydney Missionary and Bible College. He is an ordained Anglican minister with twenty-five years of pastoral and ministry training experience. He is also a director, writer, and producer for Emu Music. Rob has recently finished two books on music and singing in the Bible and is currently engaged in doctoral research in the area of sex and gender. Other recent publications include "Music, Singing and the Emotions: Exploring the Connections" (*Themelios* 37 [2012] 465–79).

Alan Thompson has been a lecturer in New Testament at Sydney Missionary and Bible College since 2005. Alan attends Petersham Baptist Church, Sydney. He is the author of *One Lord, One People: The Unity of the Church in Acts in Its Literary Setting* (LNTS; London: T. & T. Clark, 2008), *The Acts of the Risen Lord Jesus: Luke's Account of God's Unfolding Plan* (NSBT; Downers Grove, IL: InterVarsity Press, 2011), and *Luke* (EGGNT; Nashville, TN: B&H, 2016).

Donald West is the Principal of Trinity Theological College, Perth, where he also teaches Biblical Exegesis, Biblical Theology, and Christian Leadership. He is interested in the nature of biblical prayer and its implications. Prior to serving at Trinity, he served as an Anglican minister in Sydney. Don is married to Athena; they have three married daughters and five grandchildren. He enjoys encouraging men and women in various forms of word ministry, and playing the occasional game of golf.

Sharon Wood lived and worked as a missionary in the Republic of Ireland for eighteen years with European Christian Mission. She served as part of several church-planting teams in Tipperary and Waterford, finishing her time in Ireland in pastoral ministry among women in a Dublin church. She is currently studying in the area of Professional Pastoral Supervision and looks forward to supporting and equipping those in pastoral and missionary vocations.

Dan Wu is lecturer in Old Testament and Biblical Languages at Moore Theological College, Sydney. He is an ordained Anglican minister and served in pastoral ministry for several years before joining Moore. His current research interests include the concepts of honor, shame, and guilt; wisdom literature; and "up front" ministry from a performance studies perspective. He is the author of *Honor, Shame and Guilt: Social Scientific Approaches to the Book of Ezekiel* (BBRSup 14; Winona Lake: Eisenbrauns, 2016), as well as articles on the books of Romans and Psalms.

Foreword

A CONSISTENT CHALLENGE WITHIN the life of the church has been the need to resist heresy. There has, perhaps, never been a time when heresy was not an issue, and the form it has taken has varied with the times. But heresy has consistently been marked by a pattern where the life of the church was conforming to the dominant culture around it rather than holding to those points at which the proclamation of God's reign in Jesus Christ must critique that culture. This is not to say that holding to obscurantist positions that are unable to be understood by one's culture is a position the church should hold either. After all, we must always declare the gospel in a way that can be understood within a culture, even if all cultures must also stand under the critique of the gospel itself. But whenever that does not happen, heresy thrives.

It is precisely because heresy fits into the dominant culture that it can be difficult to identify. But one that has become quite important over recent decades, at least among Western churches, is the idea that because worship should always be a positive experience, there is no scope for lament, no place for believers to complain to (and sometimes even about) God. So, we quite rightly sing songs in which we offer praise and thanksgiving to God, but we lose sight of the fact that between what we might call the general praise of God and moments of thanksgiving are those times when believers have to bring their pain, petitions, and problems to God, and that thanksgiving emerges most truly when we recognize that God has responded to those moments. Thanksgiving is truly offered when it recognizes that God has seen our need and graciously addressed it—even if God chooses to act in ways different from those we would choose. Yet much of the worship offered today chooses to negotiate a path around the awkwardness of lament, offering a balm of relentlessly upbeat words—which, precisely because it does not allow the hurt to be voiced, brings no real healing.

This pattern of worship, for all that it feels comfortable and reassuring for many, must be identified as heresy. It is heresy because it functionally denies the reality of the experience of so many, refusing to allow them to voice their pain as an act of worship. This, then, is failing to recognize that Jesus has suffered for us, and so makes the act of prayer and praise a moment where believers are asked to disconnect their daily experience from their worship. But worship that is true is worship that allows us to bring the full reality of what we experience before God, knowing that his grace, which is revealed to us in Jesus Christ, addresses and transforms all our lived experience. So, even though we constantly proclaim the lordship of Christ in song, by avoiding complaint we deny the possibility of seeing how that lordship works itself out in our times of complaint. It is this subtle denial of Jesus's lordship that makes the removal of lament from our worship heresy. And it is the virtue of the essays gathered together here that they therefore lay out for us not only the importance of the recovery of lament, but also offer guidance on how that may be done.

David G. Firth
Tutor in Old Testament and Academic Dean,
Trinity College, Bristol

Preface

THIS BOOK HAD A somewhat clichéd beginning. The initial framework was sketched on the back of an envelope before being finalized over lunch at Anar's (a local Sydney hotspot). As the outline solidified and potential contributors came to mind, we began to get excited, sensing the potential helpfulness of a volume like this. In the classes we teach (and co-teach) on the Psalter, it has become clear that the psalms, though much-loved, present readers with myriad interpretative difficulties and are often more challenging than first appreciated. Also challenging is considering how the psalms should be appropriated today. One area in particular continues to generate considerable class discussion time and again: the role of lament in Christian spirituality. We have been struck by the unfamiliarity that surrounds lament, regarding both theory and practice. It is clear that lament, at least at a corporate level, is a seldom-if-ever encountered expression of faith among God's people in the Australian context, reflecting a wider condition in the Western church. Therein lies the seedbed for this exploration of lament psalms and their use in contemporary Christian contexts. Our hope is that this book will be the catalyst for many conversations about lament, and that the question might move from "Ought we to lament?" to "How can we best introduce and express lament in our Christian gatherings?"

We are grateful to Graeme R. Chatfield, series editor for the Australian College of Theology Monograph Series, for considering this collection of essays for inclusion, and to Megan Powell du Toit for her assistance behind the scenes. Our contributors too, all of them exceptionally busy people, have worked hard to produce what we think are valuable additions to the topic at hand. It is a privilege to work among like-minded colleagues who nevertheless feel free to "push back," sharpening us all in the process. Finally, it would be remiss not to mention the students whom we teach and who, by virtue of penetrating questions, teach us too.

G. Geoffrey Harper
Kit Barker
Croydon, October 2016

Abbreviations

[]	Indicates Hebrew verse number where different to EVV
ASV	*American Standard Version*
b.	Babylonian Talmud
BBRSup	Bulletin of Biblical Research Supplement Series
BDAG	Walter Bauer, Frederick W. Danker, W. F. Arndt, and F. W. Gingrich. *Greek-English Lexicon of the New Testament and Other Early Christian Literature*. 3rd ed. Chicago: University of Chicago Press, 2000.
BDB	Francis Brown, S. R. Driver, and Charles A. Briggs. *Hebrew and English Lexicon of the Old Testament*. Oxford: Clarendon, 1907.
CEB	*Common English Bible*
EGGNT	Exegetical Guide to the Greek New Testament
ESV	*English Standard Version*
EV(V)	English version(s)
HALOT	*The Hebrew and Aramaic Lexicon of the Old Testament*. 5 vols. L. Koehler, J. J. Stamm, B. Hartmann, M. E. J. Richardson, and W. Baumgartner. 3rd ed. Leiden: Brill, 1994.
IVP	Inter-Varsity Press
JSOT	Journal for the Study of the Old Testament
JSOTSup	Journal for the Study of the Old Testament Supplement Series
JPS	Jewish Publication Society
JTISup	Journal of Theological Interpretation Supplement Series
KJV	*King James Version*

LEH	J. Lust, E. Eynikel, and K. Hauspie. *A Greek-English Lexicon of the Septuagint*. 2 vols. Stuttgart: Deutsche Bibelgesellschaft, 1992, 1996.
LNTS	The Library of New Testament Studies
LXX	Septuagint
m.	The Mishnah
MT	Masoretic Text
NA[28]	*Nestle-Aland Novum Testamentum Graece*. Edited by E. Nestle, E. Nestle, B. Aland, K. Aland, J. Karavidopoulos, C. M. Martini, and B. M. Metzger. 28th rev. ed. Stuttgart: Deutsche Bibelgesellschaft, 2012.
NASB	*New American Standard Bible*
NET	*New English Translation*
NETS	*A New English Translation of the Septuagint: And the Other Greek Translations Traditionally Included under That Title*. Edited by Albert Pietersma and Benjamin G. Wright. New York: Oxford University Press, 2007.
NIB	*The New Interpreter's Bible*. Edited by Leander E. Keck. 12 vols. Nashville: Abingdon, 1994–2004.
NICOT	New International Commentary on the Old Testament
NIV	*New International Version* (2011 edition)
NIV[1984]	*New International Version* (1984 edition)
NJB	*New Jerusalem Bible*
NRSV	*New Revised Standard Version*
NSBT	New Studies in Biblical Theology
OG	Old Greek
RSV	*Revised Standard Version*
SBL	Society of Biblical Literature
TDNT	*Theological Dictionary of the New Testament*. 10 vols. Edited by Gerhard Kittel and Gerhard Friedrich. Translated by Geoffrey W. Bromiley. Grand Rapids: Eerdmans, 1964–76.

Introduction

"Weeping May Endure for a Night"
The Need to Find Lost Words

G. Geoffrey Harper and Kit Barker

> I will not say: do not weep; for not all tears are an evil.[1]

PSALM 30:5 DECLARES THAT although weeping may endure for a night, joy comes in the morning. Perhaps unsurprisingly, when this verse is quoted the emphasis tends to fall on the "joy comes in the morning" side of the equation. There is, of course, wonderful truth in that hope. Certainly, that is the case from an eschatological point of view. In his vision of the end, the apostle John asserts that the day is coming when God will wipe every tear from the eyes of those who belong to him (Rev 21:4). Yet, the question remains: How ought God's people to conduct themselves while waiting for the morning to dawn?

The Western church often seems ill equipped to answer that question. In fact, it is worth asking if the question would even be seriously entertained. One could be forgiven if, based on extensive fly-on-the-wall research carried out at Christian gatherings, the conclusion was drawn that followers of Jesus live in a world seemingly untroubled by the "slings and arrows of outrageous fortune" that are the lot of the rest of humanity. At a corporate level, the dominant rhetoric is overwhelmingly positive. Songs and sermons

---

1. Gandalf in Tolkien, *Lord of the Rings*, 1007.

exude assurance, power, and confidence. In a Facebook-*esque* manner, testimonies and stories are shaped to generate "likes." When was the last time we recounted a story of failure to our brothers and sisters or stood to sing together a song that expressed the doubts and fears we harbor? Not so, it would seem, for followers of Jesus:

> Onward, then, ye people;
> Join our happy throng.
> Blend with ours your voices,
> In the triumph song.[2]

But what happens when reality fails to match the rhetoric? The diagnosis comes back: it is cancer after all. Instead of happy retirement, early-onset dementia steals the final years of a spouse's life. A mother stands at the grave of her child. Sexual preference means that fidelity to God will entail a celibate life and years of loneliness. What then? Our churches are full of examples of "What then?" Silence. Retreat. Maintaining a façade. Seeds of disconnect that blossom into cynicism and a one-way exit out of the back door.

Faced with the reality of living in a broken world, what options do God's people have? What response should the righteous demonstrate as they inhabit the nighttime of weeping?

The answer is perhaps closer than we realize. Like every generation, we face the temptation to (foolishly) consider ourselves more advanced, more developed, than those who went before. We run the risk of falling foul of what C. S. Lewis termed "chronological snobbery."[3] Yet, perhaps our forebears understood with much greater clarity how to conduct themselves in the vale of tears. Indeed, in historical terms, the contemporary church is an oddity—for, perhaps more than any generation before us, we have ignored the psalms. Whereas the Psalter, with all its jarring words and expressions, comprised the song- and prayer-book of the people of God for millennia, we have substituted it for more "suitable" fare. One tangible result is the absence of lament in our corporate vocabulary.

It is in light of such neglect that this collection of essays had its genesis. Two convictions drive the volume. The first is that the church needs to rediscover lament. Recent history has witnessed the slow erosion of this expression of faith among God's people, particularly in Western contexts. The evidence of that loss is demonstrated by the popularly held view that

---

2. Words from Sabine Baring-Gould and Arthur Sullivan, "Onward Christian Soldiers" (1871).

3. Lewis, *Surprised by Joy*, 241.

to express lament is necessarily to take up a stance of doubt and unbelief; that verbalizing words of grief to God represents a lack of spiritual maturity rather than being an acceptable, even mandated, response to life in a broken world. The reasons for the shift are complex and will be explored in the essays that follow. The net result is that the church has deprived itself of a means to *righteously* express anguish at both individual and corporate levels. Is it any wonder, then, that we witness so many ungodly, unrighteous responses to sadness and suffering?

The second conviction is a felt need to bridge the gap that exists between biblical scholarship and the church. It seems to take a long time for developments in the academy to filter down to pulpit and pew. While this might sometimes be a blessing, it is not always the case. With respect to the Psalms, the face of scholarship has changed dramatically in the last thirty years. Form-critical analysis with its focus on psalms as individual, and often independent, units has been tempered by exploration of canonical placement and the shaping of the Psalter as a collection. New developments in literary theory have brought into greater focus the way psalms function as both human and divine discourse. The cumulative result is a greater appreciation for the theological depth and rhetorical power of these ancient poems. It is our belief that these developments can, and should, enrich the church's appropriation of the Psalter in general and of the lament psalms in particular.

The aim of this book, therefore, is twofold: to make recent developments in Psalms scholarship accessible to pastors and students, and to assuage the loss of lament in the life of the church. The resulting collection of essays has several notable features.

First, it is *intercollegial*. Most of the contributors teach at an Australian theological institution. Represented are faculty from Sydney Missionary and Bible College, Excelsia College, Moore Theological College, Morling College, Trinity Theological College, and Vose Seminary. Second, this work is *interdisciplinary*. The authors of the following essays work across a broad spectrum of fields: Old Testament, New Testament, Theology, Church History, Preaching, Music, and Pastoral Care. This diversity facilitates a rich discussion, with each discipline adding its own unique nuances to the overall exploration of the topic of lament. Third, this book is *interdenominational*. Again, this diversity is important as it allows insights from multiple church traditions to be brought to bear on a common subject. Baptist, Anglican, Presbyterian, and Uniting viewpoints find representation among the essays collected here. Fourth, although the volume represents seventeen different authors and a diversity of traditions and fields of specialization, it remains an *integrated* work. Rather than simply presenting a disparate collection of essays on the topic of lament, *Finding Lost Words* follows a conscious movement from theory to praxis, which reflects our desire to apply the resources of biblical scholarship to the life of the church. Moreover, the volume's contributors are convinced that God is offering these ancient words to his church as *righteous* responses to suffering and oppression. Consequently, each chapter contributes a unique facet to a unified call to the church to find these words again.

In short, this is a book written by the church, for the church. With its range of contributors and the institutions, fields, and denominations they represent, it aims to avoid a simplistic, parochial, and merely theoretical presentation of a complex topic. Instead, we hope that the diversity of views and approaches will facilitate a well-rounded treatment of the matter at hand, thus enabling a general applicability to a wide variety of church contexts and ministries.

The essays that follow are divided into five sections, reflecting our desire to connect theory to praxis. Part one is historical. Three essays chart the demise of lament as a mode of expression in the Western church and examine the use of lament by notable figures of centuries past. While it is one thing to note the absence of lament in the contemporary church, it is another to understand the factors that contributed to that demise. Toward that end, Rachel Ciano provides an overview of Western history that suggests possible influences that led to the loss of lament. Such loss, however, was not absolute. Two essays by Ian Maddock and Alan Thompson explore the use of lament by select church personalities well known for their preaching and pastoral ministries. At the same time, their investigation shows that appropriation of lament is not straightforward, but raises significant theological and pastoral questions. Such questions must be addressed if the contemporary church is to be convinced that lament is a righteous response and has an important place in Christian worship.

Part two tackles some of the theological questions raised by the appropriation of lament psalms, issues that often present obstacles to their use. The six essays in this section explicitly aim to alleviate some of these perceived problems and so prepare the way for utilizing these neglected portions of Scripture. A chapter by Kit Barker employs insights derived from speech act theory to wrestle with the fundamental question of how these words directed to God become God's word to his people. The following essays by David Cohen and Geoff Harper mount a case that lament does not represent a failing faith or an unhealthy dissatisfaction with God, but rather constitutes an expression of profound trust, one that is essential to our psychological and spiritual wellbeing. The remaining chapters by Kit

Barker, Don West, and David Burge address the crucial issue of how lament continues to function in light of Jesus and the New Testament.

The four essays in Part three focus on exegetical matters. If lament psalms are to be preached and otherwise used by the church, then they must be understood well. This section explores how recent developments in scholarship can aid the interpretation of these ancient Israelite poems. Dan Wu demonstrates that the lament psalms are not simply isolated prayers and songs, but need to be interpreted in context of the Psalter as a whole. Geoff Harper then offers a detailed exegesis of a well-known psalm in order to illustrate the interpretative benefits of paying heed to canonical placement. Two more essays, by Andrew Sloane and Andrew Shead, explore issues related to the interpretation of Hebrew poetry that will enable preachers and teachers alike to better appreciate the power of these ancient songs.

Part four moves to consider praxis. Four essays explore pragmatic questions of how lament psalms can be used by the contemporary church in preaching (Peter Davis), singing (Rob Smith), praying (Malcolm Gill), and pastoral care (Kirk Patston). Each author draws upon many years of ministry experience to offer important insights for the incorporation of lament in contemporary life and worship.

Part five demonstrates the use of lament. It was our desire to leave readers with examples of (and reflections on) the use of lament in the life of the church. To that end, sermons on three lament psalms are given in full-text format: Psalm 13 (Malcolm Gill), Psalm 88 (Geoff Harper), and Psalm 137 (Kit Barker). The ensuing chapter by Nick Freestone presents a lament song written by him for congregational use with words based on Psalm 88. His reflections on the songwriting process provide valuable insight into the careful thinking required to successfully blend lyrics, music, and theology. Finally, Sharon Wood's essay rounds out the volume by offering personal reflections on her journey with lament in the context of pastoral care among women.

In the end, this is a book about finding lost words—in both senses of that phrase: to *rediscover* psalms that have been marginalized in recent times, and to *find* words with which we can express personal and corporate lament to God. Thus, the volume also concerns the church's right to lament, again in both senses of the term: laments belong to the church as part of its scriptural heritage and it has a *right* to re-appropriate them. But, in submitting to laments as models of virtuous response, the church is also *right* to do so.

Bibliography

Lewis, C. S. *Surprised by Joy: The Shape of My Early Life*. C. S. Lewis Signature Classics. London: HarperCollins, 2002 [orig. 1955].
Tolkien, J. R. R. *The Lord of the Rings*. London: HarperCollins, 2001 [orig. 1954–1955].

Part I

The History of Lament

1

Lament Psalms in the Church
A History of Recent Neglect

Rachel Ciano

> It is clear that a church that goes on singing "happy songs" in the face of raw reality is doing something very different from what the Bible itself does. I think that serious religious use of the lament psalms has been minimal because we have believed that faith does not mean to acknowledge and embrace negativity. We have thought that acknowledgment of negativity was somehow an act of unfaith, as though the very speech about it conceded too much about God's "loss of control" . . . To withhold parts of life from that conversation [with God] is in fact to withhold part of life from the sovereignty of God.[1]

It is easy to forget. It is easy to forget because most of the time we are not aware we are forgetting. Our thinking drifts slowly away from that which was once so clear, until there is just a blank space or, at best, a sketchy haze of what it was we once remembered so well. For many of us, we fail to recall a time when we used a lament psalm in our church services; we have forgotten to use them. This is the case more broadly across the history of the Western church. In fact, rather than mere passive forgetfulness, the church has often been guilty of more active neglect. As Walter Brueggemann argues

---

1. Brueggemann, *Spirituality of the Psalms*, 26–27.

above, lament psalms have been neglected in churches because Christians have believed that embracing negativity is an act of unfaith and concedes too much about God's loss of control. While the tide is slowly turning, and renewed interest in studying and using the lament psalms is resurfacing, what I will present in this chapter is a proposal as to why they were forgotten and neglected in the first place, so that by being aware of this, we may be better prepared to remedy the problem and ensure that it does not occur again.

Lament Psalms and the Church: Early Church to the Reformation

The lament psalms were not always out of vogue. They were used regularly in church services in the Western church in the period up to and including the Reformation of the sixteenth century.[2] In the early church period, references to the use of lament psalms in church services are difficult to find; nevertheless, there is some helpful, suggestive evidence. In the New Testament, churches were commanded to speak and sing psalms when gathered with other believers (Eph 5:19; Col 3:16).[3] Justin Martyr records in his *First Apology* (c. AD 150) that the Old Testament was read in churches.[4] These readings no doubt included the Psalter.[5] The apocryphal *Acts of John* and *Acts of Paul*, while of uncertain origin, nevertheless reflect Christian practices of the mid-second century. In these, mention is made of Christian gatherings including hymns of lament,[6] and the psalms of David in general.[7] Tertullian also makes reference to psalms being chanted in Christian gatherings.[8]

---

2. Unfortunately, given the constraints of space, the Eastern church will not be examined.

3. For further discussion on the place of lament in the New Testament, see chapters 7–9 in this volume.

4. Justin, *First Apology* 67. See Roberts and Donaldson, *Ante-Nicene Fathers: Volume 1*, 186.

5. Justin seems to use the generic title of "prophet" to apply to the Old Testament in general (Vogel, *Primary Sources of Liturgical Theology*, 251).

6. *Acts of John* 95. See James, *Apocryphal New Testament*, 253.

7. *Acts of Paul* 9. See ibid., 576.

8. Tertullian, *On the Soul* 9. See Roberts and Donaldson, *Ante-Nicene Fathers: Volume 3*, 188.

The early church fathers such as Augustine, Jerome, Gregory of Nyssa, and Origen used the lament psalms in their lives, study, and ministry.[9] Augustine provides a helpful model of this. He saw lament as dwelling on present sufferings and eschatological hope concurrently: "Lament for things of the present, sing of what is to come in the future. Pray about what already is, sing about what you hope for."[10] Augustine preached and wrote on the lament psalms extensively; his collected sermons on the Psalms, *Enarrationes in Psalmos*, is his largest work. In it, Augustine enticed believers to the Christian practice of lament.[11] His exegesis of the psalms repeatedly insisted that his congregation use the psalms as their own words: "If the psalm prays, you pray; if it groans, you groan."[12] Augustine also used the lament psalms personally. In *Confessions* he wrote of being deeply affected and crying when reading the psalms.[13] As he lay dying, Augustine surrounded himself with penitential psalms written out on large sheets of paper hanging on the walls, and he would read them, crying constantly and deeply.[14]

In the Middle Ages, there is clearer evidence—largely because during this period the patterns of corporate worship were better documented—of the lament psalms in use, including instructions on reading, singing, and praying through the entire Psalter on a scheduled, rotational basis. Various monastic orders were at the forefront of this, documenting their heavy emphasis on the psalms in their corporate gatherings. The Benedictine order, which has been called "the most enduring, influential, numerous and widespread religious order of the Latin Middle Ages" is of particular importance in this regard.[15] Benedict instructed his order to sing the whole Psalter through every week as part of their eight church services a day.[16] He even chastised monks who could not achieve this for their extreme laxity of devotion, citing that the church fathers did in one day what he trusts his

---

9. For further discussion, see Waltke et al., *Psalms as Christian Lament*.

10. Augustine, *Enarrationes in Psalmos* 29.2.16. See Brock, "Augustine's Incitement to Lament," 186.

11. Ibid., 184.

12. Augustine, *Enarrationes in Psalmos* 30.2.3. See McCarthy, "Augustine, the Psalms," 25–26.

13. Augustine, *Confessions* 9.4.8.

14. From Augustine, *Sancti Augustini vita a Possidio episcopo* 31.1–3, cited in Brown, *Augustine*, 436.

15. Clark, *The Benedictines*, 1. This book provides a very helpful treatment of the practice and influence of the Benedictines in the Middle Ages, including their use of psalms in corporate worship.

16. Benedict, *Rule*, 18. See Cary-Elwes, *Work and Prayer*, 72–73.

lukewarm order would accomplish in a whole week![17] Over time, parish clergy became part of this routine worship practice, and Sunday Vespers (evening services) saw the laity included too. Benedict instructed that Vespers was to include the recitation of at least two lament psalms, Psalm 109 and Psalm 143.[18] The prescribed use of the psalms in the *Rule of Benedict* was elaborated on in the Carolingian, Anglo-Saxon, and Clunaic reform movements. For example, the *Regularis Concordia,* part of the Benedictine Reform in England officially sanctioned around AD 973, stipulated that the seven penitential psalms (Pss 6, 32, 38, 51, 102, 130, and 143) were to be recited before dawn (*Matins*) and at first light (*Prime*). Thus we find strong evidence of the use of lament psalms in corporate worship attended by monks, parish clergy, and lay people during the Middle Ages.

During the Reformation, lament psalms were used by the church extensively, because the whole Psalter was used extensively. Reformers such as Martin Luther, John Calvin, and Martin Bucer used the lament psalms as the basis of evangelical confession and repentance, which made them a powerful instrument in the Reformation; Luther's *Penitential Psalms* (1517) was his first original, published work.[19] Calvin preached on the Psalms every Sunday afternoon from 1547, completed his *Commentary on the Psalms* by 1557, and commissioned court poet Clement Marot to set the Psalter in meter (*Genevan Psalter,* 1562).[20] Other metrical Psalters were published in England, Scotland, and America in the sixteenth and seventeenth centuries; in fact, the first book printed in the American colonies was the *Bay Psalm Book* (1640).[21] Morning and evening prayers in the Church of England's Prayer Book made the psalms a key component, and the Psalter was sung through every month and the Old Testament read through every year in church services.[22] In 1535, Henry VIII approved the publication of Miles Coverdale's translation of the Bible, within which the Psalter, set to prose rhythm, was particularly popular.[23]

Since the Reformation, the use of the lament psalms in churches has declined. Studies of this are scarce: no one, as far as I can discover, has extensively documented why the lament psalms slowly dwindled out of corporate

---

17. Ibid.
18. Ibid.
19. Waltke et al., *Psalms as Christian Lament*, 212.
20. Ibid., 180.
21. Hustad, "The Psalms as Worship Expression," 414.
22. See, for example, the 1662 Church of England Prayer Book.
23. Waltke et al., *Psalms as Christian Lament*, 216.

usage.[24] What I offer here, therefore, are suggestions from the sweep of history as to why this may have happened. While all broad overviews of history risk being reductionistic and contain generalizations that do not represent all schools of thought within a movement, the scope of this chapter only allows a brief treatment of each period of history. Nevertheless, a survey of history reveals possible causes for the neglect of the lament psalms. It also aids an understanding of our own historical context, and therefore better enables us to correct our neglect and reclaim the lament psalms in corporate worship.

The Renaissance: Growth of Confidence in Humanity

The Renaissance of the fourteenth to seventeenth centuries celebrated a new confidence in humanity and its capabilities, spurred on by a renewed fascination with the civilizations of Ancient Greece and Rome. Renaissance scientists such as Nicolaus Copernicus (1473–1543), who advocated a heliocentric view of the world, Francis Bacon (1561–1626), who is regarded as the father of empiricism and the scientific method, and Tycho Brahe (1546–1601), who applied careful observation and empiricism to astronomy, demonstrated a new approach to science grounded in inductive reasoning based on careful observation. Leonardo da Vinci, regarded as a typical "Renaissance man," i.e., a master of many fields, devised scientific research methods to observe the natural world and movement within it, demonstrating this in his careful, observational drawings of the natural world. This approach to science laid important groundwork for the coming centuries, for it contributed to a confident humanity more certain of its capabilities to both acquire and use knowledge of the world. This attitude would, in turn, have ramifications for lament in general and lament psalms in particular.

Another important aspect of the Renaissance was its philosophical studies, based on Ancient Greek and Roman philosophy. Humanism, the intellectual basis for the Renaissance, developed. The Italian humanists' new vision of humanity, largely inspired by the assertion in Genesis that humans are created in the image and likeness of God, was "possibly the most affirmative view of human nature in the history of thought and expression."[25]

---

24. There are some discussions of why lament has been neglected—for example, Bauer, "Enquiring into the Absence of Lament," 25–43. However, Bauer writes from a theological viewpoint that examines the relationship between suffering and guilt as a means of explaining the neglect of lament in order to reclaim it, rather than the historical approach offered here.

25. Trinkaus, *In our Image*, xiv.

The Italian humanists were strongly Christian in their religious and moral concerns, but had a growing interest in reconciling this with human-centered theology, philosophy, and ethics.[26] The concept of an individual person being able to determine truth for themselves was also raised during the Renaissance. The pre-Socratic Greek philosopher, Protagoras, was one ancient philosopher studied by humanists.[27] Protagoras is particularly famous for his statement "man is the measure of all things," by which he meant, according to Plato in *Protagoras*, that individuals themselves determine truth (i.e., "measure" things), not God.[28] This concept, which would be explored much more thoroughly in Postmodernism, was revolutionary; it would further encourage self-determination and confidence in humanity, for people started to believe they could determine truth themselves.

These scientific and philosophical developments further moved the Western world's thinking towards a view that began to place humanity at the center for its ability to determine truth by observing the world. This new sense of self-confidence helped lay the foundations for God's sovereignty to be downplayed; if humanity was capable of great accomplishments by itself, then belief in God's control over the affairs of the world could diminish. Even though at this stage most still regarded God as the one who created and sustained the world and humanity in it, and regarded him as an authoritative source of revelation, in time, it would become easier to place God in varying degrees of separation from the world, even within Christendom. Modernism would take this downplaying of God's sovereignty and confidence in humanity to much fuller conclusions.

Confidence in humanity, especially as the arbiter of truth, seems to have reached its zenith in the twenty-first century. We live in an age that is supremely confident in humanity and what we are able to accomplish. However, a self-confident humanity runs antithetical to the tenor of the lament psalms. The lament psalms profess the exact opposite: humanity is utterly dependent on God and cannot forge its own destiny. The lament psalms express a contriteness and dependence on God that comes from a healthy perspective of humanity. For pray-ers of the lament psalms, confidence is placed in God to change circumstances. They know that they can do nothing

26. Trinkaus, "Protagoras," 193.

27. For a helpful discussion of this, see ibid., 190–213. Trinkaus observes similarities between Protagoras and Renaissance thinkers, and discusses how various Renaissance thinkers used his dictum "man is the measure of all things."

28. Renaissance thinker Leon Battista Alberti also used this dictum of "man being the measure" to assert the dignity of humanity and the greatness of its powers, which included contemplating the heavens and the works of God. Trinkaus, "Protagoras," 195–96.

to rescue themselves from the pit, which is why they must entreat God to do so. A buoyant and confident humanity is difficult to stress alongside the depths of darkness lamented by the psalmists. It is hard to identify with such an experience, let alone adopt the psalmists' words as if they were one's own, when confidence in one's ability to navigate life and its disasters prevails.

Modernism: Decline in Trust of God's Sovereignty

Modernism, which roughly covers the period from the Enlightenment of the mid-seventeenth century to its peak at the end of the nineteenth century, further developed thinking that had much of its beginnings in the Renaissance.[29] It was particularly Modernism's emphasis on rationalism which seems to have contributed most significantly to the decline of lament psalms in the church, as people sought to incorporate new epistemology, various aspects of science, and new developments in biblical scholarship into Christian thought and practice.

At the beginning of the Modern age, the Enlightenment (or Age of Reason; approximately 1685 to 1815) swept through Europe. This marked a revolution in epistemology; with its genesis in the Renaissance, the Enlightenment further developed rational and naturalistic ways of explaining the world. The period challenged traditional sources of authority, chiefly the Scriptures and the church, and instead emphasized that all that can be known about the world could be observed, reasoned, and explained through these means. Deism, emerging around this time, denied that God acted sovereignly in the world; the watchmaker had made the watch and now let it run without interference. The Enlightenment stressed that human reasoning was the best way to know truth and fulfillment, so much so that reason became a god—demonstrated so obviously in Revolutionary France. For example, in Notre-Dame Cathedral, Paris, on 10 November 1793, an altar to Reason was erected before which a torch of Truth burned; those assembled were directed to pay homage to an actress dressed up as the Goddess of Reason; and soon after, the cathedral was designated "the Temple of Reason."[30]

The pursuit of reason would eventually lead to the explanation of natural disasters, national crises, and individual suffering along rational and naturalistic lines as further discoveries in science were made that

---

29. Like most historical periods, start and end dates are debated. Here the movement is taken to be the period between the end of the Renaissance and the beginning of Postmodernity.

30. Baumer, *Rise of Scepticism*, 35. See also Herrick, *New Spirituality*, 75–76.

sufficiently accounted for these occurrences. This contributed to a downplaying of God's sovereignty over these affairs. Explanations for suffering could now be given without reference to God; for example, earthquakes were a result of tectonic plates shifting, high rates of death from diseases were the result of miniscule viruses and bacteria, droughts and floods were the result of increasingly predictable weather patterns. This undermined the church's confidence to use lament psalms. As people cry to the Lord in lament, they are acknowledging him as the one who is responsible for their circumstances and also as the one who is able to change them; the lament psalms are a brutal acknowledgment of God's sovereignty.[31] However, if God is not seen as completely sovereign, then lament psalms become harder to use with confidence. When Modernism's erosion of confidence in God's sovereignty was combined with the increased confidence in humanity that the Renaissance helped instill, the lament psalms inevitably lost their place in the church, for they are completely incongruent with these two thought trajectories: lament psalms are at their heart an expression of confidence in God's sovereignty, and a loss of confidence in humanity. They place God at the center of difficult circumstances, not us. It is therefore little wonder that the combination of philosophies of the Renaissance and the Modern era meant that the church started to prune the lament psalms from corporate gatherings.[32] The lament psalms had no place amid a confident humanity with a sidelined and seemingly incompetent God.

This shaving of lament psalms from corporate worship was helped along by another child of Modernity: biblical criticism. The Renaissance's affirmation of a confident humanity that is the arbiter of truth, combined with Modernism's emphasis on rationalism, resulted in biblical scholars seeking to incorporate these new ways of thinking into biblical studies. Biblical criticism emerged as the new rule for biblical authority. Form criticism in particular had ramifications for interpretation of the lament psalms. In 1925, Hermann Gunkel first classified the psalms according to type, a process repeated by others after him. This process broke the book of Psalms down into individual units, based on content and form. Psalms of Individual Lament and Psalms of Corporate Lament form part of Gunkel's categorization. While such a practice is helpful for sorting and viewing various themes and the structure of the psalms together, a pitfall of this approach is that the

---

31. See further, Harper, "Lament and the Sovereignty of God" (chapter 6 in this volume).

32. For example, despite lament psalms far outnumbering psalms of praise, the responsive readings in a widely used Presbyterian hymnal feature less lament psalms than psalms of praise or thanksgiving (Duff, "Recovering Lamentation as a Practice," 4). See also McCann, *Psalms*, 85, 188.

Psalter was divided up into individual units, and an emphasis on the Psalter as a whole was lost.

Losing emphasis on the whole Psalter meant that psalms were no longer interpreted in light of each other.[33] The juxtaposition of various types of psalms was lost: for example, the soul-crushing lament of Psalm 88 read in isolation (without, for example, the confidence in God as refuge and strength in times of trouble that Ps 46 advocates) leaves the reader with a distorted view of God's character. By interpreting psalms in isolation, lament psalms that proved difficult to interpret, or were uncomfortable, confusing, and incongruous with the accepted worldview or even faith-view, or were unpalatable in the Modern age given their themes of violent justice, became easier to neglect.[34] Even C. S. Lewis termed some of the language used in lament psalms as "contemptible" and "terrible," and argued that "[t]he hatred is there—festering, gloating, undisguised . . . we should be wicked if we in any way condoned or approved it, or (worse still) used it to justify similar passions in ourselves."[35] In terms of usage in the church, while in previous times the whole Psalter was more or less kept intact as in the *Rule of Benedict* and the *Book of Common Prayer*, it now became easier to dispense with individual psalms. This practice would eventually lead to the more selective use of individual psalms in church gatherings.

In reaction to these trends in biblical scholarship, biblical fundamentalism arose in the late-nineteenth and early-twentieth centuries. As part of this movement, dispensationalism discouraged the use of lament psalms by Christians. This is exemplified by Cyrus Scofield, arguably the most influential propagator of dispensationalism, who wrote in his introduction to the Psalms in the *Scofield Reference Bible* (1917): "the imprecatory Psalms are the cry of the oppressed in Israel for justice—a cry appropriate and right in the earthly people of God, and based upon a distinct promise in the Abrahamic Covenant . . . but a cry unsuited to the church, a heavenly people who have taken their place with a rejected and crucified Christ."[36] The *Scofield Reference Bible* is acknowledged by supporters and critics as the most influential book among evangelicals in the first half of the twentieth century: Stephen Sizer terms it "the most important single document of all Funda-

---

33. For further discussion, see Wu, "The Role of Lament in the Shape of the Psalter," and Harper, "Silence of the Lambs" (chapters 10 and 11 in this volume). While canonical criticism with its focus on final-form books of the Bible helped to mitigate the excesses of form criticism, the damage was largely done in terms of regarding psalms only as individual units.

34. See also Barker, "Lament as Divine Discourse" (chapter 4 in this volume).

35. Lewis, *Reflections on the Psalms*, 22.

36. Scofield, *Book Introduction–Psalms*, § 3.

mentalism," illustrated, for example, by the fact that half of all conservative evangelical student groups used it in the United States in the 1950s.[37] Given the extraordinary scope and influence of the *Scofield Reference Bible*, it is little wonder that in advocating the unsuitability of lament psalms for the church, it helped instill their neglect in Christian services.

The Twentieth Century Onwards

The twentieth century brought unprecedented changes to the world, and would again present challenges to using lament psalms in churches. One area of profound change was technological advancement; in the realm of warfare, technology contributed to unparalleled numbers of casualties in the wars of the last century. It was in this bloody and vicious context, especially World War Two, that the idea of suffering borne stoically was extolled as a virtue, and maintaining a "stiff upper lip" in times of danger became an integral part of contemporary British culture in particular.[38] The slogan "keep calm and carry on," which has been circulated widely in many appropriations recently, had its origins in Britain during the same period. Expressions of grief must be suppressed in such a cultural framework; excessive displays of emotion are considered "self-indulgent, even a bit selfish and unfair," while restraining displays of grief are "seen as showing great courtesy and consideration for others . . . rather than demanding attention and comfort."[39] It is not surprising to see similar sentiments expressed in contexts where there has been substantial immigration from Great Britain following World War Two, such as in Australia, New Zealand, and to a lesser extent, sections of Canada and North America.

A strong indication of this suppression of grief in favor of "staying strong" is witnessed at many contemporary funeral services, where the focus is on celebrating the life of the deceased person rather than acknowledging grief. At the most recent funeral I attended, where the death was particularly tragic and a young family was left behind, those who gathered were from the outset encouraged to set aside their grief for the duration of the service. Those who did cry were deeply apologetic, and there was an avoidance of the very event that had brought us together. In light of such encouragement in modern Western cultures—that bearing hardship with minimal emotion is virtuous—the lament psalms can appear very self-defeatist and at odds with "staying strong," and therefore their usage suffers as a result.

37. Sizer, *Christian Zionism*, 75. See also Barr, *Fundamentalism*, 6.
38. Storey, "Becoming British," 21.
39. Fox, *Watching the English*, 376.

The emergence of postmodern philosophy in the mid- to late-twentieth century, and particularly its emphasis on relative truth, has permeated nearly all aspects of the Western world and presents fresh challenges to the use of lament in churches. Relative truth has led to the authority and intrinsic value of an individual's own personal narrative. We now determine if something is "true for us," and this may be in contrast to what is true for another person. Both can co-exist, as truth is no longer external but, rather, internal and subjective. One implication of this is that the practice of using someone else's words on your behalf can be perceived as "inauthentic," and as lament psalms are not our personal story, they are not our own words, and therefore they are not true and authentic for us.

This postmodern focus on authenticity of experience pervades Western Christian culture in the twenty-first century. One example of this is seen in the emerging church movement and those churches influenced by it. Hallmarks of Western churches in the age of Modernism—rationalism, formalism, linear thought, truth, structure, and authority—are resisted in keeping with the spirit of the postmodern age.[40] Instead, in order to create an authentic experience in church gatherings, informal and fluid expression is prized, hierarchy is distrusted, and authority is shifted to the experiences of individual members of the congregation. Within this system, liturgy, which includes corporate recitation of the psalms, is deemed too formal, too structured, and inauthentic. Instead, authenticity is to be found in spontaneity. However, in rejecting formal liturgies that saw the lament psalms regularly used in churches, alternate liturgies have inevitably emerged, formal or not. They tend to focus on aspects of the experience of living as God's people that fit the current landscape of the world and the church. For example, they focus on God's perceived desire for us to live lives almost devoid of suffering. The lament psalms don't fit this paradigm, for they acknowledge the place of suffering among the people of God, which some would perceive as evidence of God's lack of favor upon them.[41]

In response to the relativism of Postmodernism and the focus on authenticity of experience and emotion, it is important to recognize that using the lament psalms actually makes for a more authentic experience of God. This is because we are able to appropriate the words of the lament psalms into our own lives, and we therefore have a ready vocabulary to utter back to God in times of distress. Our experience can be folded into the psalmist's

---

40. For a helpful discussion on the continuity and discontinuity between Modernism and Postmodernism, see Carson, *Emerging Church*, 25–36.

41. Much could be said on the lament psalms being an expression of God's love towards us—he kindly gives us these words to cry back to him.

experience so that our narratives merge in a powerful way. In addition, the focus on participation, over and against the individualism that Modernism prized, means that joining in the lament psalms together can be an authentic participatory experience that not only allows people to participate with fellow members of the congregation, but also allows them to participate with the storyline of the psalmist. Furthermore, the words of the lament psalms could be deemed some of the most "personally authentic" words uttered to God in the Bible. Their raw expression of emotion before the Lord is confronting, and if we are able to join our voice with that of the lament psalmists and join in with fellow Christians in reciting, singing, or praying them, then I have no doubt that the effect will be an authentic experience of God and an authentic experience of worshiping with his people.

Failure to acknowledge suffering as part of the life of a believer has also contributed to the neglect of the lament psalms. This is seen most clearly in the advent of the so-called prosperity gospel in some Christian circles. The prosperity gospel affords no place for suffering on the part of the genuine believer; any suffering is the result of a problem in the faith of the sufferer, and could be alleviated if the sufferer increased their faith. Lament psalms are therefore "regarded as an expression of unbelief."[42] Proponents of a prosperity gospel advocate that the Bible is a contract of faith between God and his people: God, being faithful and just, will uphold his end of the contract (i.e., his promises) if believers uphold theirs, usually through positive confession of what they want from God, with key Bible passages as the basis. That is, they ought to "name it and claim it." In this regard, Jesus "will only bring our confession of the Word to the Father. He will not bring our begging and our crying and our pleading."[43] Lament psalms are all but silenced in this system of thought. For one, they announce to God his promises, but instead ask why it appears he is not keeping them given the current circumstances of the psalmist. Furthermore, the lament psalms, which often affirm the faithfulness of the psalmist in spite of their difficult circumstances, are incongruous with a system of thought that sees suffering as the fault of the sufferer and the result of inadequate faith.

Other Christians who might shy away from a prosperity gospel can nevertheless fall into a similar erroneous belief regarding suffering—that crying out to God in lament demonstrates lack of faith. Instead, the sufferer is encouraged to meditate upon "positive" thoughts regarding God's sovereignty and his good plan in all things. In doing so, people try to protect the sovereignty of God by asserting that there is a "plan" behind the

---

42. Maré, "Pentecostal Perspective," 96.

43. Law, *Praise Releases Faith*, 94.

suffering. The way that comfort is often doled out illustrates this. A much-used sentiment in times of grief is Romans 8:28, which rightly affirms that God works in all circumstances for the good of his people. Such affirmations made by believers are often genuine, well-intentioned attempts to uphold the sovereignty of God in all situations. While the knowledge that God is sovereign over all affairs is indeed comforting in times of suffering, it seems that by putting this forward as a standard text of consolation the chance for suffering persons to truly cry out to God in lament is reduced, and any attempt by sufferers to rail against God about their circumstances is regarded as demonstrating inadequate faith in a sovereign God. However, lament *is* a genuine cry of faith, not faithlessness, for at its core is a recognition that one's own personal situation, or situation in society, is in the hands of a sovereign God; the person of faith brings their complaint *to* their sovereign Lord, instead of complaining to others about him.

Conclusion

The lament psalms were not always neglected; the early church, Middle Ages and Reformation period testify to that fact. However, over the last five hundred years or so, the use of lament psalms in the Western church's corporate gatherings has slowly dwindled. The Renaissance, with its confident view of human ability to acquire and use knowledge, laid the foundation for belief in God's sovereignty to be slowly undermined. On the back of the Renaissance, the Enlightenment's shift in epistemology that lauded reason as the best way to know truth and fulfillment further eroded people's trust in the sovereignty of God. As a sovereign God is a central tenet of the lament psalms, this movement away from trust in God's control of the world seems to have done damage to the church's confidence to use them. Furthermore, Modernism, and in particular biblical criticism, led to psalms no longer being interpreted in light of each other, and thus it became easier to dispense with individual psalms, particularly the lament psalms. In reaction, Fundamentalism arose; however, this movement also discouraged the use of lament psalms, seen so clearly in *Scofield's Reference Bible*. In the twentieth century, a stiff-upper-lip mentality, encouragement to suppress emotions of grief, a focus on personal authenticity in church services, embarrassment about questions of suffering, the prosperity gospel, and the erroneous belief that crying out to God in lament demonstrates a lack of faith, have further contributed to corporate neglect of the lament psalms.

The core affirmation of the lament psalms—that persons of faith should come to a faithful God with their complaints and beg him to act—is what we must rediscover in our own lives and in our churches if we are to honor the Lord in the fullness of our human experience in the age in which we live. To echo Brueggemann's sentiment, we cannot withhold parts of our lives from our conversation with God lest we withhold part of our life from his sovereignty. Étienne Gilson, a twentieth-century philosopher, said that "history is the only laboratory we have in which to test the consequences of thought."[44] We have seen the effects of various thought patterns on the Western world and on the church throughout history and have noted their detrimental consequences for the church's use of lament psalms. As history teaches us that we are doomed to repeat the mistakes of the past if we fail to learn from its lessons, may we take heed of our past neglect and seek to remedy the situation as best we can.

Bibliography

Augustine. *Confessions*. Peabody: Hendrickson, 2004.
Barr, James. *Escaping from Fundamentalism*. London: SCM, 1984.
Bauer, Jonas. "Enquiring into the Absence of Lament: A Study of the Entwining of Suffering and Guilt in Lament." In *Evoking Lament: A Theological Discussion*, edited by Eva Harasta and Brian Brock, 25–43. London: T. & T. Clark, 2009.
Baumer, Franklin. *Religion and the Rise of Scepticism*. New York: Harcourt Brace & World, 1960.
Brock, Brian. "Augustine's Incitement to Lament, from the *Enarrationes in Psalmos*." In *Evoking Lament: A Theological Discussion*, edited by Eva Harasta and Brian Brock, 183–203. London: T. & T. Clark, 2009.
Brown, Peter. *Augustine of Hippo*. Berkeley: University of California, 2000.
Brueggemann, Walter. *Spirituality of the Psalms*. Minneapolis: Fortress, 2002.
Carey-Elwes, Columba. *Work and Prayer: The Rule of St Benedict for Lay People*. London: Burns & Oats, 1992.
Carson, D. A. *Becoming Conversant with the Emerging Church*. Grand Rapids: Zondervan, 2005.
Clark, James. *The Benedictines in the Middle Ages*. Suffolk: Boydell, 2011.
Duff, Nancy. "Recovering Lamentation as a Practice in the Church." In *Lament: Reclaiming Practices in Pulpit, Pew and Public Square*, edited by Sally A. Brown and Patrick D. Miller, 3–14. Louisville: Westminster John Knox, 2005.
Fox, Kate. *Watching the English: The Hidden Rules of English Behaviour*. London: Hodder, 2004.
Gilson, Étienne. *The Unity of Philosophical Experience*. San Francisco: Ignatius Press, 1937.
Herrick, James. *The Making of the New Spirituality*. Downers Grove: IVP, 2003.
Hustad, Donald. "The Psalms as Worship Expression: Personal and Congregational." Review & Expositor 81 (1984) 407–24.

---

44. Moseley, *A to Z of Philosophy*, 95. For a fuller discussion, see Gilson, *Unity of Philosophical Experience*.

James, Montague. *The Apocryphal New Testament: Being the Apocryphal Gospels, Acts, Epistles and Apocalypses*. Oxford: Oxford University Press, 1953.

Law, Terry. *Praise Releases Faith*. Tulsa: Victory House, 1987.

Lewis, C. S. *Reflections on the Psalms*. London: Geoffrey Bles, 1958.

Maré, Leonard. "A Pentecostal Perspective on the Use of Psalms of Lament in Worship." *Verbum et Ecclesia* 29 (2008) 91–109.

McCann, J. Clinton. *A Theological Introduction to the Book of Psalms*. Nashville: Abingdon, 1993.

McCarthy, Michael. "An Ecclesiology of Groaning: Augustine, the Psalms, and the Making of the Church." *Theological Studies* 66 (2005) 23–48.

Moseley, Alexander. *A to Z of Philosophy*. London: Continuum, 2008.

Roberts, Alexander, and James Donaldson, eds. *The Ante Nicene Fathers: Volume 1*. Grand Rapids: Eerdmans, 1979.

———. *The Ante Nicene Fathers: Volume 3*. Grand Rapids: Eerdmans, 1978.

Scofield, Cyrus I. *Book Introduction–Psalms*. http://www.biblestudytools.com/commentaries/scofield-reference-notes/psalms-1-75/psalms-introduction.html.

Sizer, Stephen. *Christian Zionism: Roadmap to Armageddon?* IVP: Leicester, 2004.

Storey, John. "Becoming British." In *The Cambridge Companion to Modern British Culture*, 12–25. Cambridge: Cambridge University Press, 2010.

Trinkaus, Charles. *In Our Image and Likeness: Humanity and Divinity in Italian Humanist Thought*. Indiana: University of Notre Dame Press, 1995.

———. "Protagoras in the Renaissance: An Exploration." In *Philosophy and Humanism: Renaissance Essays in Honor of Paul Oskar Kristeller*, edited by Edward Mahoney, 190–213. Leiden: Brill, 1976.

Vogel, Dwight, ed. *Primary Sources of Liturgical Theology: A Reader*. Collegeville: Liturgical Press, 2000.

Waltke, Bruce K., James M. Houston, and Erika Moore. *The Psalms as Christian Lament: A Historical Commentary*. Grand Rapids: Eerdmans, 2014.

2

A Song Once Known

The Use of Psalm 77 by Calvin, Henry, Wesley, and Simeon

Ian J. Maddock

In Psalm 77:7–10, Asaph cries out "Will the Lord spurn forever, and never again be favorable? Has his steadfast love forever ceased? Are his promises at an end for all time? Has God forgotten to be gracious? Has he in anger shut up his compassion?" (ESV). Asaph's cry of dereliction is simultaneously ancient and modern, resonating with the lived experience of many past and present. They are also challenging words—not merely in terms of their poignancy, but also when it comes to the matter of how these words are to be understood and applied. Are they to be emulated as a lament that emerges from the psalmist's faithfulness? Or are they to be eschewed as expressions of the psalmist's faithlessness?

The aims of this chapter are twofold: first, to show how lament psalms such as Asaph's Psalm 77 are "a song once known," having featured prominently on the Protestant homiletical landscape since the Reformation; and second, to begin to explore the varying ways in which a representative lament psalm has been appropriated. To that end, this chapter will focus particularly on Psalm 77 and how it has been interpreted by a selection of notable Protestant preachers: John Calvin, Matthew Henry, John Wesley, and Charles Simeon. Collectively, these figures span not only the sixteenth-century Continental Reformation through to nineteenth-century

English evangelicalism, but also a range of theological and ecclesiological perspectives.

We shall observe that for Calvin, Henry, Wesley, and Simeon, Psalm 77 was not simply a song once known; it was a psalm whose message was to be preached. This shared homiletical orientation is reflected in the way their public writings on Asaph's lament either took the form of published sermons (Wesley and Simeon) or commentaries written with the (at least partial) intention of aiding those preaching on this text (Calvin and Henry). Further, each interpreted and expounded Asaph's lament as one who had absorbed many and various personal trials, whether they came in the form of personal and familial tragedy or ecclesiastical strife.

And yet we shall also observe that for all of their shared commitment to preaching the message of Psalm 77, their conclusions regarding how this difficult text ought to be understood were far from monochrome. It is these contrasting appropriations, and not chronology, that shape our approach in this chapter. We begin with Henry and Simeon, who critique the psalmist for his faithless grumbling, then turn to Calvin, who finds in Psalm 77 a lament to be emulated, and eventually consider Wesley's theological appropriation of Asaph's lament as a source of assurance.

Matthew Henry: "We Must Argue Down the Insurrections of Unbelief"

Matthew Henry's name is justifiably synonymous with his famous *Commentary on the Whole Bible* (1708–1710). Not only is his exposition still widely read today and admired for its "devotional comments, practical wisdom, warm theology and helpful insights,"[1] its fingerprints had already become evident by the mid-eighteenth century in such places as the hymns of William Cowper and Charles Wesley,[2] John Wesley's *Explanatory Notes on the Old Testament*,[3] and the sermons of George Whitefield.[4] If Henry's name is not as readily associated with suffering, it is not for lack of personal proximity to trials. Henry was born in October 1662 in the midst of circumstances in English church history that were not only momentous, but also particu-

---

1. Eveson, *Matthew Henry*, 13.

2. For example, hymns such as Cowper's "O for a closer walk with God" and "God moves in a mysterious way," and Wesley's "A charge to keep I have," reflect the influence of Henry's *Commentary* on their verse.

3. See Maddock, *Men of One Book*, 163.

4. See Crump, "The Preaching of George Whitefield," 19–28, and Packer, "The Spirit with the Word," 166–89.

larly trying for the Henry family. Just two months earlier his father, Philip Henry, was ejected from his ordained ministry in the Church of England after he, and some two thousand others like him, "dissented" from the liturgical conditions stipulated in the recently passed Act of Uniformity. Perhaps with the family's suddenly fraught ecclesiastical situation in mind, Philip Henry's diary entry as he reflected on his son's birth is tinged with lament: "We have no reason to call him Benoni [that is, "son of my sorrow"; see Gen 35:18]—I wish we had not to call him Ichabod [that is, "no glory"; see 1 Sam 4:21]."[5]

Henry's formative years at Broad Oak, Flintshire, were spent in a God-fearing, Scripture-saturated home environment. But they were also spent living under the shadow of ecclesiastical suspicion.[6] Henry's preparations for vocational ministry were influenced by this experience of religious persecution: he undertook his theological training in private, was ordained in London in 1687 in private, and his initial experience of vocational ministry at Chester was as a Nonconformist.[7] While the Act of Toleration in 1688 brought some measure of relief to Henry's exercising of his public ministry, this period of his life was beset by numerous personal tragedies. His wife of just eighteenth months, Katharine Hardware, died giving birth to a daughter in February 1689. One year later Henry married Mary Warburton. Although the couple was blessed with nine children, three were to die in infancy. The year 1693 was, in particular, a season of unrelenting mourning for Henry, losing a daughter, two of his sisters, and his former mother-in-law.[8]

And yet just two days after his daughter Mary's death, Henry was back in the pulpit preaching both morning and evening. Whatever personal grief he was experiencing, these emotions were subsumed beneath the opportunity to exhort his congregation to consider, in the wake of the death of an infant (in this case his own!), the dire impact of original sin, tempered with the comforting remembrance of God's covenantal goodness and the Christian's hope of resurrection glory. He focused, especially in his morning sermon on Job 38, upon the impropriety and impiety of questioning God's providence, mysterious as it might be. Likewise, in his evening sermon on Romans 5:14, Henry exhorted himself, as much as his flock, to

> [r]esign, and give up your dying children to God . . . Let their death bring your sin to remembrance. Did you not sin in an inordinate desire of children? Perhaps in discontent, or poverty,

5. Lee, *Diaries and Letters of Philip Henry*, 118.
6. Eveson, *Henry*, 15–27.
7. Beeke and Pederson, *Meet the Puritans*, 323.
8. Harman, *Matthew Henry*, 87.

> you have thought them too many. It may be you were over fond of them, or too indulgent. My pride, my passion, my covetousness—these slew my child. Learn to bear it patiently. Do not murmur. If I am bereaved of my children, said the patriarch, I am bereaved; not I am undone. The Shunamite said, It is well—for all is well that God doth. If a sparrow doth not fall without the will of God, then a child doth not. Comfort yourselves at such a time in God's covenant with you, and your seed. Fetch your comforts from the Lord Jesus who was dead, and is alive, and lives for evermore.[9]

Henry's public response to severe trials such as these not only offers us a rare glimpse into his interior life, it resonates with, and illuminates, his interpretative approach towards Psalm 77. His assessment of Asaph's character in the first half of the psalm is that "we have here the lively portraiture of a good man under a prevailing melancholy." Henry offers Asaph as a man with whom we can easily empathize; how "drooping saints, that are of a sorrowful spirit, may here as in a glass see their own faces."[10]

And yet in Henry's estimation, it is one thing to empathize with Asaph's "fears and apprehensions"— it is quite another thing to find in his "melancholy musings" a model fit to emulate. Henry regards Asaph's "goodness" as being incompatible with the "sorrowful complaints" that permeate his utterances in vv. 1–10, where "complaint" appears synonymous with grumbling. Indeed, Asaph's "melancholy grief" is interpreted as "an affront to God" inasmuch as he "he had no mind to hearken to those that would be his comforters."[11]

But if "despondency of spirit, and distrust of God, under affliction, are too often the infirmities of good people," then Henry also sees in Psalm 77 a model of how good men like Asaph may eventually "recover themselves." When faced with a "despondency of spirit" such as the psalmist experienced and recounted in vv. 1–10, Henry urges believers to "suppress" their complaint and argue "down the insurrections of unbelief." How might this be achieved? Principally by following Asaph's lead in Psalm 77:11–20; that is, by remembering "what God has done for his people of old." Just as it was for Asaph, so too for subsequent generations of God's people, "the due remembrance of the works of God will be a powerful antidote against distrust of his promise, for he is God and changes not."[12] In short, Henry's interpreta-

---

9. Quoted in Eveson, *Henry*, 68–69.
10. Henry, *Commentary*, 659–660.
11. Ibid., 660.
12. Ibid.

tion of Psalm 77 is that good men, such as Asaph eventually demonstrates himself to be, are not melancholy men— at least not indefinitely.

Charles Simeon: "The Complaints We Are Apt to Make"

Like Matthew Henry, Charles Simeon was no stranger to trials. Famous for his evangelistic endeavors among the Cambridge student body and for his commitment to furthering world mission (for example, through his influence upon the selection of chaplains serving with the British East India Company and his leadership in the foundation of the Church Missionary Society), Simeon's legacy also includes the vexed relationship he shared with his congregation during the fifty-four years he spent as rector of Holy Trinity Church in Cambridge between 1783 and his death in 1836. Handley Moule recounts the "long and painful . . . siege laid against Simeon's activity and influence" that characterized a parish-based ministry that was nothing if not frequently unpopular.[13]

Simeon's tenure at Holy Trinity featured many indignities, including being overlooked for the Sunday evening Lectureship by his own congregation during the first twelve years of his ministry, his churchwardens on occasion denying him access to the church premises, and a widespread refusal on the part of many parishioners to open their homes to his pastoral visits.[14] To be sure, his five decades of labor in Cambridge also included seasons of respite and even refreshment, as we might reasonably expect for such a lengthy pastorate. And yet the overwhelming impression remains: should he be given to lament, Simeon's pastoral experience surely provided fertile soil for godly sorrow in response to the difficult providences that accompanied his attempts to faithfully execute the ministry of word and sacrament.

What do we know of his reaction to these trials? If Simeon was no stranger to trials, he was not given to lament—at least not public expressions of lament. In terms of his public persona, lament was by and large, and by intention, a "song unknown." Here the testimony of one of Simeon's intimate friends, short-hand writer and publisher, Joseph Gurney, is insightful. Gurney observed how although "this experienced Christian knew well what it was to mourn and be in bitterness," Simeon was committed to maintaining a face to the world that was devoid of lament: "It was one of his grand principles of action, to endeavour at all times to honour his Master by maintaining a cheerful happy demeanour in the presence of his friends."[15]

13. Moule, *Charles Simeon*, 44.
14. Ibid., 40–49.
15. Ibid., 157.

For his own part, Simeon was adamant that for the regenerate to lament was theologically inappropriate. For those in Christ, the remembrance of the finished work of Christ precludes it. In this vein he wrote to Gurney in 1831, "My dear brother, we must not mind a little suffering. When I am getting through a hedge, if my head and shoulders are safely through, I can bear the pricking of my legs. Let us rejoice in the remembrance that our holy Head has surmounted all His sufferings and triumphed over death. Let us follow Him patiently; we shall soon be partakers of His victory."[16] Simeon affords little theological space for biblically warranted lament in his response to his own trials. No mere stoicism, much less a display of British "stiff-upper-lip" in the midst of adversity, Simeon's eschewing of lament appears to have been explicitly theologically motivated.

Perhaps Simeon had his own protracted pastoral difficulties in mind—and perhaps also his own lament-free pastoral response to those same difficulties—as he approached the task of preaching on Psalm 77:7-10, published in his *Horae Homileticae* under the title "Despondency Depicted and Reproved."[17] Here he begins with a strong, though short-lived, desire to empathize with the psalmist's plight, acknowledging that "the afflictions of Asaph were exceeding heavy" and that "he may well be considered as a mirror, wherein the Lord's people in all ages may, under their several temptations, behold the workings of their own minds."[18] Simeon observed how easily a contemporary reader might resonate with Asaph's cry: the "very strong degree of apprehension intimated" by the psalmist reflect feelings "by no means uncommon to the present day. Many in a season of darkness are led to write bitter things against themselves, and to account all their past profession a continued scene of hypocrisy and self-delusion."[19]

And yet as the title of his sermon unequivocally suggests, Simeon's willingness to empathize with Asaph's plight has definite limits. For instance, he categorizes the psalmist's cry in these verses as an evidence of impatience and unbelief under duress. If they function as a model for believers, they do so only in terms of how *not* to respond in the midst of difficult providences: "If we truly believe that God ordered every thing with infallible wisdom, and unbounded goodness, and an inviolable fidelity, we could never be put in such a consternation as is expressed in our text."[20] Simeon's verdict on

---

16. Ibid., 155–56.
17. Simeon, *Horae Homileticae*, 6:31–37.
18. Ibid., 6:31.
19. Ibid., 6:32.
20. Ibid., 6:34.

Asaph's "hard thoughts of God" is bleak: they "had no foundation in truth: they were the result only of his own weakness."[21]

Just as Psalm 77 progresses from Asaph's lament to his recalling God's redemptive faithfulness to his people, Simeon concludes his sermon by pointing to the psalmist's eventual faithfulness as emulation-worthy. Simeon observes: "Happily, however, the snare was broken," and his ungodly reaction is "effectually removed by a more attentive consideration of all that God had done for his people of old."[22] Thus for Simeon, the message and application of Psalm 77:7–10 is clear: do not grumble like Asaph! But if you do, be sure to "hear his own answer to the complaints we are apt to make."[23] He concludes, "Be watchful then, that you do not by any unhallowed dispositions 'grieve the Holy Spirit'; but endeavour to 'walk in the fear of the Lord all the day long.'"[24]

John Calvin: "This Is Not a Mere Complaint, as Some Interpreters Explain It"

Compared to Henry and Simeon, in his *Commentary on the Psalms* (1557), John Calvin offers us a distinct and divergent appropriation of Psalm 77. Here the sixteenth-century Reformer expresses not only his general evaluation of the pastoral usefulness of the psalms, but finds in the lament psalms especially, "permission and freedom granted to lay open before [God] our infirmities which we would be ashamed to confess before men."[25] Calvin is careful to distinguish between "mere complaint" (where "complaint," in a similar vein to Henry and Simeon, appears coterminous with grumbling) and godly "lament," whose object is "not to overthrow faith, but rather to raise it up."[26] Far from being an example of faithlessness, Calvin regards Psalm 77 as a model of godly lament for Christians to imitate in the midst of trials.

Like Henry, Calvin was familiar with personal grief, suffering the loss of an infant son in 1542, followed by his wife of nine years, Idelette de Bure, in 1549. For a figure known reflexively for his personal austerity and doctrinal rigidity, Calvin's heartfelt lament at Idelette's death in a letter to Peter

---

21. Ibid., 6:32.
22. Ibid.
23. Ibid., 6:36.
24. Ibid., 6:37.
25. Calvin, *Commentary*, xxxviii.
26. Ibid., 213.

Viret offers a poignant glimpse into his humanity as a grieving husband: "Truly mine is no common grief. I have been bereaved of the best companion of my life, one of who, if it had been so ordained, would willingly have shared not only my poverty but also death."[27] Like Simeon, Calvin also experienced much ecclesial strife; his tenure as Geneva's pastor between 1537 and 1564 was interrupted by a period of exile in Strasbourg as he found himself variously in, and out of, and again in, favor. Like Wesley, who by his own admission would have much preferred to "be a saunterer *inter sylvas academicus*, a philosophical sluggard"[28] than the foremost leader of a burgeoning reform movement, Calvin's preference was to live a scholarly life in anonymity, admitting that he was continually thwarted in his "one great object . . . to live in seclusion without being known."[29] He described leaving France, then Basel, seeking

> privacy and obscurity, until at length William Farel detained me at Geneva, not so much by counsel and exhortation, as by a dreadful imprecation . . . that God would curse my retirement, and the tranquility of the studies which I sought, if I should withdraw and refuse to give [pastoral] assistance, when the necessity was so urgent.[30]

And yet if Calvin's biography resonates at a number of points with those we have previously explored, his stance towards Psalm 77 offers a sharp contrast. Far from being "a mere complaint, as some interpreters explain it," Calvin interprets Psalm 77 as "a common form of prayer for the Church," one that represents "the lamentations and groanings of the chosen people."[31] Calvin saw in the Psalter as a whole, not just lament psalms such as this, a rich resource for emulation for subsequent generations of God's people. In the Preface to his *Commentary on the Psalms*, he wrote,

> I have been accustomed to call this book, I think not inappropriately, "An Anatomy of all the Parts of the Soul"; for there is not an emotion of which any one can be conscious that is not here represented as in a mirror. Or rather, the Holy Spirit has here drawn to the life all the griefs, sorrows, fears, doubts,

---

27. Quoted in Parker, *John Calvin*, 102.
28. Baker, *Letters*, 26:190.
29. Calvin, *Commentary*, xli.
30. Ibid., xlii–xliii.
31. Ibid., 205.

hopes, cares, perplexities, in short, all the distracting emotions with which the minds of men are wont to be agitated.[32]

In keeping with his attitude towards the Psalms as a corpus reflected above, one of the distinguishing features of Calvin's interpretation of Psalm 77 is the way he views Asaph's cry as an example of godly lament, one that is worthy of direct emulation. What distinguishes this godly lament from ungodly complaint? Calvin suggests that it lies in how Asaph "did not foolishly rend the air with his cries, like many who pour forth bitter cries without measure and at random under their sorrows."[33] Instead,

> Although the prophet found no solace and no alleviation of the bitterness of grief, he still continued to stretch forth his hands to God. In this manner, it becomes us to wrestle against despair, in order that our sorrow, although it may seem incurable, may not shut our mouths, and keep us from pouring out our prayers to God.[34]

That is, what sets this cry apart as a model for us to follow is that it emerges from the vantage point of faith in God; it is directed towards God and motivated by an unwavering confidence in God's faithfulness. Even in the midst of trying circumstances, Calvin observes how, "He does not properly complain or find fault with God, but rather reasoning with himself, concludes, from the nature of God, that it is impossible for him not to continue his free favor towards his people."[35]

Whereas Henry and Simeon interpret Asaph's cry as a complaint to be eschewed, Calvin appropriates Psalm 77 as a positive example of how to lament in the midst of trials. Commenting on vv. 7 and 8, Calvin summarizes, "We are . . . taught from this passage that however much we may experience fretting, sorrow and disquietude, we must persevere in calling upon God even in the midst of all these impediments."[36]

---

32. Ibid., xxxvi–xxxvii.
33. Ibid., 206.
34. Ibid., 207.
35. Ibid., 211.
36. Ibid., 208.

John Wesley: "There Are Few That Know How to Sympathize with Them That Are under This Sore Temptation"

We now turn our gaze, lastly, from sixteenth-century continental Europe to one of the most prominent leaders of eighteenth-century transatlantic evangelical revival, John Wesley. Compared to the preceding perspectives, Wesley's 1778 sermon "A Call to Backsliders" offers a unique theological and pastoral appropriation of Psalm 77. Here Wesley deals with the problem of religious despair, finding in the psalmist's cry in vv. 7 and 8 the lament of Christians whose faith has not so much foundered on spiritual presumption, but instead on "want of hope."[37] While Wesley spent much time and energy opposing antinomianism throughout his public ministry, in this sermon he demonstrates his pastoral sensitivity towards the plight of those "helpless, hopeless souls"[38] who,

> having many times fought against their spiritual enemies, and always been overcome, they lay down their arms; they no more contend, as they have no hope of victory. Knowing by melancholy experience that they have no power of themselves to help themselves, and having no expectation that God will help them, they lie down under their burden. They no longer strive; for they suppose it is impossible to attain.[39]

Although Wesley consistently emphasized that Christians ought to expect and strive after conscious experiences of pardon and assurance, he was aware that this was not a universal, much less uninterrupted, experience. Indeed, it is possible to discern an autobiographical strain in Wesley's desire to comfort those lamenting, in Asaph's words, "that God hath 'forgotten to be gracious.'"[40] Though he generally kept his interior life largely hidden from the watching world, glimpses of Wesley's own struggles with assurance occasionally reveal themselves in the midst of correspondence with his closest confidants. None was closer than his brother Charles, and nowhere does John lament more candidly than in a letter dated 27 June 1766. In the aftermath of a discouraging preaching tour of Scotland, with his marriage swiftly unraveling, and faced with the prospect of Charles himself foregoing the peripatetic lifestyle of a Methodist field-preacher in favor of a more

---

37. Outler, *Sermons*, 3:211.
38. Ibid., 3:213.
39. Ibid., 3:211.
40. Ibid., 3:213.

sedentary existence in Bristol, there is a discernible element of fragility in Wesley's admissions not often seen since his 1738 Aldersgate Street experience.[41] Just as Asaph questioned his own spiritual state before God, Wesley wrote,

> In one of my last I was saying I do not feel the wrath of God abiding on me; nor can I believe it does. And yet (this is the mystery) [I do not love God. I never did]. Therefore [I never] believed in the Christian sense of the word. Therefore [I am only an] honest heathen, a proselyte of the Temple, one of the {"God-fearers"}. And yet to be so employed of God! and so hedged in that I can neither get forward nor backward! Surely there never was such an instance before, from the beginning of the world! If I {ever have had} that faith, it would not be so strange. But [I never had any] other {"awareness"} of the eternal or invisible world than [I have] now; and that is [none at all], unless such as fairly shines from reason's glimmering ray. [I have no] direct witness, I do not say that [I am a child of God], but of anything invisible or eternal. And yet I dare not preach otherwise than I do, either concerning faith, or love, or justification, or perfection. And yet I find rather an increase than a decrease of zeal for the whole work of God and every part of it. I am {"borne along"}, I know not how, that I can't stand still. I want all the world to come to {"what I do not know"}.[42]

Wesley's commitment to preaching and printing "A Call to Backsliders"[43] constitutes his recognition that "there are few that know how to sympathize with them," lamenting not only the reality that "they cannot save themselves" but also that "God *will* not save them."[44] As a folk-theologian, one whose public writings were typically conditioned to meet the immediate pastoral needs of "the people called Methodists," Wesley here seeks to reassure those who "believe they have so provoked God that 'he will no more

---

41. Outler, *John Wesley*, 81, n. 1.

42. Telford, *Letters*, 5:16–17. The text in square brackets [] was originally written in shorthand, while the text in braces {} is a translation from the Greek. It was not uncommon for correspondents in the eighteenth century to couch potentially alarming statements in shorthand or shift to foreign languages (typically French, Latin, or Greek). Evidence of both is to be found here.

43. Wesley frequently adopted a "preach and print" strategy when it came to disseminating his sermons. Wesley preached this sermon on 20 May 1778 in Sligo, Ireland, though he also preached on Psalm 77:7–8 on August 23, 1768 at Cullompton. See Ward and Heitzenrater, *Journal and Diaries*, 22:153.

44. Outler, *Sermons*, 3:212.

be entreated.'"[45] Many onlookers, Wesley observed, were "deceived by appearances. They see men go on in a course of sin, and take it for granted, it is out of mere presumption; whereas in reality it is from quite the opposite principle—it is out of mere despair."[46]

"A Call to Backsliders" offers those lamenting their spiritual state abundant evidence of God's unfailing love. Unlike human kings whose mercy is often exhausted and whose grace has limits, God is

> God and not man, "therefore his compassions fail not." Yea, he will: not only seven times only, or seventy times seven. Nay, were your rebellions multiplied as the stars of heaven, were they more in number than the hairs of your head; yet "return unto the Lord, and he will have mercy upon you, and to our God, and will abundantly pardon."[47]

While not attempting a thorough exposition of Psalm 77, Wesley's desire to discern what constitutes valid grounds for assurance and thus offer comfort for those who think "it impossible that they should escape destruction" mirrors the trajectory of the psalm itself, especially its focus on remembrance of God's incurably faithful salvific stance towards his people.

Conclusion

In this chapter we have observed how for Calvin, Henry, Wesley, and Simeon, lament psalms such as Asaph's Psalm 77 were indeed a "song once known." Through the vehicles of either commentaries or published sermons, each demonstrated a commitment to preaching the message of Psalm 77. Further, each expounded on Psalm 77 as those who were well acquainted with what it meant to experience trial, suffering, doubt, and grief.

And yet their conclusions regarding how this challenging text ought to be understood and applied were far from identical. Is this text to be emulated as an expression of the psalmist's faithfulness? Or is it to be eschewed as an expression of his faithlessness? While all four preachers commend Asaph for remembering God's faithfulness, there are significant theological and applicatory divergences in how that remembrance ought to be manifested in the midst of suffering and trial. We have observed that, whereas Henry and Simeon conclude that our complaints are *silenced* when God's faithfulness is remembered, Calvin concludes that lament is *enabled* when

---

45. Ibid.
46. Ibid., 3:211–12.
47. Ibid., 3:217.

God's faithfulness is remembered. In contrast to these expositions of Asaph's lament, Wesley's theological appropriation of Psalm 77 serves to reassure Christians of God's salvific faithfulness in a way that nonetheless mirrors the contours of the psalm's trajectory.

Our focus here on divergent historical appropriations of a representative lament psalm demonstrates the challenges that attend this oft-neglected biblical genre. Christian appropriation of lament is not straightforward—and indeed never has been. The remainder of this volume offers theological, exegetical, and applicatory reflections on lament that encourage these songs to be known once more.

Bibliography

Baker, Frank, ed. *Letters I-II*. The Works of John Wesley: Bicentennial Edition 25–26. Nashville: Abingdon, 1980–1982.

Beeke, Joel R., and Randall J. Pederson, eds. *Meet the Puritans*. Grand Rapids: Reformation Heritage Books, 2006.

Calvin, John. *Commentary on the Book of Psalms*. Translated by James Anderson. Grand Rapids: Baker, 2005.

Crump, David. "The Preaching of George Whitefield and His Use of Matthew Henry's Commentary." Crux 25 (1989) 19–28.

Eveson, Philip H. *Matthew Henry*. Darlington: EP Books, 2012.

Harman, Allan. *Matthew Henry: His Life and Influence*. Fearn: Christian Focus, 2012.

Henry, Matthew. *Commentary on the Whole Bible*. Grand Rapids: Zondervan, 1960.

Lee, Matthew H., ed. *Diaries and Letters of Philip Henry, M.A. of Broad Oak, Flintshire, A.D. 1631–1696*. London: Kegan, Paul, Trench & Co., 1882.

Maddock, Ian J. *Men of One Book: A Comparison of Two Methodist Preachers, John Wesley and George Whitefield*. Eugene, OR: Pickwick, 2011.

Moule, Handley C. G. *Charles Simeon*. London: IVP, 1948.

Outler Albert, ed. *John Wesley*. New York: Oxford University Press, 1964.

———. *Sermons*. The Works of John Wesley: Bicentennial Edition 1–4. Nashville: Abingdon, 1984–1987.

Packer, James I. "The Spirit with the Word: The Reformational Revivalism of George Whitefield." In *The Bible, the Reformation and the Church: Essays in Honour of James Atkinson*, edited by William P. Stephens, 166–89. Sheffield: Sheffield Academic, 1995.

Parker, T. H. L. *John Calvin: A Biography*. London: Aldine, 1975.

Simeon, Charles. *Horae Homileticae*. 21 volumes. London: Holdsworth & Ball, 1832.

Telford, John. *Letters of John Wesley*. London: Epworth, 1931.

Ward, W. Reginald, and Richard P. Heitzenrater, eds. *Journal and Diaries I-VII*. The Works of John Wesley: Bicentennial Edition 19–24. Nashville: Abingdon, 1988–1997.

3

"Consolation for the Despairing"
C. H. Spurgeon's Endorsement of Lament Psalms in Public Worship

Alan J. Thompson

As the preface indicates, one of the aims of this book is to encourage the rediscovery of the lament psalms in the life of the church. At first glance, Charles Haddon Spurgeon (1834–1892), the famously successful preacher from the nineteenth century, may seem like an unlikely candidate to help us with this project. His life and ministry have become legendary and Spurgeon has often been called "the Prince of Preachers."[1] The growth of New Park Street Baptist Church after Spurgeon, "the boy preacher," became the pastor at nineteen years of age—from 230 members to approximately six thousand at each service in the Metropolitan Tabernacle—is widely known. This phenomenal growth, together with Spurgeon's renowned personal oversight of numerous other ministries such as the Pastor's College, an orphanage, a Colportage Society, and his prolific writing, has meant that his story has often been told with an accent on the extent and successes of his ministry and a sense of wonder at what God can do.[2]

---

1. See the excellent overviews of Spurgeon's life and ministries in Drummond, *Spurgeon*, and Nettles, *Living by Revealed Truth*. I am grateful to Zack Eswine, Christian George, David Music, and Tom Nettles for taking the time to read and provide feedback on a previous draft of this essay.

2. Morden, "Suffering," 307, makes this observation. For Spurgeon's many

Spurgeon's life, however, was also characterized by much suffering and anguish.[3] Serious effects of kidney disease, the stress of needing funds for the many ministries he oversaw, concern for the wellbeing of his frequently ill and bed-ridden wife, Susannah, as well as his own insomnia and depression, were regular features of his life. Spurgeon spoke openly about his physical, emotional, and spiritual anguish, including his depression.[4] Spurgeon's depression related in part to the physical suffering he endured, but is also traceable to his distress over the Surrey Gardens Music Hall tragedy in October 1856 when seven people died and many others were injured because of a prankster's shout of "fire." The sight of seeing the crowd fleeing in panic and people trampled to death at one of his services haunted Spurgeon for the rest of his life.[5]

Given this life-long experience of suffering in various forms, it is perhaps not surprising to find that Spurgeon regularly preached on what we today call the lament psalms.[6] Spurgeon obviously loved the psalms, as his twenty-year, seven-volume "magnum opus" commentary on the Psalter, *The Treasury of David*, makes clear. Spurgeon also loved applying the psalms to the needs of his flock. Far from avoiding lament, Spurgeon sought to help his congregation appreciate the value and benefits of lament psalms in their own personal lives and in their congregational worship. This chapter will show, therefore, that Spurgeon brought before his congregation the value and benefits of these psalms of sorrow by (1) explaining that it is good and necessary to hear lament psalms in church; (2) encouraging the congregation to follow the pattern of the lament psalms in taking their cries and sorrows to the Lord; (3) reassuring the congregation that such laments are the experience of all true believers; and (4) helping the congregation to apply the pattern of the lament psalms in congregational singing. Thus, as we sample Spurgeon's sermons and "expositions" on lament psalms our focus

---

benevolent ministries see Drummond, *Spurgeon*, 393–441; Nettles, *Living by Revealed Truth*, 339–92.

3. In addition to Nettles, *Living by Revealed Truth*, 595–665, see Morden, "Suffering," 306–25.

4. See also Eswine, *Spurgeon's Sorrows*, and Skoglund, *Bright Days, Dark Nights*.

5. Nettles, *Living by Revealed Truth*, 597–99; Morden, "Suffering," 309–10.

6. As well as preaching a sermon, Spurgeon often read a passage of Scripture along with verse-by-verse comments. These "expositions" were often published at the end of his weekly sermons in *The Sword and the Trowel*. Spurgeon often preached numerous times on the same lament psalm. For example in *MTP* there are at least four "expositions" and another four sermons on Psalm 77 (a psalm that Spurgeon believed reflected his own experience; see Morden, "Suffering," 311), and four expositions and three sermons on Psalm 39.

will not be on his exegesis of the psalms, the content of his sermons, or even his teaching on a theology of suffering. Rather, we will observe how this nineteenth-century, psalm-loving, suffering shepherd used lament psalms in church life and showed his congregation the value and benefits of these psalms of sorrow.[7]

Spurgeon Oriented His Congregation to the Benefits of Sorrowful Psalms

Spurgeon recognized that many in the congregation would prefer to have more joyful topics for sermons and therefore needed to be oriented to the benefits of reflecting on grief and sorrow in the lament psalms. Thus, often in the introductions and conclusions to his sermons or expositions of these psalms, Spurgeon explains to his congregation that it is good to reflect on such psalms. For instance, in his sermon on Psalm 39:6–8 Spurgeon opens with the following:

> These are solemn words. Sometimes we have a more joyful theme than this; but I believe that, spiritually, as well as naturally, it is better to go to the house of mourning than to the house of feasting. A meditation of a quiet kind, on things not as they are in fiction, but as they prove to be in fact, is always salutary. There is a great mass of sorrow in the world; and all of us meet with something every now and then to calm our spirit, and cool our blood. So, tonight . . . by the blessing of God's Spirit, we may go away even more lastingly refreshed than if our hearts were made to leap for joy by meditation upon some transporting theme.[8]

In another introduction to this psalm he refers to the variety of life's experiences and how David's psalms reflect those experiences. Sometimes David was very joyful and he wrote joyful psalms. Sometimes, however, "he was very sad, and then he touched the mournful string." "This is a very sorrowful Psalm," Spurgeon noted, "but" he quickly adds, "it is full of teaching." Spurgeon concludes this exposition by affirming, "So, you see, this is a sweet Psalm after all; it is a bitter sweet, a sweet bitter, a Psalm that tends

---

7. The following survey primarily refers to Psalms 25, 31, 39, 42, 69, 70, 83, 88, and 120 (Psalm 77 is not examined here as its use in Christian history is the focus of Ian Maddock's chapter in this volume).

8. Spurgeon, *MTP*, vol. 40, 49 ("Earth's Vanities and Heaven's Verities"; preached November 7, 1889). See also his introductory and concluding comments to his broader exposition of this psalm (ibid., 58, 60).

towards our spiritual health."⁹ In these introductions and conclusions we get the sense that Spurgeon acknowledges the reluctance of some to hear an exposition on sorrow and mourning and reassures them that there is much to gain from such expositions.

On other occasions Spurgeon orients his congregation to the lament by providing possible justifications for the psalmist's lament before expounding the text. For example, in introducing his sermon on Psalm 120:5, Spurgeon notes that his outline is: "on this occasion, first, to say *a word or two in justification of the psalmist's complaint;* secondly, *to justify God's dealings with us in having subjected us to this dwelling in the tents of Mesech;* and thirdly, *a few words, by way of comfort, to those who are sad at heart, by reason of those ill times, and those ill places, in which they abide.*" Then, as he begins his first point justifying the psalmist's complaint, he declares: "I will say, and must say, that it is not only excusable, but scarcely needs an apology, for that Christian man sometimes to cry out, 'My soul is weary, I am almost weary of my life.'"¹⁰

Many times Spurgeon anticipates a potential objection from some in the congregation to a sermon that focuses on sorrow. He often explains that his own calling as a shepherd of the flock and his responsibility to comfort those in the congregation who are in grief or despair is the reason why he must speak on a lament psalm.¹¹ In the introduction to his exposition of Psalm 88, Spurgeon explains:

> I think that this is the darkest of all the Psalms; it has hardly a spot of light in it. The only bright words that I know of are in the first verse; the rest of the Psalm, is very dark, and very dreary. Why, then, am I going to read it? Because, it may be, there is some poor heart here that is very heavy; you cannot tell out of this great crowd how many sorrowing and burdened spirits there may be amongst us; but there may be a dozen or two of persons who are driven almost to despair.¹²

---

9. Spurgeon, *MTP*, vol. 40, 572–76.

10. Spurgeon, *MTP*, vol. 48, 242. Emphasis original. See also ibid., 457 (on Ps 42:6). Spurgeon also followed the pattern of the psalmists in noting the many and varied potential causes of sorrow and depression, including physical and constitutional elements, and thus the many potential helps for sorrowful saints. See Eswine, *Spurgeon's Sorrows*; Skoglund, *Bright Days, Dark Nights*.

11. E.g., Spurgeon, *MTP*, vol. 19, 685 ("Consolation for the Despairing," on Ps 31:22; preached December 7, 1873).

12. Spurgeon, *MTP*, vol. 41, 478–80. Later in this exposition, Spurgeon again notes: "This subject may not interest some of you, just now; but it is here, so we must mention it; and it may be wanted even by you one of these days . . . The day may

Spurgeon recognizes that his calling is not only to minister to those in the congregation who may be presently going through these sorrows, but also to prepare others for the time when they will experience such grief. This is the way he introduces his sermon on Psalm 88:7, with an eye toward those who think it may be inappropriate to have a "discourse upon sorrow." It is worth quoting this introduction in full:

> It is the business of a shepherd not only to look after the happy ones among the sheep, but to seek after the sick of the flock, and to lay himself out right earnestly for their comfort and succour. I feel, therefore, that I do rightly when I this morning make it my special business to speak to such as are in trouble. Those of you who are happy and rejoicing in God, full of faith and assurance, can very well spare a discourse for your weaker brethren; you can be even glad and thankful to go without your portion, that those who are depressed in spirit may receive a double measure of the wine of consolation. Moreover, I am not sure that even the most joyous Christian is any the worse for remembering the days of darkness which are stealing on apace, "for they are many." Just as the memories of our dying friends come o'er us like a cloud, and "damp our brainless ardours," so will the recollection that there are tribulations and afflictions in the world sober our rejoicing, and prevent its degenerating into an idolatry of the things of time and sense. It is better for many reasons to go to the house of mourning than to the house of feasting . . .; it will work thee no ill. It may be, O thou who art today brimming with happiness, that a little store of sacred cautions and consolations may prove no sore to thee, but may by-and-by stand thee in good stead. This morning's discourse upon sorrow may suggest a few thoughts to thee which, being treasured up, shall ripen like summer fruit, and mellow by the time thy winter shall come round.[13]

Thus, Spurgeon often orients his congregation to the benefits of these lament psalms, explaining that it is good to examine these psalms of sorrow. It is an opportunity and indeed obligation of Spurgeon's as their shepherd to comfort the afflicted and strengthen others for the day of affliction. These psalms are, however, not only beneficial to reflect on, they direct us in expressing grief.

---

come when you will turn to this Psalm with the two eights to it, and find comfort in it because it describes your case also." A similar explanation is found in the conclusion to this exposition.

13. Spurgeon, *MTP*, vol. 19, 13 ("For the Troubled"; preached January 12, 1873).

Spurgeon Encouraged his Congregation to Follow the Pattern of the Psalmists by Taking Their Cries to the Lord

Many times Spurgeon explained the benefit of lament psalms by encouraging his congregation to follow the example of the psalmists in expressing their grief. "We all know," Spurgeon reasoned in his exposition of Psalm 39, "that, unless our grief can find expression, it swells and grows till our heart is ready to break. We have heard of a wise physician who bade a man in great trouble weep as much as ever he could. 'Do not restrain your grief,' he said, 'but let it all out.' He felt that only in that way would the poor sufferer's heart be kept from breaking."[14]

Spurgeon also spoke specifically of the tears of those expressing their sorrow. In "Consolation for the Despairing" (on Ps 31:22) Spurgeon notes that, "when David feared that he was cut off from God, he was wise enough to take to crying. He [David] calls prayer crying." Spurgeon then extols the benefits of such an expression of grief from this lament psalm: "Crying is the language of pain; pain cannot cumber itself with letters and syllables and words, and so it takes its own way, and adopts a piercing mode of utterance, very telling and expressive. Crying yields great relief to suffering. Everyone knows the benefit of having a hearty good cry: you cannot help calling it 'a good cry,' for, though one would think crying could never be especially good, yet it affords a desirable relief. Red eyes often relieve breaking hearts."[15]

The element of the psalmists' laments that Spurgeon particularly emphasizes, however, is that they expressed their grief to the Lord. Spurgeon encourages his congregation, therefore, to see from these lament psalms that their expression of sorrow is more than a hopeless exercise of merely expressing grief. In "Consolation for the Despairing" Spurgeon adds that "according to our text this cry was addressed to the Lord . . . It is important to observe that he cried to the Lord, even though he thought himself cut off from hope . . . Ah, soul, if thou be in despair, yet resolve to pour out thy heart before thy God."[16] For those who say "Oh, I cannot pray," Spurgeon replies, "My dear friend, can you cry? . . . If you cannot say it in words, tell it with your tears, your groans, your sighs, your sobs . . . Never is a child in such a bad plight that it cannot cry. It never says, 'Mother, it is so dark I cannot see to cry'; no, no, the child cries in the dark. And are you in the dark,

---

14. Spurgeon, *MTP*, vol. 57, 46.

15. Spurgeon, *MTP*, vol. 19, 693 ("Consolation for the Despairing"; preached December 7, 1873).

16. Ibid., 693–94.

and in terrible doubt and trouble? Then cry away, my dear friend, cry away, cry away; your Father will hear and deliver you."[17]

Spurgeon regularly applies the example of the psalmist's expression of sorrow before the Lord to the sorrowful believer in his congregation. In his sermon on Psalm 25:19, Spurgeon observes that David asked the Lord "to look, not only upon the trouble, but also upon the misery which the trouble caused him." "So here," Spurgeon continues, "we may bring before God's notice, not only our trial, but the inward anguish which the trial occasions us."[18] This parallel between the psalmist and the grieving believer in Spurgeon's congregation is made regularly throughout the sermon. "It was to God that David took his sorrow . . . Observe then, *we must take our sorrows to God.*" Spurgeon contrasts this with taking our sorrows to our neighbors and instead urges that we must make it a rule to bring them before God first: "Your little sorrows you may take to God, for he counteth the hairs of your head: your great sorrows you may take to God, for he holdeth the world in the hollow of his hand. Go to him, whatever your present trouble may be, and you shall find him able and willing to relieve you." Again, later in the same sermon, Spurgeon tenderly urges the sorrowful (and even suicidal) believer to take their grief to God:

> We may further say that *the most sorrowful and the most sinful are welcome to the Lord Jesus.* The most sorrowful may come; I mean those in despair, those who are at their wits' ends, those poor souls who, through superabundant difficulty are ready to do the most unreasonable things—ready, it may even be, to give way to that wicked, Satanic temptation of rushing from this present life into a world unknown by their own hand. Go, sorrowful one, go now to Jesus, whose tender heart will feel for you . . . first and foremost, in a flood of tears, reveal your case to the great invisible helper. Kneel down and tell him all that racks your spirit and fills your tortured mind, and plead the promise

---

17. Ibid. It is also true that Spurgeon noted David's own faults, particularly when David himself identified them, such as, "I said in my haste" (Ps 31:22). On this occasion Spurgeon notes, "it is well to follow David, but it is better to follow David's son; . . . Do not let us imitate David in his speaking in haste, or in his saying, 'I am cut off from before thine eyes;' but at the same time let us take care that we closely copy him in confessing conscious fault, as he here does; in crying to God in the hour of trouble, as he tells us he did; and also in bearing witness to the exceeding goodness of God, notwithstanding our faultiness, as he here bears witness when he says, 'Nevertheless thou heardest the voice of my supplications when I cried unto thee.'" Spurgeon, *MTP*, vol. 27, 158 ("A Hasty Expression Penitently Retracted").

18. Spurgeon, *MTP*, vol. 13, 157 ("A Troubled Prayer").

that he will be with you, and you shall find him true though all else be false.[19]

In his many expositions and sermons on Psalm 39:4, Spurgeon observes that David's expression of grief begins with "Lord." He encourages his congregation to follow this same pattern. "That was a good beginning of David's speech," argues Spurgeon. "When we turn our burning words towards God, and not towards men, good will come of them. David's hot heart finds a vent Godward. This was the wisest thing that he could do, cry unto his God, 'Lord.'"[20] Similarly, in preaching on Psalm 39:4 Spurgeon exhorts, "if we are the subjects of the same infirmity as these godly men of old, we must flee where they fled for strength to grapple with these infirmities and overcome them. We must look to the strong for strength . . ."[21] In this sense Spurgeon often spoke of prayer as the resort of the Christian "in every plight."[22] Thus, Spurgeon recommends the lament of the psalmist in Psalm 69:14 because "You cannot be in any condition of poverty, or sickness, or obscurity, or slander, or doubt, or even sin, but still it is true that your God will welcome your prayer at any time and in every place." Even in extreme weakness, Spurgeon urges his hearers, "although you can scarcely bend your knee, and are almost afraid to utter words once dear to you, yet your soul desires, pants, hungers, thirsts, and that is the . . . very marrow and essence of prayer. Sobs and looks are prayers."[23]

In his sermon, "Heman's Sorrowful Psalm" (on Ps 88), Spurgeon notes that Heman "seems to have been brought about as low as a man can be brought." Nevertheless, even in this, "the darkest of all the Psalms," Spurgeon observes, "there was this fact in his favour, he continued praying." Thus, far from being a negative example, Spurgeon urged his audience, "if you would pray aright, you will do wisely to copy the writer of this Psalm; and first, *tell the Lord your case*."[24] In pouring out their sorrows before the

---

19. Ibid., 165. Emphasis original.

20. Spurgeon, *MTP*, vol. 55, 21. See also Spurgeon, *MTP*, vol. 40, 573 (both are expositions).

21. Spurgeon, *MTP*, vol. 60, 325–26 ("Brief Life is Here Our Portion," on Ps 39:4). Emphasis original. Spurgeon later again speaks of the lament psalm as instruction ("let us go to God with the prayer of the Psalmist").

22. Spurgeon, *MTP*, vol. 11, 299 ("The Believer Sinking in the Mire," on Ps 69:14).

23. Ibid. Spurgeon often speaks of our various weaknesses and inability to manage the griefs of life on our own as an encouragement to take our sorrows to the Lord. E.g., page 289 in this sermon, and Spurgeon, *MTP*, vol. 48, 464 ("Sweet Stimulants for the Fainting Soul," on Ps 42:6; preached "in the winter of 1860").

24. Spurgeon continues by noting the example of Heman. "In this Psalm, Heman makes a map of his life's history, he puts down all the dark places through which he

Lord, Spurgeon encourages his congregation that "Your eyes shall aid you with their liquid pleas, your breath shall assist you as you sigh and sob, every part of your being shall help you as you stretch out your hands unto God. The best prayer is, like a cry, the most natural expression of the sorrow and the need of the heart. Come like that to God . . . The psalmist says that he cried day and night *before God* . . . Praying is not whistling to the winds, it is crying before God—speaking to God."[25]

For Spurgeon, not only does God hear the grieving cries of his people, God is the only one we can cry to because in his sovereignty these trials ultimately come from God.[26] Thus, in his sermon "For the Troubled" (on Ps 88:7) Spurgeon notes that Heman not only cries out to the Lord, "he traces all his adversity to the Lord his God. It is God's wrath, they are God's waves that afflict him, and God makes them afflict him." Spurgeon speaks of secondary causes and "the more immediate agent of our grief." Yet, he urges the believer to remember that "all that thou art suffering of any sort, or kind, comes to thee from the divine hand." Thus, the call to "cast your burden on the Lord" is something that is easier to do "when you see that the burden came originally from God."[27]

Confidence in God's sovereignty and power, however, was no deterrent to earnest prayer. In fact, in addition to the cries and pleas of the psalmists, Spurgeon often noted their earnest engagement with God in prayer. In the introduction to his sermon on Psalm 39:12 Spurgeon observes, "If you read the whole verse, you will see that David used these words as an argument in prayer." This pattern is also to be emulated by the grieving believer. "It is a grand thing to be able to argue with God in prayer . . . it is by well-grounded arguments that we must wrestle with him until we prevail. Expectancy puts in the wedge, but it is solid argument that drives it home. When we want to obtain any mercy from the Lord, we must support our plea by reasons drawn from his nature, his promises, and the experiences of his children as recorded in his Word." After noting the examples of Luther and the apostle

---

has travelled. He mentions his sins, his sorrows, his hopes (if he had any), his fears, his woes, and so on." Then Spurgeon urges, lay "your case before the Lord. Go to your chamber, and shut to your door, and tell the Lord all about yourself. Do you lack words? Well then, use no words."

25. Spurgeon, *MTP*, vol. 41, 469–71 ("Heman's Sorrowful Psalm"; preached September 25, 1887).

26. See Morden, "Suffering," 311, 313. See also, Harper, "Lament and the Sovereignty of God" (chapter 6 in this volume).

27. Spurgeon, *MTP*, vol. 19 (1873), 13–24 ("For the Troubled"; preached January 12, 1873). Spurgeon also explains that God's "judicial anger" and punishment for sin have been laid upon Christ in the believer's place (18).

Paul, Spurgeon then adds, "Let it be so with you also, beloved; besiege the throne of grace with the most powerful arguments you can find in the heavenly armoury ... "[28] Similarly, after noting how the psalmist pleads with God in Psalm 88, Spurgeon concludes his exposition of the psalm by commending the psalm as an example of persevering prayer. The psalmist is "a pattern to us" in continuing to pray "even when he did not seem to be heard."[29]

Spurgeon therefore often encouraged his congregation to see the benefit of lament psalms in providing a pattern to follow in the expression of their grief. He encouraged them to follow this pattern and take their sorrows to their sovereign Lord and Savior.

Spurgeon Reassured His Congregation That Such Laments Are the Experience of True Believers

In addition to regularly encouraging believers to follow the pattern of the psalmists in pouring out their griefs to the Lord, Spurgeon regularly reassures his congregation that such psalms show that these sorrows and trials are no sign of their inferior status. Along with numerous references to David as a type of Jesus as "the man of sorrows, and acquainted with grief,"[30] Spurgeon regularly refers to the examples of Luther, Bunyan's *Pilgrim's Progress*, and his own personal weakness to reassure his congregation that the cries of these lament psalms are common in the lives of Christians. While recognizing that there are more than laments in the Psalter, and that there are more emotions than sorrow in the Christian life, Spurgeon encouraged his congregation to see that one significant benefit of the lament psalms is that they help to assure the sorrowing and burdened believer that "somebody else has been just where you are."[31]

In his sermon on Psalm 69:14 Spurgeon draws a deliberate link between the psalmist and the experiences of believers to reassure his congregation.

28. Spurgeon, *MTP*, vol. 57, 37 ("Strangers and Sojourners"; preached November 5, 1863).

29. Spurgeon, *MTP*, vol. 41, 480.

30. Spurgeon, *MTP*, vol. 48, 249 (on Ps 120:5). See, e.g., "Tears have ever had great prevalence with God. Christ used these sacred weapons when, 'with strong crying and tears,' he prayed to his Father in Gethsemane." Spurgeon, *MTP*, vol. 57, 48 (exposition of Ps 39:10–12). Likewise in his introduction to the exposition of Psalm 39 as a "sorrowful Psalm," Spurgeon calls David "the type of Christ, in whose great heart the joys and sorrows of humanity met to the full." Spurgeon, *MTP*, vol. 40, 572. Cf. also Morden, "Suffering," 313–14.

31. Spurgeon, *MTP*, vol. 41, 478 (introduction to the exposition of Psalm 88).

"True believers, beloved, are sometimes in deep mire, and in fear of being swallowed up." Spurgeon then notes, "This was the state and condition of the Psalmist when he wrote this psalm." This then becomes the basis for his outline of this sermon.[32] Later in this same sermon Spurgeon regularly notes his own struggles with doubts and temptations, and that these are in fact the regular experience of ministers as well.

> If I were only to reveal my own struggles and conflicts with Satan, I might stagger some of you; but this I know, that no Christian minister will ever be able to enter into the trials and experiences of God's people, unless he has stood foot to foot with the arch fiend, and wrestled with the prince of hell. Martin Luther was right when he said that temptation and adversity were the two best books in his library.[33]

Similarly, in his sermon, "Consolation for the Despairing" (on Ps 31:22), Spurgeon reassures his congregation that despair is not the lot of just some disobedient or unbelieving Christians:

> Yet this bitter sorrow has been endured by not a few of the best of men. If it could be said that only those Christians who walk at a distance from Christ, or those who are inconsistent in life, or those who are but little in prayer, have felt in this way, then, indeed, there would be cause for the gravest disquietude; but it is a matter of fact that some of the choicest spirits among the Lord's elect have passed through the Valley of Humiliation, and even sojourned there by the month together. Saints who are now among the brightest in heaven, have yet in their day sat weeping at the gates of despair, and asked for the crumbs which the dogs eat under the master's table. Read the life of Martin Luther . . . Do not condemn yourself, my dear sister, do not cast yourself

---

32. E.g., "*first, that the true believer may be in the mire, and very near sinking; secondly, that the true believer may be in such a condition that God alone can deliver him;* and thirdly, that in whatever condition the believer may be, *prayer is evermore his safe refuge.*" Spurgeon, *MTP*, vol. 11, 289–90 ("The Believer Sinking in the Mire"). Emphasis original.

33. Ibid., 293. See also the reference to this saying of Luther's in the sermon "For the Troubled" (on Ps 88:7), Spurgeon, *MTP*, vol. 19, 22. See also Spurgeon, *MTP*, vol. 42, 548 ("Shame Leading to Salvation," on Ps 83:16; preached October 31, 1886) where Spurgeon speaks movingly of how many of his close friends have died suddenly, and his exposition of Psalm 120 (Spurgeon, *MTP*, vol. 58, 480) where Spurgeon identifies with the distress and helplessness of being slandered, and acknowledges that cries to God are the only source of strength.

away, my dear brother, because your faith endures many conflicts, and your spirits sink very low.[34]

Spurgeon shows his congregation that these sorrowful psalms are beneficial in large part because they reassure the grieving believer that they are not alone, nor are their sorrows a sign of inferior status. Rather, they provide reassurance that even "the best child of God may be the greatest sufferer."[35]

Spurgeon Encouraged the Use of Lament Psalms in Congregational Worship

Spurgeon recognized of course that there are many joyful psalms and reasons to sing for joy. In keeping with Spurgeon's repeated explanations of the benefits of lament psalms and reasons for preaching on the lament psalms, however, it is not surprising that Spurgeon also recognized the value of lament psalms in congregational singing as part of the congregation's worship. Thus, when he introduces his sermon, "For the Troubled," Spurgeon directs his congregation to notice that from this passage "we learn that sons of God may be brought so low as to write and sing psalms which are sorrowful throughout, and have no fitting accompaniment but sighs and groans . . . their songs are generally like those of David, which if they begin in the dust mount into the clear heavens before long; but sometimes, I say, saints are forced to sing such dolorous ditties that from beginning to end there is not one note of joy."[36]

Similarly, when introducing his sermon "Consolation for the Despairing" (on Ps 31:22) he argues that he has scriptural warrant for speaking to a congregation that is mostly filled with "joyous hearts" on a psalm that is largely sorrowful because it was intended for public worship. The reason for this is because this psalm, "as do several others which are even more full of grief," bears the inscription, "To the chief Musician." Spurgeon concludes: "If, therefore, griefs which to the full could only be known by a few, were

---

34. Spurgeon, *MTP*, vol. 19, 688 ("Consolation for the Despairing"; preached December 7, 1873).

35. Ibid. 14 ("For the Troubled"; preached January 12, 1873). Similarly, this sorrowful psalm teaches that "the best of God's servants may be brought into the very lowest estate" (13). It is also true that at times Spurgeon's application comes across as harsh. In his sermon "A Call to the Depressed" it appears that he changes tone from sharp critique to tender understanding in the last quarter of the sermon. See Eswine, *Spurgeon's Sorrows*, 52–53.

36. Ibid. ("For the Troubled").

nevertheless to be made the subject of public psalmody, I am quite sure they ought not to be passed over in public ministry."[37]

Although Spurgeon's preaching ministry is widely known, it is less commonly known that he took a special interest in music and even composed some hymns.[38] Spurgeon compiled the hymnal *Our Own Hymn-Book* for his own congregation (combining Isaac Watts's *Psalms and Hymns* and John Rippon's *Selection of Hymns*). This in itself is evidence of Spurgeon's interest in singing all the psalms, including lament psalms. The first part of the hymnal (titled "The Spirit of the Psalms")[39] consisted of psalms or paraphrases of all one hundred and fifty psalms along with seventy alternate versions, making a total of two hundred and twenty psalms to sing.[40] Spurgeon's personal interest in singing psalms is further evidenced in that he authored fourteen of these psalms and slightly edited another one (on Psalm 120).[41] Interestingly, of these fifteen psalms, eight of them are (what we label today as) lament psalms.[42]

The psalms and hymns that were sung from the hymnal are often listed at the end of each sermon or exposition in *The Metropolitan Tabernacle Pulpit Sermons*. Sometimes Spurgeon's own psalm composition that is based on the lament psalm that he preached is also sung. Thus, on the occasion of the sermon ("Earth's Vanities and Heaven's Verities") and exposition on Psalm 39, the congregation sung Spurgeon's hymn on that psalm. The following are two of the verses:

> 3 What is there here that I should wait,
> My hope's in Thee alone;
> When wilt Thou open glory's gate
> And call me to Thy throne?
>
> 4 A stranger in this land am I,
> A sojourner with Thee;
> Oh be not silent at my cry,
> But show Thyself to me.

37. Spurgeon, *MTP*, vol. 19, 686.
38. See Music, "Hymnody," 174–81; Nettles, *Living by Revealed Truth*, 260–67.
39. The second part was simply called "Hymns."
40. Music, "Hymnody," 176. A similar emphasis on the psalms is found in the successor to this hymnal used at the Metropolitan Tabernacle today (*Psalms and Hymns of Reformed Worship*; see the preface by Peter Masters).
41. Spurgeon wrote a further ten hymns and edited four other hymns.
42. Although the hymnal was adopted by other Baptist churches of the time and remained in use at the Metropolitan Tabernacle long after his death, Spurgeon's own compositions did not become popular.

Likewise, when the sermon "Consolation for the Despairing" was preached (see Spurgeon's reference to the inscription of this psalm above), one of the hymns sung was Spurgeon's on Psalm 70. Three of the four verses of that composition are as follows:

> 1 Make haste, O God, my soul to bless!
> My help and my deliv'rer Thou;
> Make haste, for I'm in deep distress,
> My case is urgent; help me now.

> 3 Make haste, for I am poor and low;
> And Satan mocks my prayers and tears;
> O God, in mercy be not slow,
> But snatch me from my horrid fears.

> 4 Make haste, O God, and hear my cries;
> Then with the souls who seek Thy face,
> And those who Thy salvation prize,
> I'll magnify Thy matchless grace.

A similar acknowledgment of sorrow and distress is seen in Spurgeon's adaptation (from the Scotch Psalter of 1641) of Psalm 120.[43]

> 3 My soul distracted mourns and pines
> To reach that peaceful shore,
> Where all the weary are at rest,
> And troublers vex no more.

> 5 But as for me my song shall rise
> Before Jehovah's throne,
> For He has seen my deep distress,
> And hearken'd to my groan.

Although other examples could be given, these verses show many of the themes highlighted in Spurgeon's sermons and expositions of lament psalms. In this way, Spurgeon not only spoke about the benefits of lament psalms and encouraged grieving believers similarly to express their sorrows to the Lord, he led the congregation in following the instructions of the psalmists to express these laments corporately in song.

---

43. See above on Spurgeon's exposition and sermon "The Sojourn in Mesech."

Conclusion

In seeking to recover lament psalms in church life today we have in Charles Spurgeon a model of how this may be done. Although faltering in places himself, he nevertheless encouraged his congregation to see the benefits of these psalms. As part of his ministry of shepherding the flock he anticipated potential objections to sorrowful themes, so he oriented his congregation to the benefits of applying these psalms to the sorrowful in their midst and in anticipation of their own seasons of grief. Spurgeon also helped his congregation to see the benefit of these psalms in teaching them how to express their sorrow and in providing them with a model for taking their cries and pleadings to the sovereign Lord as the only One who can help. Spurgeon also drew attention to the benefit of lament psalms by reassuring sorrowful believers from these psalms that they are not alone. Such distresses are not the only experience of believers; but all true believers do experience them in various ways. They anticipated Christ's own suffering, and such sorrows are also the experience of all who follow him. Finally, since these are songs directed to musicians, they are meant for public worship. This is something Spurgeon encouraged with the use of psalms in congregational singing and his own compositions based on lament psalms. In this, the congregation immediately applied the encouragements of the sermon and not only sang songs of joy, but also corporately took their cries and pleadings to the sovereign Lord and Savior on the basis of his promises in his word.

Bibliography

Drummond, Lewis. *Spurgeon: Prince of Preachers*. Grand Rapids: Kregel, 1992.
Eswine, Zack. *Spurgeon's Sorrows: Realistic Hope for Those Who Suffer from Depression*. Fearn, Ross-Shire: Christian Focus, 2014.
Masters, Peter, ed. *Psalms and Hymns of Reformed Worship*. London: The Wakeman Trust, 1991.
Morden, Peter J. "C. H. Spurgeon and Suffering," *Evangelical Review of Theology* 35 (2011) 306–25.
Music, David W. "C. H. Spurgeon and Hymnody," *Foundations* 22 (1979) 174–81.
Nettles, Tom. *Living by Revealed Truth: The Life and Pastoral Theology of Charles Haddon Spurgeon*. Fearn, Ross-Shire: Mentor, 2013.
Skoglund, Elizabeth R. *Bright Days, Dark Nights: With Charles Spurgeon in Triumph over Emotional Pain*. Grand Rapids: Baker, 2000 [reprint Wipf & Stock, 2014].
Spurgeon, Charles H., ed. *Our Own Hymn-Book*. London: Passmore & Alabaster, 1866.
———. *The Metropolitan Tabernacle Pulpit Sermons*. London: Passmore & Alabaster, 1861–1917 (abbreviated *MTP*).
———. *The Treasury of David*. London: Marshall Brothers, n. d.

Part II

The Theology of Lament

4

Lament as Divine Discourse
God's Voice in Our Cry

Kit Barker

Finding one's voice in the psalms has a long and distinguished history. Yet we, as modern readers, often find their words confusing, confronting, and bearing little resemblance to life in the twenty-first century. While their words of passion, anguish, and joy resonate with the full spectrum of human experience, the raw confidence of lament that challenges God's "inactivity" or calls for the destruction of an enemy are words we do not readily adopt either in our gatherings or in our solitary moments.[1] Yet, these words are offered to God's people for precisely that purpose. We are invited to pray them in similar situations. To ignore these words and abandon this practice creates a fracture in our relationship with God in moments when it is most critical. To neglect this practice in our corporate worship fails to model a robust faith to those who are suffering and fails to stand with them in their pain. An important step in recovering this practice is to understand how the psalms function not only as human words to God, but as divine discourse, God's words to us. I am convinced that if we gain an appreciation of how

---

1. Many of the psalms of lament employ imprecation where the psalmist calls for divine judgment upon his enemy. I briefly address this issue in chapter 7 of this volume. For a fuller discussion of whether this language should be appropriated by God's people today, see Barker, "Psalms of the Powerless."

God speaks through these prayers, then many of our barriers to appropriating lament will be removed.

It has long been recognized that the psalms occupy a unique place in Christian Scripture. For those who believe that the Scriptures are the word of God, the psalms offer a curious conundrum. Dietrich Bonhoeffer famously asked, "The Holy Scripture is the Word of God to us. But prayers are the words of men. How do prayers then get into the Bible? . . . are these prayers to God also God's own word?"[2] The psalms are not like other parts of Scripture. When the author of Leviticus or the apostle Peter call readers to "Be holy," it is easy to see that God is also calling us to "Be holy." However, when it comes to psalms in general, and lament psalms in particular, this connection between what the human author is doing and what God is doing with these words is not as clear. When the psalmist cries, "How long, O Lord? Will you forget me forever? How long will you hide your face from me?" (Ps 13:1–2),[3] is God asking the same question? Is he echoing the cry of complaint? Does God need salvation from his enemies? Alternatively, is it possible that the way in which the psalms function as divine discourse requires greater nuance? Is it more complicated than simply acknowledging a direct correspondence between what the human author is doing with the psalm and what God is doing with the same psalm? I believe it is. My aim in this chapter is to clarify the major ways that God has spoken and continues to speak through these ancient prayers. In doing so, my hope is that we will gain a renewed appreciation of this gift of lament and accept the invitation to find our words in theirs.

What the Psalmist Is Doing with Lament

Speech Act Theory

In order to unpack what God is doing with the lament psalms, it is first of all necessary to understand what the human author was doing with them. At first glance, what the psalmists were doing with lament may seem obvious. The psalmists were crying out to God for him to act on their behalf, to deliver them from their enemies, and to not neglect them (Ps 13:1–2). These are common cries throughout the psalms of lament. Yet, I think the human authors are *doing far more* with lament than simply making a desperate cry to God, and it is here that the answer to our question resides. What else are the psalmists doing with the psalms?

---

2. Bonhoeffer, *Psalms*, 13–15.
3. All biblical quotations are taken from the NIV unless otherwise stated.

To aid us in this discussion I am going to introduce some terminology from communication theory, in particular, from speech act theory. The benefit of speech act theory is its ability to describe in detail what we do when we communicate and how we generate meaning with the words, sentences, and texts that we write. This will help us discover the rich communication of the psalms by expanding our appreciation of what the authors are doing with them.

In speech act terms, a communicative event can consist of a *locution*, *illocution*, and *perlocution*. The locution is the words that are uttered or written, the illocution is what the author or speaker is doing with those words, and the perlocution is the affect that this produces in the audience. The meaning of a text is located in the illocution (i.e., what the author was doing with the words, sentences, and text he or she produced).[4]

An illustration may help to clarify how this works. Suppose I say to my children, "It's cold outside." The locution is simple. It's a sensible sentence and one commonly uttered. What the utterance *means*, however, is not so simple. If my daughter had asked me, "What's the weather like today?" then the sentence is nothing more than a simple *assertion*. However, imagine my eldest son is about to leave for school wearing only a shirt and pants when the temperature outside is eight degrees Celsius. My statement, "It's cold outside," is not merely, or even primarily, an assertion. Rather, it's a *request* that he put on something warmer before he leaves. Alternatively, if my youngest son had just asked me to have a water fight on the lawn, my locution, "It's cold outside," is at the very least a *protest* and more likely a *rejection* of his kind request. Context creates meaning. Thus, the words we say and the sentences we create can *mean* innumerable things because we can *do* innumerable things with them in different contexts. We have already seen this in the example of Psalm 13 above. When the psalmist questions God asking, "Will you forget me forever?" he is not suggesting that God has actually forgotten him or that God is unaware of his plight. Rather, this is a common way for the psalmist to ask God why he is taking so long to act and save him from this situation. In fact, the question is really functioning as a challenge to God: "Why are you letting this happen to me?" By locating meaning in the illocution, speech act theory demonstrates the need for us to ask *what an author was doing* with the words, sentences, and text he has written.

---

4. There are, of course, authors who object to meaning being located in the illocution and would prefer the meaning of a text to include the perlocution, the response of the audience. For a defense of meaning as located in the illocution, see Wolterstorff, *Divine Discourse*; Vanhoozer, *First Theology*; Barker, "Divine Illocutions in Psalm 137."

Moreover, *authors almost always do more than one thing* when they communicate and it is the sum of these actions (illocutions) that constitutes the meaning of a text.[5] Furthermore, while the meaning of the locution, "It's cold outside," is the sum of the illocutions performed by it, some illocutions will be primary (e.g., the request: "Put on something warmer"), and some will be secondary or attendant (e.g., the assertion: "It's cold outside"). Interpretations of texts that account for this richness of meaning are said to provide a "thick" description (as opposed to one that is "thin" and reductionistic).[6] Providing an adequately thick description of a text is, therefore, necessary for understanding its meaning. Furthermore, identifying the range of illocutions present in a text will also aid us in understanding how a text functions as divine discourse.

Levels of Meaning

We have noted that texts are complex and can contain multiple illocutions within a given sentence or paragraph, yet this is not the full extent of their complexity. Texts can also perform illocutions at higher literary levels such as that of the chapter or book as a whole. Allow me to illustrate from the book of 1 Samuel. In 1 Samuel 31, the Philistine army descends upon Israel prompting Saul to commit suicide on Mount Gilboa. Subsequently, the Philistines behead Saul, strip him of his armor, and hang his body in Beth Shan. At the level of the chapter, the author is making historical assertions about these events: what happened when, who did this, who said what, etc. In its immediate context the story is a sad picture of the unnecessary death of Saul and particularly that of Jonathan, his son. In the context of the immediate chapters it is placed in contrast to David's great feats of salvation and military success, consequently highlighting the change of kingship in the rise of David and the fall of Saul. At the level of the book, Saul is compared to others who have similarly fallen over and lost their heads (i.e., Dagon and Goliath), thus casting Saul as one of the enemies of God (see 1 Sam 28:16). Furthermore, when seen in light of Hannah's song in chapter 2, the death of Saul is a reflection of the so called "reversal" theme in Samuel which anticipates that the arrogant will be brought low by Yahweh and that kingship will be a mechanism of blessing and judgment (1 Sam 2:1–10; 8:10–18). Therefore, a "thick" description of 1 Samuel 31 will not only attend to the illocutions of chapter 31 in isolation, but will also seek to understand what the author is doing with this chapter in the context of the entire book.

5. Vanhoozer, *First Theology*, 178.
6. Ibid., 179.

What does this have to do with psalms of lament? In the past, the Psalter has been treated as a collection of individual prayers and poems with little or no connection to one another. In recent years, however, Psalms scholarship has recognized that the intentional shaping of the Psalter contributes to its overall message. While the exact nature of this shaping and its intended message continue to be debated, it is now widely held that each psalm cannot be interpreted in isolation.[7] They must, at the very least, be seen in the context of the whole and may take on additional meaning in light of their particular placement within the five Books of the Psalter. Just as 1 Samuel 31 is best interpreted in light of the rest of Samuel, in order to fully appreciate what the author was doing with a psalm, we need to understand how individual psalms function as part of the Psalter. While this discussion will be advanced in following chapters, a summary of the primary illocutions of the Psalter (the main actions that the authors are performing through the book as a whole) will help us to see not only what the human author is doing with lament but also how we might construe lament as divine discourse.

The Primary Illocutions of the Psalter

The introduction to a book should aid a reader in understanding what to expect from its contents and how to read it. This is true of the Psalter. In recent years, Psalms 1 and 2 have been recognized as its introduction.[8] In these opening psalms we encounter the primary illocutions of the Psalter, which alert us to its contents and provide us with a reading strategy.[9] Firstly, Psalms 1 and 2 present the reader with a number of *declarations*: the contrasting destinies of the wicked and the righteous, the sovereignty of Yahweh, Yahweh's king as his representative and the only place of refuge, and meditation on Yahweh's instruction (torah) as the defining quality of the righteous. However, Psalms 1 and 2 are more than a series of declarations; they are examples of wisdom psalms, and as such they *invite* the reader to a life of wisdom, a life of righteousness marked by loyalty to Yahweh and his king.

---

7. For further discussion, see Wu, "The Role of Lament in the Shape of the Psalter," and Harper, "Silence of the Lambs" (chapters 10 and 11 in this volume).

8. Childs, *Introduction to the Old Testament as Scripture*; Futato, *Interpreting the Psalms*; Miller, *Interpreting the Psalms*.

9. While the introduction of Psalms 1 and 2 performs primary illocutions, there are other ways that the Psalter performs primary illocutions that I will not have time to address in this chapter. For a detailed discussion, see Barker, *Imprecation as Divine Discourse*.

The primary illocutions and corresponding reading strategy formed by Psalms 1 and 2 are supported by the Psalter's other literary features, in particular, the division of the Psalter into five Books and the climactic declaration in Book IV that "Yahweh reigns." I have commented elsewhere on these features:

> The shaping of the Psalter into five books, the repeated presence of *tôrâ* psalms and the introduction provided by Psalms 1 and 2 are evidence that the Psalter is to be read as divine instruction.
>
> Psalm 1, with its invitation to blessing and life through a meditation on *tôrâ*, is implicitly an invitation to mediate on the contents of the Psalter. It is here that blessing will be found through an engagement with God and his instruction ... Through this connection to Psalm 2, the invitation to righteousness and blessing in Psalm 1 becomes an invitation to be loyal to the king and an invitation to take refuge in him.
>
> Fundamentally, as mentioned above, the Psalter *invites*. It is an invitation to meditation, to blessing, to life, to submission to Yahweh and his king, and to refuge. The fact that most of the Psalter is then comprised of prayers and songs that are directed to Yahweh indicates that it *invites imitation*. It *offers* these responses as appropriate, even "righteous" (Ps 1:5–6), responses to readers who find themselves in similar situations.[10]

The *invitation to imitate* the psalms is directly connected to the *declaration that Yahweh reigns*.[11] The sovereign rule of Yahweh over all peoples and powers not only establishes the basis and necessity of praise, but it also provides the foundation for lament. Consequently, the psalms of lament are not an embarrassment, nor are they the response of a sub-Christian spirituality. Lament is not merely allowed or tolerated by the Psalter. Lament is fundamentally affirmed. These psalms are offered to God's people as the right way to respond to their pain and suffering and to the pain and suffering of others. Silence (i.e., the absence of prayer) is never anticipated or affirmed. When we vocalize our cry, our complaint, and our frustration to God we recognize God for who he is. He is the sovereign Lord who reigns over all. He "watches over the way of the righteous" (Ps 1:6) and "searches" (Ps 139:1) the hearts of men and women. Thus, the Psalter offers these words to God's people as righteous words, words that reflect a deep and active faith, a faith that does not turn its back on God even when it feels like God has turned his back on us (Ps 13:1).

---

10. Barker, "Psalms of the Powerless," 213–14.
11. For additional discussion in support of this thesis, see Mays, *The Lord Reigns*.

The heights of praise and depths of lament and every expression in between are presented as righteous responses to the reign of Yahweh. He is sovereign. He has promised to protect and deliver his people, to vindicate their faith, and to dwell among them forever. The realization of these promises rightly results in the praise of his people and the absence of such realization prompts the desperate cry of lament. Both are responses of deep faith, one acknowledging the gracious gifts of Yahweh, and the other acknowledging that he alone is the King who can change the situation and bring deliverance. Yahweh alone is responsible for what happens in his kingdom. Yahweh alone can save. Yahweh alone must save. The voice of praise and the cry of lament are evidence that the psalmist has not abandoned God in his delight or in his despair. This is a faith that continues to commune with God in every situation. Praise and lament are the antithesis to self-reliance and idolatry. "Day and night" (Ps 88:1) the prayers of the psalmist come before God, because he is sure that God not only hears him, but he delights in him, and will prove faithful to all that he has promised.

What God Is Doing with Our Lament

Clarifying the Conundrum

The precise way in which the psalms function as God's word, as divine discourse, poses a unique challenge. Unlike other parts of Scripture where the illocutions of the human author can be sensibly understood as God's own illocutions (e.g., the *command* to "Be holy" and the *declaration* that "Jesus is Lord" can both be understood as God's own speech acts), the psalms contain speech acts that are not so sensibly applied to God. For example, the psalmist's *declaration*, "I know my iniquity," and his corresponding *request* to God to "cleanse me from all my sin" (Ps 51:2–3) are difficult to attribute to God, to say the very least.

Certainly, illocutions within the psalms are rightly applied to Jesus as the New Testament authors demonstrate—for example, the opening cry of Psalm 22, "My God, my God, why have you forsaken me?" and perhaps much of the remaining content of Psalm 22 as well. However, this clearly does not account for a majority of the psalms, nor does it exhaust the way in which the psalms can function as divine discourse.[12] In fact, suggesting that the psalms function as divine discourse because Jesus speaks them and he is divine largely misses the point.[13] It is true that if they are the words of Jesus,

---

12. See my discussion in chapter 7 of this volume.
13. Contra Waltke, "Canonical Process Approach," 13–16.

then they are "divine illocutions"; however, this exegetical "back flip" to attempt to solve our conundrum does little justice to what we mean when we declare Scripture to be the word of God. Scripture is not simply words that Jesus spoke or words that God speaks, though it is at least that. Scripture is fundamentally the word that God speaks to all his people. So while it is certainly true that some of the psalms can rightly be attributed to Jesus, this does not explain how they function as Scripture. In order for us to affirm the psalms—and the lament psalms in particular—as divine discourse, we need to clarify how they function as God's speech acts directed to his people. This does not discount the fact that they may also be the words of Jesus directed to his Father, but it acknowledges that they must be more than that.

This entire discussion is, of course, predicated on the belief that Scripture is the word of God. God in his wisdom decided that these texts, including these psalms of lament, should constitute his word to his world, both then and now. The apostle Paul notes not only that "all Scripture is God breathed" (2 Tim 3:16), but that "everything that was written in the past was written to teach us so that through endurance and the encouragement of Scripture [the Old Testament] we might have hope" (Rom 15:4).[14] Thus, we return to the question at hand: How do these ancient laments function as Scripture? Where is God's voice in their cry?

Proposing a Solution

I believe the solution to this question is found in the complexity of speech acts in play within a psalm, or, as described earlier, in a "thick" description of the psalm. Most helpful for resolving our conundrum is the recognition that a text contains illocutions at multiple levels: the level of the sentence or phrase, the level of the pericope, and also at the level of the text as a whole. Elsewhere, I have suggested, "When we understand that the psalms provided patterns of prayer, a fuller range of illocutions is uncovered. The meaning of the Psalm must be understood in terms of its total communicative act."[15]

As I have noted, there are times when it makes no sense to attribute particular illocutions within the psalm directly to God. However, the psalm can still be counted as divine discourse by recognizing that God *does things with it* at higher levels. Thus, I suggest that it is possible (and necessary for understanding the psalms as divine discourse) to attribute to God those illocutions that occur at the level of the psalm and the Psalter.

---

14. In Romans 15:4, Paul refers to the lament of Psalm 69.
15. Barker, *Divine Illocutions*, 10.

Allow me to return to Psalm 13 to clarify how I understand psalms of lament to function as divine discourse. The psalmist opens with the bold cry, "How long, O Lord?" He expresses his frustration that God has seemingly ignored his plight so that those who wish to harm him are prevailing. The desperation of the psalmist is seen in the repeated cry in v. 3, "Look on me and answer, O Lord my God," where the addition of "my God" adds weight to his complaint. His current experience is that "his God" is not answering him, and that his life is in danger. However, the final words of the psalm express confidence in God's salvation and the intent to praise God for it.

It is clear that God cannot be performing the illocutions that the psalmist is performing at this level in the text. God is not questioning his own "forgetfulness." God is not charging himself with turning his face away; neither is God expressing confidence in his own promise of salvation. At these lower levels, most of what the psalmist is doing cannot be sensibly attributed to God. However, as we have noted, focusing solely on illocutions within the psalm does not produce an adequate description of its meaning. In order to provide a "thick" description of this psalm's meaning we need to appreciate how its inclusion in the Psalter provides further illocutions at higher levels. As I discussed above, these higher-level illocutions are formed, in part, by the introduction of Psalms 1 and 2, which cast the Psalter as a collection of righteous responses to varying circumstances. Therefore, at this higher level, there are a number of primary illocutions that become common (or generic) to the psalms contained within in it.

A thick description of Psalm 13 will therefore pursue levels of meaning both within the psalm *and* at the level of the Psalter. As we have noted, it is not sensible to attribute to God the illocutions of the psalmist within Psalm 13.[16] However, Psalm 13 can be understood as divine discourse by recognizing and identifying illocutions that occur at the level of the psalm as a whole. In the context of the Psalter, Psalm 13 is *offered* to readers as a righteous response to situations of continued threat and oppression. The ambiguity of the psalm allows for and anticipates a variety of future applications as the enemies are left unnamed and the exact nature of the situation remains unknown. Thus, a common or "generic" illocution of Psalm 13, and many other psalms, is an *invitation* to "pray like this" in similar situations. More specific to this psalm is the *reminder* that even though God appears to have ignored the psalmist, God hears his cry and will bring salvation. Addition-

16. In some cases it might be sensible and warranted to acknowledge God's appropriation of illocutions at this level. This is more common in the wisdom psalms (e.g., "the way of the wicked will perish," Ps 1:6) and more obviously when God is recorded as speaking in the first person within the psalm ("I have installed my King in Zion," or perhaps more ambiguously, "Kiss the Son," Ps 2:6, 12).

ally, the *declaration* of God's *ḥesed* ("steadfast love") and the expectation of rejoicing in his salvation are intended to *create hope*. Thus, Psalm 13 is God's word to his people as God appropriates the illocutions of the psalm at this "higher" level of the text. While God does not appropriate every illocution within the psalm, he *affirms* the illocutions of the psalmist at these lower levels and *declares* them to be righteous. At the higher level, God *invites* readers to respond in similar fashion, *reminding* them that he does in fact hear them; he is "steadfast in love" and he will bring about their salvation.

There is one further set of illocutions, occurring at the level of the psalm as a whole, that I believe God appropriates and which is critical to our understanding of the function of lament. The superscription to Psalm 13, and to many other psalms, includes the direction "For the choirmaster."[17] While Psalm 13 is an example of an individual lament, its inclusion in the Psalter means that it is not only offered to individual readers but to the community as whole. This reflects the intention that it be used in communal worship as a response to the sufferings of individuals with it. By collectively voicing Psalm 13, the community *affirms* these words as a righteous response, *acknowledges* the need to cry out to God for help, *stands* with those among them who are suffering, and *cries out* with them and for them when perhaps they do not have the strength to cry out for themselves. The corporate expression of lament thus *gives license* to its private expression, *liberating* this voice for those who are suffering. It is here that the psalms of lament also function as divine discourse. God speaks through these psalms to his people, *calling upon them to cry out to him with those who have cause to cry*.

Conclusion

The psalms function as divine discourse in unique ways. While God often does not appropriate the illocutions of the psalmist at levels within a psalm, he does appropriate those at the level of the whole psalm and at the level of the Psalter. Firstly, with respect to illocutions working within a psalm, God *affirms* the stance of the psalmist. Secondly, at the level of the psalm and Psalter, God *offers* the psalms as righteous responses to varying situations.

Lament is, therefore, not an embarrassment in the lives of God's people but a profound act of faith and righteousness. Lament recognizes that Yahweh reigns and no one else. He is the one to whom prayers should rise. He is the only one who has the power to save. He is the one ultimately responsible for what happens in his kingdom. Lament does not represent a

---

17. Psalm 13:1 in the MT.

weak or failing faith; rather, it demonstrates a commitment to God when God himself appears to be absent.

God speaks in our cry. Strangely, the cry of the psalmist at God's silence becomes God's own voice to his people *declaring* that he hears their cry. God *offers* these words to his people as righteous responses to their sufferings and as righteous responses to the suffering of those among them. Our collective voicing of these psalms not only imitates God's affirmation of lament, but is also an act of corporate obedience. In the psalms of lament God *calls* his people *to stand* with those who suffer, *to cry out* with them, and *to remember* that he alone is worthy of their praise and their lament.

Bibliography

Barker, Kit. "Divine Illocutions in Psalm 137: A Critique of Nicholas Wolterstorff's 'Second Hermeneutic.'" *Tyndale Bulletin* 60 (2009) 1–14.
———. *Imprecation as Divine Discourse: Speech Act Theory, Dual Authorship, and Theological Interpretation*. JTISup 16. Winona Lake: Eisenbrauns, 2016.
———. "Psalms of the Powerless." In *Stirred by a Noble Theme: The Book of Psalms in the Life of the Church*, edited by Andrew G. Shead, 205–29. Nottingham: Apollos, 2013.
Bonhoeffer, Dietrich. *Psalms: The Prayer Book of the Bible*. Minneapolis: Augsburg, 1970.
Childs, Brevard. S. *Introduction to the Old Testament as Scripture*. Philadelphia: Fortress, 1979.
Futato, Mark D., and David. M. Howard. *Interpreting the Psalms: An Exegetical Handbook*. Grand Rapids: Kregel, 2007.
Mays, James. L. *The Lord Reigns: A Theological Handbook to the Psalms*. Louisville: Westminster John Knox, 1994.
Miller, Patrick. D. *Interpreting the Psalms*. Philadelphia: Fortress, 1986.
Vanhoozer, Kevin. J. *First Theology: God, Scripture & Hermeneutics*. Downers Grove: IVP, 2002.
Waltke, Bruce K. "Canonical Process Approach to the Psalms." In *Tradition and Testament: Essays in Honor of Charles Lee Feinberg*, edited by Charles L. Feinberg, John S. Feinberg, and Paul D. Feinberg, 5–15. Chicago: Moody, 1981.
Wolterstorff, N. *Divine Discourse: Philosophical Reflections on the Claim That God Speaks*. Cambridge: Cambridge University Press, 1995.

5

"Why O Lord?"

Lament as a Window to the Human Experience of Distress

DAVID J. COHEN

WITHIN THE LITURGICAL TRADITIONS of the church, general use of the psalms has been consistent from ancient times up to today. However, in the evangelical setting, which is my context, psalms are used sparingly and selectively in both corporate worship and personal devotion. Sadly, in the evangelical setting the situation is even more acute when one considers the use of lament psalms. Of course, the Psalter is recognized as the hymnbook of Second Temple Judaism. But, subsequently, it was also adopted for use by the early church, which begs questions about the place of psalms generally, and lament psalms more specifically, within contemporary church life. The latter, lament psalms, is the focus of the following exploration.

In recent decades, fresh appraisals of lament psalms have emerged with a growing recognition of their importance in both corporate worship and personal devotion. These appraisals have arisen in part because lament psalms have fallen into disuse in some settings and are misunderstood in others. Most of these explorations naturally lead to a key question, "What then ought we to do with these psalms?" This question is, by nature, inherently both theological and pastoral, and *assumes* that we ought to use them. In distinguishing theological and pastoral here I am in no way suggesting that the term *theological* implies something theoretical while *pastoral* implies something practical. Rather, the distinction reminds us that thinking theologically about an issue, in this case the use of lament psalms, is always inextricably linked to pastoral praxis involving their use. The two perspectives rightly belong together, informing each other interdependently.

For some, the validity of using lament psalms, assumed in my question above, may seem justified: such psalms ought to be used for personal devotion because they are beneficial.[1] However, for others, especially those who are less familiar with lament psalms, there may be doubts for various reasons. In order to explore the potential benefits of using lament psalms, I will address two underpinning questions. The answers to these questions will, I hope, stimulate some awareness of these potential benefits. We will discover that lament psalms offer us a deeper appreciation of the relational nature of distress and the way in which a healthy engagement with distress can promote growth. This, in turn, provides a window into our understanding of the broader human experience of distress, and a pathway for engaging practically with distress as people of faith.

In broad terms, I am proposing that the *way in which* the relationships are portrayed and voiced in lament psalms is intimately connected to the potential for change in the person using these psalms. The first question is, "What do the relationships portrayed in lament psalms tell us about the experience of distress for the psalmist?" The second question, related to the first, is, "What changes seem to occur for the psalmist in recognizing these relationships?" We will explore each question in turn and I hope to show the interconnectedness of the responses. At the close of the chapter I will suggest some implications for our understanding of the human experience of distress. In addition, we will reflect on how these psalms offer a pattern of engagement with the distress that we inevitably encounter at various points in our lives.

The Relationships in Lament Psalms

Even a cursory reading of most lament psalms alerts us to the presence of three characters: the psalmist, God, and an enemy. The psalmists themselves are the most obvious, mainly because they are the ones speaking/praying the psalm. God is also present as a character within lament psalms, as the one who is addressed by the psalmist, although it should be noted that God does not speak or act directly within these psalms. The final character present in

---

1. I am not ignoring the value of these psalms in a communal context. However, it is beyond the scope of our current exploration. Many issues raised here have relevance for both individual and communal contexts nonetheless.

lament psalms is an opponent. Opponents are most often vividly referred to as enemies of the psalmist, although they are seldom specifically identified by name. These three characters are not present in isolation from each other. Rather, they engage with each other to create a *dialectic space* where the psalmists both voice and wrestle with their experiences of distress.

I use the phrase *dialectic space* for two reasons. First, lament psalms are shaped in the form of dialectic in that they embrace the tradition of protest or argument, as well as often expressing praise to God. Second, by using dialectic form these psalms focus on the dissonance caused by experiences of distress rather than ignoring or avoiding the issue. In so doing, a space is opened which offers opportunity for both articulation of, and reflection on, the distress being experienced.

Claus Westermann, viewing the psalmist as the central character, provides a helpful beginning point by describing the relationships between the three characters. He identifies them as psychological (the psalmist's relationship with himself),[2] theological (the psalmist's relationship with God), and social (the psalmist's relationship with his enemies).[3] As lament psalms consist almost exclusively of psalmists speaking about themselves, God, and their enemies, it is correct to see the psalmist as the central character. However, it ought to be noted that at times the psalmist does quote God, and often quotes the words of the enemy.[4] This forms the basis for recognizing the three relationships we will explore below in depth.

The "Psychological" Relationship

In considering the "psychological" relationship, we observe how psalmists in distress view themselves. The view of oneself could be described as self-awareness, which ultimately contributes to an evolving self-image. Throughout the course of most lament psalms, self-awareness seems to increase and self-image develops as the psalmists engage with their experience of distress rather than disavowing it.

One example of this is when the psalmist sometimes identifies himself by using the Hebrew term translated as "poor, needy, afflicted or weak." While revealing self-awareness, it is also indicative of the distressed person's sense of disempowerment.[5] Conversely, at various other points psalmists

---

2. Although the term "intrapsychic" is perhaps more appropriate here, "psychological" is Westermann's preferred way of describing this notion.
3. Westermann, *Praise and Lament*, 30.
4. E.g., Psalms 12:5; 13:4.
5. Mays, *The Lord Reigns*, 30.

describe themselves as being faithful, or even innocent, also suggesting self-awareness but perhaps a more positive self-image in this instance.

Taken together, these kinds of contrasts suggest that the psalmists' self-awareness grows and their self-image changes, perhaps developing through the process of engaging with distress.[6] Lament psalms implicitly signal that disavowing one's distress is not ideal for people of faith. It is the self-disclosure of thoughts and feelings associated with distress that offers insight into the experience of distress and contributes to the impetus for the change.

The "Theological" Relationship

The second relationship evident within lament psalms is between the psalmist and God, or what Westermann called the "theological" relationship.[7] Despite the continual cries of distress from the psalmists there is still an acknowledgment of divine presence with them *in* the distress.[8] However, this belief in God's presence is expressed in a broad variety of ways. Divine presence—or, paradoxically, the lack thereof—is variously described as wrathful, rejecting, forgetting, and hiding, among other descriptors.[9] Interestingly, lament psalms verbalize these beliefs *to God* rather than simply *about* God, which contributes to the dialectic mentioned above.

There is a striking dissonance between these fragmented, negative perceptions and the clear plea for response from a God who—the psalmist, at least, believes—*can* do something helpful. In an attempt to understand this incongruity, Kathleen Farmer describes the psalmists' calling out to God as proactive in nature, saying,

> They do not wait passively for God to notice their pain and come to their aid. Rather, they cry out as an act of faith in the steadfast love of the one they confidently trust will not reject them for what they feel or say.[10]

Farmer makes a crucial remark here about lament psalms, particularly with her second observation. From the psalmists' perspective, their relationship

---

6. E.g., Psalm 4:3.

7. Of course lament psalms do not record a verbal response from God, yet there is an implicit understanding that God has spoken and continues to speak in the situation.

8. Even in Psalm 22:1 where a feeling of abandonment is expressed it is still, incongruently, expressed to God.

9. E.g., Psalms 13:1; 88:7.

10. Farmer, "Psalms," 140.

with God is such that nothing seems out of bounds. The dialectic with God is free to contain whatever thoughts and emotions emerge from the distressed person's reflection on their experience.

It is also important to notice that the dialectic voices authentic stress and anxiety that needs an outlet somewhere. The chosen outlet for the psalmist is mainly, and perhaps even only, the divine-human relationship (recognizing, of course, that this occurs in both individual and communal contexts).[11] In other words the dialectic, as an expression of relationship with God, voices an experience that, at some point, recognizes the potential for God to be the primary change agent. As part of this recognition, the psalmists, not infrequently, juxtapose their actions with the action or inaction of God. For example, they sometimes portray themselves as faithful alongside an implicit protest that God is not being faithful.[12] This kind of self-affirmation and challenge to God's faithfulness may also be indicative of the visceral experience of trusting God and doubting God amid distress. While this is a perception, it is, no doubt, felt deeply.

The contrast between how the psalmists perceive themselves and how they perceive God could also be viewed as an attempt to find some kind of leverage. Any leverage gained, it is hoped, might then result in a favorable response from God. Either way, lament psalms consistently record the psalmists steadfastly looking towards God as the only hope for resolution of the situation. This appeal to someone while in distress reveals what seems to be an instinctual desire for those who are distressed to seek help from someone or something outside themselves. Of particular interest here is that the psalmists seek help through strident protests and requests offered to God.

The "Social" Relationship

The third relationship in lament psalms is with those who surround the psalmist. In this regard there are both positive and negative influences. On the positive side, Erhard Gerstenberger argues convincingly for the significance of the community ("kinsfolk") to the person who is engaging with distress.[13] While his added proposal of a "ritual expert" with a salvation

---

11. Mays, *The Lord Reigns*, 27–30. As a reinforcing image to the idea of divine sufficiency, Mays argues that the idea of God's kingship is a given for the psalmist facing distress and, therefore, acknowledgment of God's ability to change the situation is significant.

12. E.g., contrast Psalm 13:1–2, with its implicit protest against God's silence and inaction, with Psalm 13:5a, where the psalmist affirms that his trust in God is firm.

13. Gerstenberger, *Psalms*, 14.

type oracle being present in lament is speculative, it does highlight some important principles in responding to distress. First, it underlines the importance of people being present to support the distressed person: in this case, the faith community ("kinsfolk"). Second, the presence of a "ritual expert" assumes that the practice of lament is a regular activity with associated ritual actions, which are specific to the event, performed by a priestly figure. Third, taken together, the presence of the community and a "ritual expert" accepts lament as normative for people of faith. Finally, while the experience of distress is personal for the individual, it seems that the faith of the psalmist insisted on the experience not being private.

Although some who are associated with the psalmist are characterized as supportive, there are clearly also those who oppose the psalmist, and their presence is obvious in the text of most lament psalms. These opponents are, more often than not, labeled as enemies. The nature of the confrontation that results in distress is not clearly described and the enemy is rarely named. Observing this, John Day suggests, "this is just what we should expect of psalms that were constantly being used in the liturgy of a variety of people."[14] It may also be that the person who is experiencing distress cannot precisely identify who the enemy is. For the contemporary reader of the psalms, however, the enemy's anonymity shifts our focus to the *function* of the enemy.

In relationship terms, identifying the presence of an enemy stresses both the isolation of the distressed person from God and/or the community and the power, felt or real, of the enemy. While there is rarely a suggestion of physical confrontation, the isolating effects of the enemy on the distressed person are palpable. It is also worth noting that the enemy is not always identified as other people; sometimes God can be viewed in this way as well.[15] While certainly not unimportant, the identity of the enemy seems to be of lesser significance than the fact that there *is* an enemy.

More troubling than the presence of an enemy, for some, is the way in which the psalmist speaks about their enemy with the use of imprecation. Although this element is sometimes placed in the "too hard basket," it is critical for recognizing the role of lament.[16] For Christians, expressing violence through imprecation can be viewed as contrary to Jesus's teaching and other parts of the New Testament. However, it needs to be acknowledged that imprecation is *an expression of emotions and thoughts* that can be, al-

14. Day, *Psalms*, 29.

15. E.g., Psalm 35:11–12. See also Harper, "Lament and the Sovereignty of God" (chapter 6 in this volume).

16. E.g., Psalms 10:15–16; 55:15.

though unpalatable, a natural response to those who are viewed as enemies. It is important to stress that imprecation is a calling on God to act forcefully *for* the psalmist *against* their enemy rather than the psalmist himself taking violent action. While we rightly condemn violence, the presence of imprecation recognizes feelings provoked by injustice and a desire to respond in some way to the one who has offended.

Imprecation provides a safe space and a safe way for these feelings to be expressed without resorting to actual violence of some kind, while empowering the one lamenting. It provides empowerment by allowing people to enter into dialectic with those who caused their distress while opening an avenue for God to act on their behalf. It is also another way in which confidence can be expressed in a God who is perceived to be able to help. So, in this sense, imprecation can be considered an expression of trust in God. Interestingly, whether God actually acts on the psalmist's demand seems immaterial for the psalmist. It is the presence of the imprecation in the dialectic, and therefore its function—rather than the outcome—that is important.

So, how can we summarize the function of the enemy within psalms of distress? We have noted how the psalmists wrestle dialectically with themselves and God because of distress. The enemy offers a third direction for the dialectic, recognizing the need for venting of emotion about, or even to, the source of distress. It could also underline the importance of lament in validating the experience of being conflicted by distress. Together these expressions shape self-awareness and self-image through the lens of the perceived enemy.

It seems that, amid personal distress, the psalmist can ignore neither those who support *nor* those who oppose. However, it is particularly those who oppose the psalmist who expose internal conflict. Perhaps it is dialectic directed toward the enemy that contributes most to heightening self-awareness, prompting the deeper questions about self-image to break the surface of the person's experience. By stimulating this conflict, the enemy becomes a potential catalyst for the spiritual growth of the person in distress. In so doing, an acknowledgment of "social" relationships (both positive and negative) contributes to the "psychological" relationship discussed above.

Relationship, Dialectic, and Aspects of Change

The dialectic between the psalmist, God, and the enemy underscores the co-existent relationship between them and creates a space around which the psalm is shaped. This space, in turn, forms a basis for changes in the psalmist that can be observed within lament psalms themselves. In doing so, lament psalms not only offer a unique window into the lived experience of a distressed person but also the possibility of navigating distress. The potential changes underline the capacity of lament psalms to shape people's experience of distress and also to form their sense of relationship with God. Rather than disavowing their distress, this formation occurs as people embrace their experience *within* a faith context and fearlessly confront God with their struggle. This leads Walter Brueggemann to suggest that, "while the experience shaped the pattern of expression, it is also true that the pattern of expression helped shape the experience, so it could be received, understood and coped with."[17]

We have now reached a point of appreciating the nature of the relationships within lament psalms and how their dynamics interconnect to produce a dialectic space. When this space opens, it reveals three specific aspects of change for the psalmist, which we will now explore. The aspects of change are as follows:

1. Level of distress
2. Sense of empowerment
3. Sense of relationship with God.

Level of Distress

Distress refers to an experience that has been caused by forces either external or internal to a person. The thoughts, feelings, and behaviors that occur in response to a particular level of distress typically display as stress and anxiety. As one reads through lament psalms, both stress and anxiety are obvious in varying degrees. For example, in Psalm 22:1 we hear a high level of distress in the form of a question, "My God, my God, why have you forsaken me?" However, just a little later in v. 22 we read, "I will tell of your name to my brothers and sisters, in the midst of the congregation I will praise you." At this point the level of distress has seemingly decreased, or even dissipated completely.

It would be simplistic to suggest that lament psalms consistently display a dramatic movement like this from a high level of distress to a lower level of distress for the psalmist. However, movement in this general direction is obvious within most lament psalms.[18] Likewise, it would be far too

---

17. Brueggemann, *The Psalms*, 69.
18. Westermann, *Praise and Lament*, 266. Of course, Westermann notes that the

simplistic to suggest that using a psalm such as this would *automatically* move a person from a high level of distress to a lower one. However, what it does suggest is that movement in a particular direction is possible, and even perhaps predictable.

Observing this movement in these psalms raises an important question as to possible causes. It seems that the psalmist being able to speak openly and honestly about their relationship within themselves (psychological), with God (theological), and with others (social) contributes to this shift and possibly even precipitates it. Interestingly, the exact nature of the distress is rarely identified and seems to be of little importance. The key in reducing stress and anxiety produced by distress is in the person finding a voice for their experience. This is what lament psalms provide.

Some, then, have concluded that praying lament psalms is a form of "religious coping . . . associated with reduced stress and other forms of improved mental health."[19] One way of understanding how this happens is that a "turning to religious faith brings an omnipotent and ever-present Partner to one's life, lending a greater sense of control, which is a critical element to decreasing . . . stress."[20]

In lament psalms, the invocation and complaint (typically toward the beginning of the psalm) are evidence of a high level of distress. The confession of sin/affirmation of innocence and the plea (which is always present) are also signs of a high level of distress. However, the plea that God would do something in response to the situation does seem to signal the beginning of a change, with an increasing sense of hope for divine action. When the psalmist expresses trust in God and hope for the future, a reduction in the level of distress becomes evident within the movement of most lament psalms.

Sense of Empowerment

The observations made by Janice Meisenhelder and John Marcum above alert us to a second potential change for a distressed person using lament psalms: a growing sense of empowerment. A significant aspect of experiencing distress is the loss of a sense of control, and feelings of disempowerment in the situation. This loss raises questions about where power lies

---

Psalter as a whole moves from an emphasis on lament to an emphasis on praise. See further the essay by Dan Wu in this volume.

19. Meisenhelder and Marcum, "Responses of Clergy," 548. This conclusion is based on earlier studies by Koenig, McCullough, and Larson.

20. Ibid., 553.

and whether it is possible for a sense of personal empowerment to emerge from the crucible of distress. The experience of disempowerment through distress seems to be a typical part of most people's experiences. For the psalmist, a sense of equilibrium is found in a balanced empowerment that acknowledges God's action but does not abrogate personal responsibility. This is important to emphasize, because

> A common secular perspective on religion assumes that believing God is an active agent in one's life requires relinquishing a sense of personal or internal control.[21]

Contrary to this, empirical research suggests that people who pray do not abrogate personal responsibility, but rather discover the sense of equilibrium in empowerment.[22] So, in contrast to the view that religious people "relinquish" personal agency in response to distress, this reinforces the significant place of prayer in discovering a realistic balance between an expectation of God's action and personal responsibility. An earlier study suggested that "individuals reporting a deeper sense of change of state in prayer are particularly low in this [external locus of control] trait."[23] So it could be argued that those who pray lament psalms not only become more collaborative with God in their situation, but also take greater personal responsibility for their distress. Laurence Jackson and Robert Coursey sum up the desired outcome best, concluding that "effective coping is achieved via personal control *through* God."[24]

So, using lament psalms enables a person to recognize and acknowledge feelings of disempowerment amid distress, and also to imagine a new sense of self-empowerment *with* God. This gradual discovery of empowerment in the face of distress is evident through the progression of many lament psalms.[25] As with the decreasing levels of distress explored above, this is not to suggest that using a lament psalm means that self-empowerment is automatic. However, it does illustrate a process for becoming aware of feelings of disempowerment and then beginning to gain a sense of self-empowerment.

A final observation about the nature of empowerment needs to be reiterated here. The efficacy of lament psalms, as with other genres, also needs

---

21. Jackson and Coursey, "The Relationship of God Control," 399.

22. Ibid., 407. These conclusions are also supported by Furnham, "Locus of Control," 130–36, in his literature review of research on this issue. He surmises that numerous studies demonstrate the same result.

23. Richards, "The Phenomenology," 361.

24. Jackson and Coursey, "The Relationship of God Control," 399.

25. E.g., Psalms 13, 22, 105.

to be considered in connection with ritual, as suggested above. Christina Mitchell notes that empowerment (or "locus of control" as she calls it) "is a learned approach to assigning cause to outcomes."[26] This being the case suggests that using lament psalms in a regular way for both personal devotion and corporate worship will reinforce a healthy balance between personal empowerment and confidence in God to act.

Sense of Relationship

The third potential change for a person using lament psalms is in their sense of relationship with themselves, and between themselves and God. While the divine-human relationship could be viewed as different from any human-to-human relationship, there are some parallels. Todd Hall, with others, agrees "that psychological and spiritual functioning are inextricably related because people relate to God through the same psychological mechanisms that mediate relationships with other people."[27]

In essence these observations highlight that both psychological and spiritual maturity are embedded in the experience of relationships. In addition, they point out the interconnectedness between human relationships and relationship with God. It can be concluded then that "the quality of one's relationship with God is . . . highly related to the quality of relationship with others."[28] The way in which lament psalms cover the full gamut of relationships ought not to be downplayed here.

These observations and conclusions suggest two important perspectives on the relationships. First, while some may seek to distinguish divine-human and human-human relationships substantively, they cannot be separated in terms of their implications for the maturation of the distressed person of faith. In other words, if a person in distress is to navigate their experience successfully, such navigation must include grappling with relationships with oneself, others (including enemies), and God. If a person's sense of relationship with God is contingent on their relationship with others, then it also infers that any process that addresses *both* divine-human and human-human relationships will ultimately strengthen a person's relationship with both God and others.[29]

26. Mitchell, "Internal Locus of Control," 21.
27. Hall et al., "An Empirical Exploration," 304.
28. Ibid., 310.
29. On the other hand, Hall et al. also suggest that individuals with "disturbed relationships with other people" are more likely to display a more "pathological relationship with God" (Ibid., 311).

A heightened sense of relationship with God and others may also lead to increased meaning making and a deepening of spirituality. A primary impetus for growing spirituality in lament psalms is recognizing "a conflictual drive which threaten[s] self-identity," which we discussed in detail above.[30] This conflictual drive, obvious in lament psalms and far from being a negative factor, contributes to an "integrated spiritual experience [which] tends to move an individual away from the importance of need-satisfaction."[31]

Reflections

There is no doubt in my mind that the lament psalms offer us a window into the human experience of distress in unique ways. In them we find affirmed that the experience of distress is multifaceted, deeply exposing, and potentially refining for those who engage with it. But it remains for us to return to the questions posed at the beginning of this chapter to see what answers we may have gained. We will begin with the two underpinning questions I suggested we ask and then see how they address the primary question with which we began our exploration.

We first asked, "What do the relationships portrayed in lament psalms tell us about the experience of distress for psalmist?" It seems self-evident that lament psalms expose the relational nature of distress for all human beings. Distress affects us to the very core of our humanity, and ideally it is not experienced or processed alone. A person of faith is reminded through these psalms that God is attentive to our laments in the same way that God is attentive to our praises. Another way of expressing this is to say that our praises *and our laments* together form our worship as we bring all our lived experience before God.

We then posed the question, "What changes seem to occur for the psalmist in recognizing these relationships?" In acknowledging each relationship through these psalms, the psalmists illustrate the power of authenticity and the usefulness of dialectic in opening a space for change. The changes evident chiefly relate to the psalmists' level of distress, their sense of empowerment, and their sense of relationship with God. While primarily descriptive in form, these powerful psalms offer an invitation for people of faith to walk and talk with the psalmists through these psalms amid their own unique experiences of distress. As a result, those using lament psalms are alerted to their connection with themselves, God, and their enemies. While perhaps at first a reactionary cry for divine intervention, using these

30. May, "The Psychodynamic," 84.
31. Ibid., 85.

psalms takes on a more profound trajectory by providing a pathway for greater reflection, meaning making, and, ultimately, transformation.

Finally, we move to the primary question I posed at the beginning of our exploration, "What then ought we to do with these psalms?" If what I suggested holds true, then the answer is simple. We must use these psalms for all they are worth! They encompass a wonderful reflection on the lives of faithful people who encountered various distressing circumstances. It remains for us to continue to read or sing these psalms, making them our own prayers and finding a voice amid the vicissitudes of life. If you have forgotten about lament psalms until now, or if you have never known them before, then the invitation is open. Come and encounter this collection of prayers within the Psalter. May we "not cease from exploration, and the end of all our exploring will be to arrive where we started and know the place for the first time."[32]

Bibliography

Brueggemann, Walter, and Patrick D. Miller. *The Psalms and the Life of Faith*. Minneapolis: Fortress, 1995.

Day, John. *Psalms*. Sheffield: JSOT, 1990.

Eliot, T. S. *Four Quartets*. London: Faber, 2001.

Farmer, Kathleen A. "Psalms." In *The Women's Bible Commentary*, edited by Carol A. Newsom and Sharon Ringe, 145–52. Louisville: Westminster John Knox, 1992.

Gerstenberger, Erhard S. *Psalms: With an Introduction to Cultic Poetry: Part I*. Grand Rapids: Eerdmans, 1988.

Hall, Todd W., et al. "An Empirical Exploration of Psychoanalysis and Religion: Spiritual Maturity and Object Relations Development." *Journal for the Scientific Study of Religion* 37 (1998) 303–13.

Jackson, Laurence E., and Robert D. Coursey. "The Relationship of God Control and Internal Locus of Control to Intrinsic Religious Motivation, Coping, and Purpose of Life." *Journal for the Scientific Study of Religion* 27 (1988) 399–410.

May, Gerald G. "The Psychodynamics of Pastoral Care." *The Journal of Pastoral Care* 31 (1977) 84–90.

Mays, James L. *The Lord Reigns: A Theological Handbook to the Psalms*. Louisville: Westminster John Knox, 1994.

Meisenhelder, Janice B. and John P. Marcum. "Responses of Clergy to 9/11: Posttraumatic Stress, Coping and Religious Outcomes." *Journal for the Scientific Study of Religion* 43 (2004) 547–54.

Mitchell, Christina E. "Internal Locus of Control for Expectation, Perception, and Management of Answered Prayer." *Journal of Psychology and Theology* 17 (1989) 21–26.

Richards, Douglas G. "The Phenomenology and Psychological Correlates of Verbal Prayer." *Journal of Psychology and Theology* 19 (1991) 354–63.

---

32. Eliot, *The Four Quartets*.

Westermann, Claus. *Praise and Lament in the Psalms.* Translated by Keith R. Crim and Richard N. Soulen. Atlanta: John Knox, 1981.

6

Lament and the Sovereignty of God
Theological Reflections on Psalm 88

G. GEOFFREY HARPER

In order to spare the laity all "difficulties" he has deserted both the lectionary and the appointed psalms and now, without noticing it, revolves endlessly round the little treadmill of his fifteen favourite psalms and twenty favourite lessons. We are thus safe from the danger that any truth not already familiar to him and to his flock should ever reach them through Scripture. But perhaps your patient is not quite silly enough for this church—or not yet?[1]

LAMENTS ARE UNCOMFORTABLE. THE vivid and sometimes vindictive language used to express profound emotional anguish can stir up long-buried feelings for readers, feelings that many would rather keep buried. For others, especially for Western readers, the openness of the psalmists to bewail their lot is frankly embarrassing. But beyond all this, the Psalter's laments are theologically disquieting. Ought not mature Christian spirituality to be permeated with the victory that is ours in Christ? Where is the place for these ancient expressions of discontent that even presume to complain to God? Did the psalmists not learn the secret of being content in all circumstances? Did they not know that God is sovereign, that he works all things

---

1. Lewis, *Screwtape Letters*, 82–83.

for the good of those who love him? What then are we to do with these poems, which propagate such seeming *un*spiritual and *dis*believing concerns?

Perhaps more than most, Psalm 88 confronts readers with these very questions. The psalm is an anguished and bitter cry to God, made without reprieve, that ends (in Hebrew at least) with the word "darkness." Lewis's "little treadmill" suddenly looks appealing. Yet with any part of the Bible that we functionally excise, we do so to our detriment. So too with Psalm 88, for this most uncomfortable of psalms is theologically rich. Indeed, the theological perspective it offers provides an invaluable window into the nature and function of lament—not only for ancient Israel, but also for the contemporary church. In order to explore the insights this psalm has to offer, I first make some general observations about lament as a genre before taking a more detailed look at Psalm 88.

The Shape of Lament

Biblical laments have a certain "shape." This realization has proven to be one of the more beneficial aspects of the legacy bequeathed to Psalms scholarship by Hermann Gunkel. The primary goal of Gunkel's form-critical approach to the Psalter was the identification of the particular *Gattung*, or form, of each psalm within the collection. In fact, many of the labels so frequently used today to classify psalms both in commentaries and in popular parlance—hymn, lament, royal, etc.—can be traced to the influence of Gunkel's pioneering work.[2] While form criticism has its downsides, most notably its focus on psalms as individual units without due consideration for their canonical placement,[3] it also offers some valuable insights.

One of these is the window that is opened into the generic nuances of particular psalms. In all great literature the mark of true genius becomes evident in an author's ability to follow the conventions of genre closely enough so as to produce a recognizable piece, yet to also diverge enough from those expectations so as to be original. Thus getting a handle on the normal or anticipated "shape" of biblical laments can aid us in our task as interpreters because we can more easily see where, and begin to ask why, the author of a particular psalm has exercised his or her poetic license in given ways. I will explore some of this exegetical potential with respect to Psalm 88 below. Before I do that, however, it is important to clarify what we should expect.

---

2. See Gunkel and Begrich, *Introduction*.

3. Gunkel disavowed any ordering principle in the Psalter and accordingly advocated that the "researcher first has to disregard the context in which the items came to us more or less accidently" (ibid., 3).

The following elements are typical of lament psalms:[4]

1. An appeal or cry for help directed to God
2. Reference to God's past deliverance (usually only in communal laments)
3. The lament proper with a three-way focus on God, the lamenter(s), and the enemy (or enemies)
4. Confession of trust
5. A double petition for God's intervention—*on behalf of* the psalmist, and *against* the enemy
6. Assurance of being heard (usually just in individual laments)
7. A vow to offer praise, or even enacted praise if the petition has already been answered

As can be observed from the above, laments generally evidence a movement from initial distress to a note of hope, or praise. There are of course variations to this pattern,[5] but it is repeated often enough to be regarded as the norm.

The characteristic shape of lament psalms is illustrated well by Psalm 13. The psalm opens with an appeal: "How long, O Lord?" (v. 1a).[6] The lament proper, which follows, involves the interfusion of God, psalmist, and enemy: "Will you forget me forever? How long will you hide your face from me? How long must I take counsel in my soul and have sorrow in my heart all the day? How long shall my enemy be exalted over me?" (vv. 1b–2). Lament in turn provokes a double petition (for and against): "Consider and answer me, O Lord my God; light up my eyes, lest I sleep the sleep of death, lest my enemy say, 'I have prevailed over him,' lest my foes rejoice because I am shaken" (vv. 3–4). Verse 5 confesses trust. "But I have trusted in your steadfast love; my heart shall rejoice in your salvation." The psalm ends with a vow to praise Yahweh because the psalmist's petition has been answered. "I will sing to the Lord, because he has dealt bountifully with me" (v. 6). The movement is thus exactly as expected. Accordingly, Adele Berlin notes, "the reader of this psalm, if identifying with the speaker, traverses the same emotional path from despair to hope."[7]

---

4. Adapted from Westermann, *Praise and Lament*, 52–81.
5. For examples, see Villanueva, "Preaching Lament," 67–74.
6. All biblical quotations are taken from ESV unless otherwise stated.
7. Berlin, "Hebrew Poetry," 314.

In light of the standard shape of lament just outlined, Psalm 88 is decidedly odd. First, a number of expected elements are missing. There is no confession of trust; nor is there any assurance that petition has been heard. Furthermore, even though the psalmist is oppressed, he makes no mention of "foes" or "enemies." Most strikingly, instead of ending with a vow to praise Yahweh, the psalm ends (literally) with "darkness." Second, the movement is unusual. While the majority of laments move from lament to praise, and even those that don't still have some kind of movement (alternation between lament and praise, for example), Psalm 88 attests no movement at all. The psalm, from beginning to end, sits resolutely in the place of lament. What we are to make of this I will explore below, but this lack of movement is perhaps one of the reasons Psalm 88 is so seldom preached, or even read, in church. Who, after all, wants to remain in the place of lament? To sit in darkness with the psalmist, without any comforting chink of light? Yet these odd features of Psalm 88 prove to be exegetically important; more than that, they are theologically significant. To better see how this is the case requires a closer look at Psalm 88.

Exploring Psalm 88

Needless to say, a comprehensive exegesis of Psalm 88 is well beyond what I can hope to accomplish here. For more detailed analysis, interested readers should consult the standard commentaries. Instead, my focus will be on salient features of this psalm that provide the exigency for the theological reflections I make in the following section.

The Situation Faced

The first notable feature concerns the circumstances that provoke the lament. Psalm 88 opens with a plea for help. "O Lord, God of my salvation; I cry out day and night before you" (v. 1). However, while the psalmist's cry to God is clearly evident, the exact reasons provoking the appeal are not.

Throughout, a veritable litany of woes is bemoaned. In v. 3 the psalmist declares that his soul is full of troubles. These troubles, moreover, have brought him close to death: "my life draws near to Sheol. I am counted among those who go down to the pit" (vv. 3b–4a). This idea of imminent demise is revisited in vv. 10–12, where the psalmist asks a series of rhetorical questions in which words connected with death occur in quick succession. Do "the dead" or "the departed" praise Yahweh? Is Yahweh known in "the grave," "Abaddon," "the darkness" or "the land of forgetfulness"?

Physical symptoms are hinted at—the psalmist has no strength (v. 4), and his eyes grow dim (v. 9). Emotional or spiritual turmoil is also conveyed through feeling overwhelmed by God's wrath (vv. 7, 16). Furthermore, the problem faced is both continual—the psalmist is surrounded "all day long" (v. 17)—and has a long history—he declares he has been "afflicted and close to death from my youth up" (v. 15). The affliction in turn has also caused relational estrangement: "You have caused my companions to shun me; you have made me a horror to them . . . You have caused my beloved and my friend to shun me" (vv. 8, 18).

Not surprisingly, even a brief survey of the commentaries suggests multiple diagnoses. For Mitchell Dahood, Psalm 88 is the "lament of a desolate man in mortal illness."[8] Walter Brueggemann and William Bellinger suggest that "acute social isolation" compounds any physical threat to life.[9] Elmer Leslie adds the "excruciating mental pain" that stems from abandonment.[10] Robert Alter even posits that perhaps, like Job, the psalmist's fortunes have met with disaster.[11] Of course, these suggested causes are not mutually exclusive. What Psalm 88 demonstrates is the ambiguity surrounding historical and contextual details that characterizes the psalms more broadly. These poems are intentionally vague and, therefore, by virtue of this feature, have the ability to transcend time and space and so become applicable to multifarious situations in the lives of God's people. The lament voiced in Psalm 88 is a suitable response to a wide range of distressing life situations.

The Response of the Psalmist

A second point to note, and in contrast to determining the exact nature of the situation faced, is the unambiguity of the psalmist's response—he cries out to Yahweh for rescue. The appeals made are impassioned. The verb צעק ($ṣ'q$, "to cry out" v. 1) is a strong word. Elsewhere, the term denotes exclamations evoked by oppression (Judg 4:3), looming destruction (Exod 14:10), and even rape (Deut 22:27). Hence, as Michael Goulder notes, the lament of Psalm 88 is "not a dignified prayer, but protracted wailing."[12] Similarly, v. 2

---

8. Dahood, *Psalms II*, 302. See, similarly, Preuss, "Psalm 88," 71.
9. Brueggemann and Bellinger, *Psalms*, 379.
10. Leslie, *Psalms*, 397.
11. Alter, *Psalms*, 310.
12. Goulder, *Sons of Korah*, 204.

implores Yahweh to attend to a "loud, resounding cry" (רִנָּה, *rinnâ*).[13] Moreover, the psalmist's heavenward petition is made regularly. "Day and night" he wails (צעק, *ṣʿq*) to Yahweh (v. 1); "[e]very day" he calls (קרא, *qrʾ*) upon him (v. 9). Even in the morning his prayer rises to God (v. 13). Regularity is tinged with desperation. So pressing is the situation that all the rhetorical stops are pulled out in order to provoke Yahweh's deliverance. The pervasive language of death noted above functions towards this end. The psalmist declares to Yahweh that he stands in the very gates of *Sheol* and is about to take his place among the dead. Whether real or metaphorical, the imminence of death is used to stimulate divine action. This is also the way the rhetorical questions in vv. 10–12 work. The implied answer in each case is "no"—the dead are beyond Yahweh's reach; the psalmist will only be able to praise God if he remains alive.[14] The force of the appeal is clear: "save me now, because it's about to be too late!" Thus the psalmist acts as a model believer. In the face of suffering (whatever the exact cause) he turns to God in passionate, persistent prayer. There is not even a hint of sullen silence.

A Darker Reality

Psalm 88 is the prayer of a model believer. The situation may be desperate but the response is a cry to Yahweh who, in the very first verse, is hailed as the "God of my salvation." And yet the very devotion of the psalmist raises a disturbing question. Why does he need to cry out *day and night*? To plead with his God *every* day? The uncomfortable answer that begins to dawn—for reader and psalmist alike—is that Yahweh remains unmoved. Heartrending wails seem to have fallen on deaf ears. By all accounts, if v. 15 is anything to go by, this is an asked-for deliverance that has failed to materialize not just in the midst of a recent "rough patch" but across an entire lifetime. The "God of my salvation" has manifestly not saved.

Thus, at the heart of this psalm, compounding and relativizing all other reasons for lament, is an overwhelming sense of divine abandonment. It is an abandonment that is made all the more distressing by the knowledge that Yahweh *can* save (v. 1) but that he simply seems to have chosen not to. Indeed, six expressions that characterize Yahweh's usual action are

---

13. *HALOT* 3:1247. There is a degree of irony in the language used. As Norman Wagner elucidates, רִנָּה (*rinnâ*, "loud cry") is more usually associated with joyful shouts made in cultic contexts (Wagner, "רִנָּה in the Psalter").

14. At points like this it is important to remember the reality of progressive revelation. For a helpful treatment of the Old Testament understanding of *Sheol* and what happened to the dead, see Johnston, *Shades of Sheol*.

listed—wonders, praise, steadfast love, faithfulness, wonders, righteousness (vv. 10–12)—but all this does is reinforce the incongruity of the psalmist's position.[15] In this case, orthodox theology exacerbates, rather than alleviates, suffering. For make no mistake, the psalmist is orthodox. The prayer of Psalm 88 is, from beginning to end, uttered in the context of relationship—seen, for instance, in the utilization of God's covenant name throughout. Yet in light of this existing relationship the question posed in v. 14 is made all the more poignant. "O Yahweh, I cry to you; in the morning my prayer comes before you. O Yahweh, why do you cast my soul away? Why do you hide your face from me?" (vv. 13–14 ESV [adapted]). There is more than a hint of betrayal expressed in the query.

But Psalm 88 gets darker still. It is not just God's *absence* that is bemoaned, but God's antagonistic *presence*. This becomes clear in the use of second person forms throughout Psalm 88—language that is both striking and disturbing. In a manner that assaults twenty-first century Christian sensibilities, the psalmist accuses Yahweh directly:

> *You* have put me in the depths of the pit,
>   in the regions dark and deep.
> *Your* wrath lies heavy upon me,
>   and *you* overwhelm me with all *your* waves. *Selah*
> *You* have caused my companions to shun me;
>   *you* have made me a horror to them.
> . . .
> Afflicted and close to death from my youth up,
>   I suffer *your* terrors; I am helpless.
> *Your* wrath has swept over me;
>   *your* dreadful assaults destroy me.
> They surround me like a flood all day long;
>   they close in on me together.
> *You* have caused my beloved and my friend to shun me (vv. 6–8, 15–18, emphasis mine).

It is here that an already disquieting psalm becomes unbearable. If only the psalmist had blamed his circumstances, or his parents, or society, that would be better than this. At least then it would be the psalmist and his God facing trouble together. Instead, the repeated use of "you" lays the blame for experienced suffering squarely at Yahweh's feet. Moreover, the lack of movement in the psalm leaves these pained accusations hanging without rejoinder. And so the psalm ends in the next colon literally, emotionally,

---

15. Brueggemann, *Message of the Psalms*, 80. Regarding the direct contrast this creates with the promises of Psalm 85, see Hossfeld and Zenger, *Psalms 2*, 397.

and perhaps even spiritually, in "darkness." Working together, the absence of movement, the psalmist's unheard cries, and the use of "you" all drive to one crushing reality. Whereas in the other laments the psalmists are afflicted and oppressed by forces variously labeled as "foes" or "enemies," Psalm 88 is different. Here, God is the enemy.

Theological Reflections on Psalm 88

What are we to make of this darkest of laments? What possible place could it have in our private reading—let alone a corporate gathering or (perish the thought) a children's Sunday School lesson? Surprising as it may seem, Psalm 88 is theologically rich. In fact, this strained prayer provides a window into the nature and role of biblical lament that proves essential for contemporary readers. I offer reflections in relation to three particular areas.

Psalm 88 as Reality Check

First and foremost, Psalm 88 functions as a reality check. There are seasons in life that begin and end in lament. Some prayers for deliverance, faithfully and persistently offered though they may be, go unanswered. Facing uncomfortable truths such as these may well provide a necessary corrective for our theological frameworks, because individual Christians, as well as the communities they represent, often functionally reflect an over-realized eschatology. Such over-realization is not limited to those who submit to a so-called prosperity gospel, but is regularly encountered in the implicit (or sometimes explicit) expectations of others. It is seen when uttering words of lament is understood to reveal an unspiritual or at best immature faith; when expressing grief, sadness, or doubt is seen to conflict with genuine Christian spirituality. As a result, such "negative emotions" are given no quarter in our gatherings where even funerals are re-labeled as "celebrations" and we applaud those who "remain strong" in the face of heartrending loss. Psalm 88 offers a forceful corrective to the naïve optimism that is at times reflected in this kind of reasoning. On the contrary, this psalm allows, even encourages, us to name things for being as bad as they are.

Yet there are also those who need no reminder. In fact, for many readers of this psalm, and maybe for some readers of this essay, the very words that strike fellow believers as confronting and problematic are strangely comforting. That comfort stems from the realization that others have also uttered words like these. Others too have wailed and cried out in a darkness that will not end. There is relief in knowing one is not alone, even while feeling shunned and excluded from divine and human companionship. It is not surprising, then, to find similar expressions of grief being uttered by God's people. Nicholas Wolterstorff, for instance, lost his son in a climbing accident. Like the psalmist, Wolterstorff felt, acutely, the gap between his experience and the God he thought he knew. He lamented accordingly:

> I am at an impasse, and you, O God, have brought me here. From my earliest days, I heard of you. From my earliest days, I believed in you. . . . Noon has darkened. And fast as she could say, "He's dead," the light dimmed. And where are you in the darkness? I learned to spy you in the light. Here in this darkness I cannot find you. If I had never looked for you, or looked but never found, I would not feel this pain of your absence. Or is it not your absence in which I dwell but your elusive troubling presence?[16]

The realization that others occupy the same darkness as that experienced by the psalmist in Psalm 88 reveals a further function of biblical laments. These poems and prayers give access to the thoughts and feelings of those who find themselves in the midst of severe crisis. Psalm 88 reflects the kinds of words someone in severe pain would utter, or maybe has uttered. Thus, those who happen to dwell in the light are afforded invaluable insight into the inner turmoil of those who are suffering, which ought, in turn, to inform pastoral care. Once again, Wolterstorff is insightful.

> But please: Don't say it's not really so bad. Because it is. . . . If you think your task as comforter is to tell me that really, all things considered, it's not so bad, you do not sit with me in my grief but place yourself off in the distance away from me. Over there, you are of no help. What I need to hear from you is that you recognize how painful it is. I need to hear from you that you are with me in my desperation. To comfort me, you have to come close. Come sit beside me on my mourning bench.[17]

With its hefty dose of reality, Psalm 88 can teach us to sit on that bench.

Psalm 88 as Response of Faith

A second point I want to draw attention to is that Psalm 88 constitutes a response of faith, not unfaith. This is important to state, precisely because the language and ethos of Psalm 88 seems so at odds with many iterations

---

16. Wolterstorff, *Lament*, 69.
17. Ibid., 34.

of contemporary Christian spirituality. Yet, lament, just as much as praise, is a righteous response. While the Psalter's hymns rightly praise Yahweh for who he is, and the thanksgiving psalms rightly thank God for his acts of deliverance, lament psalms rightly bemoan the absence of fulfillment with respect to divine promise.

This dynamic is clearly seen in the opening psalms of the Psalter. Psalm 1 boldly asserts that the one who meditates upon *torah* will be blessed (1:1–2). Psalm 2 adds another layer to that promise by connecting blessing with the rule of the Davidic king whom Yahweh has installed on the throne. Yet the very next psalm, a psalm of David no less, laments the many foes that have arisen to oppress. Where now are the lofty promises of Psalms 1 and 2? Where is the foretold blessing?

This dissonance between claim and realization forms the engine room of lament. The psalmists, too, know of the tension between the already and the not yet. In light of this, they cry out to God. Hence, it is precisely because they continue to believe that Yahweh is faithful and dependable that the psalmists offer their petitions. If Yahweh was merely capricious, as were the other gods of the ANE, then lament would be superfluous. The very fact that laments are voiced to Yahweh is therefore testimony to a determined faith that clings on even in the absence of evidence or, as in the case of Psalm 88, even in light of seeming evidence to the contrary. Here, though the psalmist feels betrayed, Yahweh is nevertheless "God of *my* salvation." Psalm 88 demonstrates that expressing grief, even anger, to God is not an immature or unspiritual thing to do; it is not a slippery slope towards atheism. Rather, to lament is a righteous act carried out in full assurance of faith. The unspiritual response is to cease communication with God, or to begin muttering discontent to ourselves and to others. There is a world of a difference between complaining *to* God and complaining *about* God.

Perhaps unsurprisingly, we see this aspect of faith being modeled by Jesus. In the Garden of Gethsemane, Jesus willingly submitted himself to his Father's will and to the ordeal ahead. Yet, suffering on the cross, Jesus did not sing a hymn. He did not feel compelled to demonstrate faith by crying out "Praise God!" Rather, taking up the words of Psalm 22:1, he lamented his fate. "My God, my God, why have you forsaken me?" The Gospel writers record his words in Aramaic to make sure we understand this comes verbatim from his lips.[18] Lament, just as much as praise, is a response of faith.

This being the case, we may well need to adjust our theological horizons. Praise is not the only godly response to suffering. Lament too is an act

---

18. Brueggemann, *Into Your Hand*, 17.

of faith. In fact, it is the expected response of the suffering person who has truly meditated upon torah.

Psalm 88 and the Sovereignty of God

The third area I want to reflect on concerns the relationship between lament and the sovereignty of God. Ironically, it is one of the more challenging aspects of Psalm 88—the psalmist's accusing use of "you" with respect to Yahweh—that unveils a significant theological point. In the Israelite conceptual universe, this use of second person language is not surprising. Indeed, to attribute suffering to Yahweh is a necessary consequence of belief in one God (see 1 Sam 2:6–7; Ps 105:25; Isa 45:6–7). Barry Webb's observation, made in connection with Lamentations, is thus equally applicable to Psalm 88.

> Here we make contact with an angst which is at the very heart of Israelite religion with its uncompromising monotheism. For if there is but one God, who is sovereign over all things, no final explanation for anything is possible other than that he is behind it, and there is nowhere else to run but into the arms of the very One whose anger you have aroused.[19]

Thus the unrelenting use of "you" throughout Psalm 88 is not only an explicit complaint to Yahweh but is also an implicit recognition of his sovereignty.

The mimetic function of the psalms drives home the importance of this theological point. By mimetic I mean that the psalms are presented to readers as models to be emulated. The prayers and songs of the Psalter display a variety of righteous responses to varying situations that God's people have faced, and will continue to face. Moreover, at the level of how the Psalter functions as divine word, God invites readers to take up the words of the psalms and use them to articulate their responses to him.[20] In this way, the Psalter functions to shape God's people ethically. As the words of individual psalms are appropriated and offered back to God, they begin to conform the pray-er to the values encoded within.[21]

Psalm 88 also functions this way. As I argued in the last section, even this darkest of laments constitutes a righteous response. Therefore, God invites his people to also take up these words and to use them in commensurate circumstances. It is here that the use of "you" in Psalm 88 is most

---

19. Webb, *Festal Garments*, 64.

20. On this, see Kit Barker's essays in this volume. See further, Barker, *Imprecation as Divine Discourse*.

21. Consult the very helpful treatment offered by Wenham, *Psalms as Torah*.

sharply felt, as God invites his people to vocalize lament *in this manner*—irrespective of their sensibilities. Indeed, Psalm 88 perhaps goes further than mere invitation. Rather than simply suggesting an option for how people *might* vocalize their response to severe suffering (if they happen to feel like it), Psalm 88 indicates this is how godly sufferers *must* respond. When the darkness descends, when life seems to be drawing near to *Sheol*, this is how those in dire straits *must* speak to Yahweh.

But why must God's people pray this way? Theologically, there is much at stake. To shy away from using second person forms, to avoid assigning blame to God by charging other people or circumstances—no matter how laudable the motive—in the end detracts from Yahweh's absolute rule and authority. Webb is right: "no final explanation for anything is possible other than that he is behind it."[22] That is why complaint uttered with the direct and confronting use of second person language is necessary. It affirms and declares God's sovereignty—often one of the first divine characteristics to drop out of view as sufferers' lives seem to spiral out of control. Thus, by virtue of requiring pray-ers to talk like this, Psalm 88 conditions them theologically. Against any pseudo-pious reticence, Psalm 88 leads its readers to utter the words, "*you* have put . . . *you* overwhelm . . . *you* have made" (vv. 6–8 [emphasis mine]) and, by so doing, to acknowledge Yahweh's unremitting control even in the bleakest of circumstances.

Conclusion

Psalm 88 is confronting. Its lack of movement, unrelenting language and expression, and resolute determination to keep pray-ers in the place of darkness mean this psalm is seldom among people's favorites. Yet, in the end, the aspects of Psalm 88 that contemporary readers find most unpalatable may actually be what they require most. Certainly, the need is apparent. Against the alarming attrition rate experienced in churches, often linked to existential crises of varying sorts, Psalm 88 offers an alternate model. Instead of the retreat from fellow believers and from God, that is so often the case, Psalm 88 invites Christians to imitate a better response, to develop and exercise a robust, theologically sound retort to suffering. Lament does not question or deny God's sovereignty—it appeals to it. Thus, Psalm 88 ought not to be jettisoned in a misguided attempt to preserve Christian orthodoxy. Rather, laments such as this are indispensable for the life of faith in a broken world. Indeed, if we are ever tempted to

---

22. Webb, *Festal Garments*, 64. Of course, there is complexity here. For further discussion, see Carson, *How Long*, esp. 177–203.

eschew Lewis's warning and retreat to a "little treadmill" of "fifteen favourite psalms," we would do well to ensure Psalm 88 is among them.

Bibliography

Alter, Robert. *The Book of Psalms: A Translation with Commentary*. New York: W. W. Norton & Company, 2007.

Barker, Kit. *Imprecation as Divine Discourse: Speech Act Theory, Dual Authorship and Theological Interpretation*. JTISup 16. Winona Lake: Eisenbrauns, 2016.

Berlin, Adele. "Introduction to Hebrew Poetry." In *NIB* 4:301–315.

Brueggemann, Walter. *Into Your Hand: Confronting Good Friday*. Eugene, OR: Cascade, 2014.

———. *The Message of the Psalms: A Theological Commentary*. Minneapolis: Augsburg, 1984.

Brueggemann, Walter, and William H. Bellinger. *Psalms*. New Cambridge Bible Commentary. New York: Cambridge University Press, 2014.

Carson, D. A. *How Long, O Lord?: Reflections on Suffering and Evil*. 2nd ed. Grand Rapids: Baker, 1990.

Dahood, Mitchell. *Psalms II. 51–100: Introduction, Translation, and Notes*. Anchor Bible 17. Garden City: Doubleday, 1983.

Goulder, Michael D. *The Psalms of the Sons of Korah*. JSOTSup 20. Sheffield: JSOT Press, 1982.

Gunkel, Hermann, and Joachim Begrich. *Introduction to Psalms: The Genres of the Religious Lyric of Israel*. Translated by J. D. Nogalski. Mercer Library of Biblical Studies. Macon: Mercer University Press, 1998 [orig. 1933].

Hossfeld, Frank-Lothar, and Erich Zenger. *Psalms 2: A Commentary on Psalms 51–100*. Edited by Klaus Baltzer. Translated by Linda M. Maloney. Hermeneia: A Critical and Historical Commentary on the Bible. Minneapolis: Fortress, 2005.

Johnston, Philip S. *Shades of Sheol: Death and Afterlife in the Old Testament*. Leicester: Apollos, 2002.

Leslie, Elmer. A. *Psalms: Translated and Interpreted in the Light of Hebrew Worship*. Nashville: Abingdon, 1949.

Lewis, C. S. *The Screwtape Letters*. C. S. Lewis Signature Classics Edition. London: HarperCollins, 2002 [orig. 1942].

Preuss, H. D. "Psalm 88 als Beispiel alttestamentlichen Redens vom Tod." In *Der Tod— ungelöstes Rätsel oder überwundener Feind*, edited by A. Strobel, 63–79. Stuttgart: Calwer, 1974.

Villanueva, Federico G. "Preaching Lament." In *"He Began With Moses . . .": Preaching the Old Testament Today*, edited by Grenville J. R. Kent et al., 64–84. Nottingham: IVP, 2010.

Wagner, Norman E. "רָנָּה in the Psalter." *Vetus Testamentum* 10 (1960) 435–41.

Webb, Barry G. *Five Festal Garments: Christian Reflections on the Song of Songs, Ruth, Lamentations, Ecclesiastes and Esther*. NSBT 10. Leicester: Apollos, 2000.

Wenham, Gordon J. *Psalms as Torah: Reading Biblical Song Ethically*. Grand Rapids: Baker, 2012.

Westermann, Claus. *Praise and Lament in the Psalms*. Translated by Keith R. Crim and Richard N. Soulen. Atlanta: John Knox, 1981 [orig. 1965].

Wolterstorff, Nicholas. *Lament for a Son*. Grand Rapids: Eerdmans, 1987.

7

Finding Our Words in His
Christology and Lament

Kit Barker

If there are questions regarding the appropriation of lament in Christian practice, the answers must be found in Christology. How does Christology affect our interpretation of lament? Although some suggest that Christology reduces the function of lament so that it no longer has a place in Christian practice, I will argue that Christology expands the function of lament in a way that offers these words back to God's people as their own.

The aim of this chapter is twofold. Firstly, I will critique popular christological interpretations of lament. Secondly, I will offer a theological interpretation of Psalm 69, by providing a brief discussion of the psalm in its original context and highlighting how Christology shapes a Christian reading of this text.

Contemporary Christological Interpretations
Christ Is the Only Legitimate Appropriator of Lament

In my earlier chapter, I concluded that lament functions as divine discourse in that God offers these words to his people as righteous responses to their sufferings and as righteous responses to the suffering of those among them.[1] Some scholars, however, disagree with the idea that the psalmist's words of lament should become our words. Rather, they see lament psalms as either prophetic pointers to the sufferings of Christ or words that are primarily those of Christ in his suffering. Either way, they are not intended to be our words. Bruce Waltke represents this perspective when he says,

> [Christ] alone is worthy to pray the ideal vision of a king suffering for righteousness and emerging victorious over the hosts of evil. As the corporate head of the church, he represents the believers in these prayers. Moreover, Christians, as sons of God and as royal priests, can rightly pray these prayers along with their representative Head.[2]

For Waltke, the lament psalms are fundamentally the words of Christ. Christians can only pray them if the words are understood as Christ's words, and not their own. Waltke believes that a personal, Christian appropriation of lament is a misguided application of these psalms and is based upon an individualistic, Western interpretation that would be totally "foreign" to Israelite readers.[3]

Hans-Joachim Kraus is similarly adamant that the psalms are no longer words for God's people to adopt. He asserts,

> From the NT perspective, only through the suffering of Jesus as the servant of God has the mystery of the message of Psalm 69 been revealed. For Christians, the essential content of *this psalm will henceforth be accessible in no other way*. The fulfillment "fills" the kerygma of this OT psalm that transcends all individualism; it enters the inexhaustible profundity of the expressions of suffering of a song which, in its powerful proclamation, stands beside Isaiah 53 and Psalms 22 and 118.[4]

Both Kraus and Waltke believe that the psalms of lament should now be understood solely as the prayers of Christ. As they suggest, it is important to recognize that the New Testament portrays Christ as the speaker in the

---

1. "Lament as Divine Discourse" (chapter 4 in this volume).

2. Waltke, "Canonical Process Approach," 16.

3. Ibid., 13. He suggests that the intertestamental period might be responsible for the loss of a messianic interpretation and that this required rectification (15–16). For a defense of democratization as a primary function of the Psalter, see Grant, *King as Exemplar*, 22–23.

4. Kraus, *Psalms 60–150*, 65 (emphasis mine). See also Hays, "Can the Gospels Teach Us," 414–15.

psalms and specifically in certain lament psalms. However, it has not been demonstrated that Christ is the only one who can legitimately pray these words. Such reductionism robs the church of powerful and important words. Furthermore, it is unclear how many of the psalms continue to maintain any relevance to the new covenant community when appropriation by Christ seems unlikely. For example, how are we to understand the admission of guilt and the cry of penitence in the lament of Psalm 51? If the psalms are not our words—and they surely cannot be attributed to Christ—then whose are they? More importantly, how are they God's words to us today?

I suggest that it is not necessary to choose between christological fulfillment and personal appropriation. Rather, I will argue that the christological fulfillment of lament both affirms its previous function and offers these words anew to the church.

Christ Fulfills and Authorizes Lament

Many others have noted that the christological fulfillment of the psalms should not result in a reduction of their relevance. They suggest that the continuing function of the psalms is not limited to either a proclamation about Christ or a presentation of his voice, but exhibits a more complex function.[5] Jamie Grant describes this function in the following manner:

> First, the evangelists present Jesus adopting the psalms as his own prayers; secondly, the psalmic references to YHWH, and his works, are presented as being equally applicable to Jesus himself; and thirdly, the psalms are presented as having a prophetic role, predicting especially the trials and sufferings of Christ.[6]

James Mays agrees and notes further that the function of the psalms as Christ's prayers does not preclude them being our prayers as well. Christ's appropriation of the psalms reinforces their original function as words offered to God's people. In discussing Psalm 22, Mays argues that Jesus was doing exactly what the psalm intended of its audience, and that in doing so, Jesus validated its original function.

> Psalm 22 was composed for liturgical use. What one hears through it is not the voice of a particular historical person at a certain time but one individual case of the typical. Its language

---

5. E.g., Futato and Howard, *Interpreting the Psalms*; Miller, *Interpreting the Psalms*; Grant, "Singing the Cover Versions"; Villaneuva, "Preaching Lament"; Nasuti, "God at Work."

6. Grant, "Singing the Cover Versions," 29.

> was designed to give individuals a poetic and liturgical location, to provide a prayer that is paradigmatic for particular suffering and needs. To use it was to set oneself in its paradigm.
>
> That is first of all what Jesus does in his anguished cry to God when he begins to recite the psalm. He joins the multitudinous company of the afflicted and becomes one with them in their suffering. In praying as they do, he expounds his total identification with them. He gives all his followers who are afflicted permission and encouragement to pray for help. He shows that faith includes holding the worst of life up to God.[7]

As Mays suggests, the fulfillment of the psalm in the life of Jesus does not preclude further appropriation by his followers. On the contrary, Jesus stands in solidarity with the psalmist and those who suffer like him, both vindicating their past responses and providing a model for the future.[8]

I suggest that Grant and Mays offer helpful insights into the christological interpretation of lament. The function of lament is not reduced to Christology; rather, Christology expands its function. The psalms are not only the words of Christ, but words about Christ. They are about Christ as they prophesy concerning his sufferings and vindication, but they are also about Christ because they are about Yahweh. The New Testament declaration "Jesus is Lord" reverberates over the psalms as it does the rest of the Old Testament. So the psalms are about Christ because they are about Yahweh.

Christ fulfills the psalms of lament, resulting in new ways of reading them: he fulfills the role of Yahweh in the psalms; he fulfills the suffering of the psalmist in his own suffering; and Christ's appropriation of lament encourages its continued appropriation by his followers.

Theological Interpretation of Psalm 69

Having outlined two very different approaches to lament, I suggest that a theological interpretation of lament (i.e., "what God is doing with lament")[9] will establish that lament continues to be offered by God to his people. The validation of this claim is best accomplished through a discussion of

7. Mays, *Psalms*, 106.

8. Villaneuva offers a similar explanation: "Now, on the cross, Jesus continues to teach them how to pray. By praying the Psalms, and especially the lament psalms, Jesus points the way further into the heart of God where all our sufferings are validated, accepted and embraced. Praying the lament psalms makes us one with Jesus in taking the sufferings and brokenness of our world" ("Preaching Lament," 80).

9. In speech act terms this asks the question, What illocutions is God performing by way of the text in today's context?

a particular psalm. I have chosen Psalm 69 as it raises particular questions regarding christological fulfillment and is also quoted at length by a number of New Testament authors. My discussion will begin with a discussion of what God *was doing* with Psalm 69 in its original context. Having established this, I will assess how Christology informs our interpretation of what God *is doing now* with Psalm 69 and so offer a theological interpretation of the psalm.

Psalm 69 "Back Then"

Historical Context

Psalm 69 is an individual lament. The exact situation in which the psalmist finds himself is uncertain, yet it is clear that he suffers false accusation, abandonment by loved ones, and physical threat. The reason for his suffering is unclear, yet it is apparent that he suffers through no fault of his own (v. 4). Rather, he is suffering righteously on account of his zeal for Yahweh (vv. 7–9). His suffering, though protracted, is now acute, and death appears imminent. The psalmist associates himself with the עָנִי (*'ānî*, "poor," v. 29 [30]) and אֶבְיוֹנִים (*'ebyônîm*, "needy," v. 33 [34]), creating an expectation of vindication and divine deliverance. Reference to David in the broader collection and here in Psalm 69 presents the psalmist as a righteous responder. He both represents the people and leads the people in their response to Yahweh.

Self-Involving Language

The word of God is powerful. God uses it to change and shape us with each genre having a peculiar force. One way that psalms exert this force is with their self-involving language.[10] By self-involving, I refer to the way in which the psalms *impose* their voice upon us as readers. As we read a psalm, we are forced to adopt the voice of the psalmist. We may or may not be conscious of this and we may or may not agree with the sentiment or the emotion of the psalmist. Nonetheless, the language of the psalm is imposed upon us. We are, in the very reading of the psalm, invited to imitate the psalmist. Thus we have the opportunity to adopt the stance of the psalmist or to reject it.

---

10. For discussion, see Sloane, "Weeping with the Afflicted" (chapter 12 in this volume).

Boldness

Biblical lament is not simply crying out about some misfortune, as lament is often understood in common parlance. Biblical lament is to cry out *to God*, often with a boldness that is at odds with modern sensibilities. The language of lament occurs across a spectrum: from imperatives requesting deliverance, to questions regarding God's apparent inactivity, and bold assertions regarding God's complicity. Psalm 69 offers us such words for desperate times—words to maintain a dialogue with God, words that honor him in times of distress, honest words, bold words, words we need when we need them most.

Each strophe of Psalm 69 opens or closes with a desperate call to God for deliverance. The psalmist states that his "eyes have failed" as he waits for God to act (v. 3), that God has "concealed" his face from him (v. 17), and that ultimately God himself is not only the source of salvation, but the cause of suffering (v. 26).[11] The psalm is presented to the reader and community as a righteous response to suffering. It portrays a deep and unrelenting faith that will not give up on God even when it appears God has given up on them (e.g., "turned his face away").

Innocence and Loyalty

The self-involving language of Psalm 69 challenges readers to consider their own "innocence" and whether they are committed to suffering for God's honor. The psalmist reminds Yahweh that he is innocent, that he is hated "without cause" (v. 4), is unjustly charged with theft (v. 4), and that he ultimately suffers as a result of loyalty to God (v. 8). While the psalmist is adamant that his current situation is not a result of his sin, he does not claim to be without sin. In fact, he openly admits his own "folly" and "guilt" (v. 5), acknowledging that Yahweh is fully aware of them. He is certainly a sinner, but he is innocent with respect to the charges laid against him.

Thus, the psalm asks of its readers whether they can echo these words and claim to suffer innocently for their faith. Furthermore, readers are confronted with the steadfast loyalty of the psalmist (vv. 7–13), and are asked once again whether they would be willing to suffer this much for God.

---

11. See Harper, "Lament and the Sovereignty of God" (chapter 6 in this volume) for further discussion.

Imprecation

A significant obstacle to appropriating psalms of lament is that they often include words of imprecation (i.e., where the psalmist cries out to God for their enemies to be judged). Psalm 69 is a case in point. Verses 23–29 contain some of the strongest words of imprecation found in Scripture: "Pour out your wrath upon them, and your fiery anger overtake them. May their camp become desolate, and in their tents may no one dwell . . . Let them be wiped from the book of life."[12] With these words the psalmist calls for his enemies to be destroyed, their progeny annihilated, and for their destruction to endure beyond the grave. Are we to echo these words?

I have tackled this topic in detail elsewhere, but as any defense of lament must account for the language of imprecation, I summarize that discussion here.[13] Imprecation is a difficult issue. It is difficult to know whether it was right for the psalmist to enact, difficult to reconcile with other portraits of God's character, and certainly difficult to know how to apply it today. However, I believe a deeper understanding of the nature of imprecation and the context in which it occurs can alleviate much of this difficulty.

Firstly, imprecation is often misunderstood as vengeance and cursing. It is neither of these. In fact, imprecation is the antithesis to both. Vengeance says, "I will enact reciprocal violence (and maybe a little extra) against the offender." Imprecation says, "I commit this injustice to you, O Lord, and will not take the matter into my own hands." Imprecation is, first and foremost, prayer. It is directed to God and commits the cause of the oppressed to him. Imprecation "surrenders retribution" to Yahweh.[14] As prayer, imprecation is also vastly different from cursing. Cursing is a direct action against the other. In cultures where it is practiced, it is considered an act of violence. The words are intended to work. They are intended to have an adverse effect upon the person to whom they are directed. Imprecation, by contrast, is directed to God. While it may cry out for justice by requesting acts of violence, it does not enact them and ultimately leaves both the decision and the action to God.

Secondly, imprecation is an act of faith. It recognizes that God is sovereign over all circumstances and all people. Like lament more generally, imprecation is based on the conviction that God rules, and that the problems in this world are his problems (e.g., Pss 2; 46; 97). He is the one to whom we should come when faced with injustice and oppression. In fact, he is the

---

12. Unless otherwise noted, translations are my own.

13. For more detail on how imprecation functions today, see Barker, "Psalms of the Powerless."

14. Here I adapt the title of Firth's monograph, *Surrendering Retribution*.

one who has promised to save and deliver. Imprecation is therefore an act of faith in the promises of God, faith that he will bring justice and vindicate his people.

Lastly, and perhaps more surprisingly, imprecation is an act of loyalty to Yahweh. It is a declaration of "whose side we're on." There are only two "sides": those with Yahweh and those against Yahweh, those who are righteous and those who are wicked, those who "kiss the Son and find refuge" and those who are "destroyed" (see Pss 1 and 2). Imprecation acknowledges that the wicked are fundamentally the enemies of God. While they may also be our enemies or the enemies of our loved ones, they are primarily God's enemies. Imprecation sides with God against the enemy and calls for God's rule to be acknowledged and his name to be honored (Ps 139:19–22). Psalm 69 is no exception. Here we see the psalmist cry out for justice against his enemies, but we also see that the psalmist is "suffering for [God's] sake" (v. 7), and that the "reproaches" that "fall upon" him are those actually directed at God (v. 9).

Expectation

Lament is based on the character of Yahweh. It assumes that he is listening, he cares, and he is able to save. Lament acknowledges that the world is not as it should be and that it cannot remain this way forever. Lament expects change. Psalm 69 concludes with such expectation. In the midst of continual suffering (v. 29), the psalmist is confident that change will come. He anticipates praising Yahweh for salvation (v. 30) and that all God's people will be vindicated and dwell safely with God (vv. 35–36). This hope is based on God's character and his promises. In an earlier strophe, the psalmist "reminded" God of God's own character, of his חֶסֶד (ḥesed), אֱמֶת ('ĕmet), and רַחֲמִים (raḥămîm)—"loyal love, compassion, and faithfulness" (vv. 13, 16). Reminding God of his own qualities forms part of the psalmist's plea for salvation, but it also brings the psalmist, and his audience, hope of a different future. Lament has its basis in the character of God and cries out to him to save, because that is who God is. He is the one who saves.

Summary

What was God *doing* with Psalm 69 "back then"? A few primary actions are evident. Broadly speaking, God *invites* readers to imitate the psalmist's response to suffering and persecution. God also *questions* readers as to whether they are zealous for his glory and whether they are willing to suffer innocently for this zeal. Furthermore, God *reminds* readers of his faithfulness, loyalty, and compassion, which assures them of their vindication, should they remain loyal to God. Finally, God *commends* these bold and desperate words to his people as their righteous response to suffering for his sake.

Psalm 69 in the New Testament

Having discussed what God *was doing* with Psalm 69, we now consider how Christology shapes what God *is doing* with the psalm. Multiple references to Psalm 69 in the writings of John, Luke, and Paul provide us with an important picture of how Christology should inform our reading of this psalm.

John's use of Psalm 69 places Jesus in the narrative of the psalmist. Parallels between the psalmist's circumstances and those of Jesus were clear not only to John but also to the other disciples. After the cleansing of the temple, John notes that the disciples remembered the words of Psalm 69:9—"Zeal for your house consumes me"—implying that the psalm applies prophetically to Jesus. Moreover, it is likely that the application of v. 9 to Jesus suggests that the whole psalm applies to him more generally. This alerts the reader that the zeal of Jesus sets him on the path of the psalmist, a path where unjust suffering is imminent.

This association of this psalm with the life of Jesus is maintained throughout John's Gospel with the next occurrence found in 15:25. Here we find Jesus applying Psalm 69 to his experience of opposition as a fulfillment of v. 4, "They hated me without cause." The third and final reference to Psalm 69 in John occurs in the final moments of Jesus's life. In John 19:28–37, Jesus asks his executioners for a drink. The text states that this request "was to fulfill Scripture." The request itself was not the fulfillment; rather, by asking for a drink, Jesus was aware that the response of the soldiers would place them in the role of the enemies in Psalm 69.[15] Predictably, the soldiers played along, giving Jesus a sponge full of "wine vinegar." The word used to describe the drink in all four Gospel accounts is ὄξος, which refers to either "sour wine" or "vinegar,"[16] and is the word used to translate חֹמֶץ (*ḥōmeṣ*)

---

15. While some have suggested that Psalm 22 is the referred text (e.g., Brown, *John*), Brawley argues convincingly that the surrounding context supports intertextuality with Psalm 69. He notes that on either side of the offer of vinegar are images used in the fulfillment of Scripture. In these cases, it is not the act of Jesus that is the focus, but the actions of his persecutors. Therefore, the fulfillment of Scripture in 19:28 is not the declaration of "thirst" but the action of the soldiers in giving Jesus a drink. Brawley, "An Absent Complement," 438–39.

16. BDAG (574) suggests that this cheaper version of wine was popular among

in the LXX (68:22; MT 69:22). This drink, rather than acting as a sedative, "prolonged life and therefore pain" and should be understood as an act of sadism rather than compassion.[17] Thus, Jesus's request for a drink is both precipitated by his real thirst and also by his knowledge that the reception of a drink will evoke the narrative of Psalm 69.[18] By evoking the psalm in this way, Jesus casts himself in the role of the psalmist and the soldiers and Jewish leaders as his unnamed enemies.

That both Jesus and the disciples recognize his experiences as the fulfillment of Psalm 69 does not exhaust either its meaning or its application. If we return for a moment to John 15 where Jesus states he suffers "without cause" we see that Jesus applies the psalm to himself and also to his disciples. If he has suffered, those who follow him should expect the same; "If they persecuted me, they will persecute you also" (v. 20). I have commented elsewhere on the implications of this for our reading of Psalm 69:

> With his reference to Psalm 69, Jesus places both Himself and His disciples within the narrative of the psalmist. In this pericope, Jesus prepares his disciples for the conflict and suffering ensured by their faithfulness to him (15:18; 16:1-4). Their suffering is to be expected because the world hated both him and the Father (15:18, 23). Therefore, rather than present Psalm 69 as solely fulfilled in the suffering of Jesus, John is affirming that those disciples who faithfully follow Jesus also enter the paradigm of the psalm.[19]

John's use of Psalm 69 both acknowledges its fulfillment in the life and death of Jesus and affirms its continuing application for his followers.

---

soldiers because it more effectively quenched thirst; however, its usage in this scene indicates malice. Carson notes that this drink should not be confused with the earlier drink offered to Jesus while on his way to be crucified as Mark refers to this drink as ἐσμυρνισμένον οἶνον ("wine mixed with myrrh"). Carson, *John*, 620.

17. Köstenberger, *John*, 550. See also Wilson, *Psalms*, 955. Brawley notes the different uses of this drink across the four Gospel accounts. While Matthew and Mark both view the drink as an act of compassion, Luke portrays it as an act of mockery. Brawley, "An Absent Complement," 436.

18. Carson concludes, "John wants to make his readers understand that every part of Jesus' passion was not only in the Father's plan of redemption but a consequence of the Son's direct obedience to it ... And either way, the hermeneutical assumption is that David and his experiences constitute a prophetic model, a 'type', of 'great David's great son.'" Carson, *John*, 619-20; so also Köstenberger, *John*, 550; Ridderbos and Vriend, *John*, 616.

19. Barker, *Imprecation as Divine Discourse*, 201-2.

In similar fashion, Luke records Peter's use of Psalm 69 (and Ps 109) to explain the death of Judas in Acts 1. Here Peter recognizes that Judas plays the role of the unnamed enemy against whom the psalmist imprecates, "May his camp become desolate, and let there be no one to dwell in it" (Acts 1:20 ESV). This use of Psalm 69 (and Ps 109) offers a christological interpretation similar to that found in John's Gospel. Jesus is the innocent and loyal servant of Yahweh who suffers unjustly at the hands of the wicked. Judas, in turn, represents a fulfillment of the unnamed enemy against whom the psalmist imprecates. These associations result in unexpected implications. Casting Judas in the role of the enemy implies that Jesus is the one who imprecates against him.[20] Christ is the imprecator. He is pictured as crying out to God for his enemy to be destroyed.

The last reference to Psalm 69 occurs in Romans 15. In this case, Paul is encouraging the church to emulate the character of Jesus. Paul quotes from Psalm 69:9 and, again, I have commented on this elsewhere:

> This quotation of Psalm 69 is significant because it accomplishes two things. Firstly, . . . the Psalm continues to be applied to Jesus as the righteous sufferer. Secondly, the example of Jesus as the righteous sufferer is offered to the church as a model for them to imitate. In this way, Paul is inviting his readers to identify with both Jesus and the psalmist and place themselves in the narrative of Psalm 69.[21]

The christological application of Psalm 69 in the New Testament demonstrates a consistent pattern. Jesus is cast in the role of the psalmist and various enemies of God's kingdom are cast in the role of the unnamed enemy in the psalm. The reader of the New Testament is, therefore, encouraged to read Psalm 69 as the words of Jesus, and as a model for how to respond to oppression and suffering. Yes, Jesus fulfills Psalm 69, but he does not exhaust its fulfillment or application. His appropriation of the psalm is offered to his people so that they might know how to respond rightly when faced with similar circumstances.

---

20. This is also the case in Romans 11, where Paul casts Israel as the enemy of God and the object of imprecation in Psalm 69 (Rom 11:20).

21. Barker, *Imprecation as Divine Discourse*, 208. So Moo, *Romans*, 869: "Paul therefore implicitly appeals to Jesus' giving of himself in service to others as a model to imitate." See also Schreiner, *Romans*, 747; Morris, *Romans*, 499.

Psalm 69 as Divine Discourse

In light of its New Testament usage we are now in a position to think about how Psalm 69 functions today. Before we do so, let us return briefly to the function of Psalm 69 in its original context. God used the psalm to call people to imitate the psalmist when suffering in a similar manner. He affirmed the words of the psalmist and offered them to his people as a righteous response.[22] Thus, God encouraged readers to imitate the psalmist's wholehearted commitment, despite the consequences. Furthermore, God reminded readers of his character: his faithfulness, love, and compassion. Knowing this, readers were encouraged to cry out with the same honesty and boldness when faced with oppression. Likewise, they were encouraged to acknowledge their sinfulness but also to suffer innocently, "without cause." They should, in fact, have expected suffering because of their faith in God. They were reminded that God is present, is faithful to his promises, and will vindicate his people.

How does Christology complete our theological interpretation of Psalm 69? Simply put, what is God *doing today* with Psalm 69? I believe much of what God *did back then*, he continues to do today. The richness of what God is doing today is not limited to, or truncated by, Christology; rather, a theological interpretation of Psalm 69 is filled out and expanded by Christology. Our examination of New Testament usages of Psalm 69 revealed a range of christological fulfillments: the voice and narrative of the psalm finds a (climactic) fulfillment in Jesus; the unnamed enemies of the psalmist find fulfillment in those opposed to God's kingdom (namely Roman soldiers, unbelieving Israel, and Judas Iscariot); and finally, if we exhibit the same passion and loyalty as the psalmist, his suffering will likely become our own.

These conclusions suggest that contemporary readings of lament that limit its function to the words of Christ have grossly underestimated how Christology completes such a reading. As noted, it is clear that the New Testament presents lament as words about Christ and as the words of Christ. However, even this form of christological fulfillment does not account for all of the psalms or even all of Psalm 69. While much of this psalm can be attributed to Christ, it is difficult to see how the acknowledgment of guilt could be appropriated by him. Christological fulfillment is, therefore, not simply an attribution of the words of the lament to Christ. Though this is part of the fulfillment, there is more: Christ fulfills the suffering of the psalmist in

---

22. As I discussed in chapter 4 of this volume, God does not "request salvation" like the psalmist, yet the psalm remains God's word in that he affirms the psalmist's response and offers it to us as a righteous response.

his own suffering and Christ climactically appropriates the words of lament, even words of imprecation. However, Christ's appropriation of lament is not its end. Rather, his appropriation authorizes, legitimizes, and invites a similar appropriation by his followers. Thus, God continues to speak through these psalms by inviting his people to pray like this when faced with similar circumstances. He offers these words as a righteous response to horrific oppression, reminding us that he is the God who is faithful, loyal, and compassionate; he is the God who saves. Christ found, in the psalms of lament, words he needed when he needed them most. He offers them now to his people who find themselves in desperate need. May we find in these words *his* words—and our own.

Bibliography

Barker. Kit. "Psalms of the Powerless: A Theological Interpretation of Imprecation." In *Stirred by a Noble Theme: The Book of Psalms in the Life of the Church*, edited by Andrew G. Shead, 205–29. Nottingham: Apollos, 2013.

———. *Imprecation as Divine Discourse: Speech Act Theory, Dual Authorship and Theological Interpretation*. JTISup 16. Winona Lake: Eisenbrauns, 2016.

Belcher, Richard. P. *The Messiah and the Psalms: Preaching Christ from All the Psalms*. Fearn: Mentor, 2006.

Brawley, Robert. L. "An Absent Complement and Intertextuality in John 19:28–29." *Journal of Biblical Literature* 112 (1993) 427–43.

Brown, Raymond E. *The Gospel According to John (XIII–XXI)*. Anchor Bible 29A. Garden City: Doubleday, 1970.

Carson, D. A. *The Gospel According to John*. Leicester: IVP, 1991.

Dahood, Mitchell J. *Psalms II. 51–100: Introduction, Translation, and Notes*. Anchor Bible 17. Garden City: Doubleday, 1966.

Futato, Mark D., and David M. Howard. *Interpreting the Psalms: An Exegetical Handbook*. Grand Rapids: Kregel, 2007.

Grant, Jamie A. "Singing the Cover Versions: Psalms, Reinterpretation and Biblical Theology in Acts 1–4." *Scottish Bulletin of Evangelical Theology* 25 (2007) 27–49.

———. *The King as Exemplar: The Function of Deuteronomy's Kingship Law in the Shaping of the Book of Psalms*. Academia Biblica 17. Atlanta: SBL, 2004.

Hays, Richard B. "Can the Gospels Teach Us How to Read the Old Testament?" *Pro Ecclesia* 11 (2002) 402–18.

Kraus, Hans-J. *Psalms 60–150: A Commentary*. Minneapolis: Fortress, 1993.

Köstenberger, Andreas J. *John*. Baker Exegetical Commentary on the New Testament. Grand Rapids: Baker, 2004.

Mays James L. *Psalms*. Interpretation. Louisville: John Knox, 2011.

Miller, Patrick D. *Interpreting the Psalms*. Philadelphia: Fortress, 1986.

Moo, Douglas J. *The Epistle to the Romans*. The New International Commentary on the New Testament. Grand Rapids: Eerdmans, 1996.

Morris, Leon. *The Epistle to the Romans*. Grand Rapids: Eerdmans, 1988.

Nasuti, H. P. "God at Work in the World: A Theology of Divine-Human Encounter in the Psalms." In *Soundings in the Theology of Psalms: Perspectives and Methods in Contemporary Scholarship*, edited by Rolf A. Jacobson, 166–72. Minneapolis: Fortress, 2011.

Ridderbos, Herman. N., and J. Vriend. *The Gospel According to John: A Theological Commentary*. Grand Rapids: Eerdmans, 1997.

Sander, Otto. "Leib-Seele-Dualismus im Alten Testament." *Zeitschrift für die alttestamentliche Wissenschaft* 77 (1965) 329–32.

Villaneuva, Federico G. "Preaching Lament." In *Reclaiming the Old Testament for Christian Preaching*, edited by Grenville J. R. Kent et al., 64–84. Downers Grove: IVP, 2010.

Waltke, Bruce K. "Canonical Process Approach to the Psalms." In *Tradition and Testament: Essays in Honor of Charles Lee Feinberg*, edited by John S. Feinberg and Paul D. Feinberg, 3–18. Chicago: Moody, 1981.

Wilson, Gerald H. *Psalms*. New International Version Application Commentary. Grand Rapids: Zondervan, 2002.

8

The Shape and Function of New Testament Lament

Donald West

THE AIM OF THIS chapter is to set out the shape and function of petitionary prayer in the New Testament with a particular focus on lament. I begin by observing three distinctive emphases of New Testament petitionary prayer and discussing how these aspects impact upon prayers of lament. I then offer a theological framework that allows us to comprehend and apply the distinctive emphases of the New Testament petitionary prayer material, with particular consideration given to Jesus's prayer in the Garden of Gethsemane.

Distinctive Emphases of New Testament Petitionary Prayer

The prayer of lament is a type of petitionary prayer found throughout the Bible in which supplicants plead with God to rescue them from various forms of distress. This form of prayer is especially common in the Old Testament, where petitioners pray to God confident of being heard because of God's "steadfast love" (חֶסֶד, ḥesed; e.g., Pss 5:7; 6:4; 13:5; 17:7; 25:6, 7).[1] This qual-

---

1. In biblical parlance, divine "hearing" does not mean mere listening, but includes acting in response to a request. "Hearkening" is probably a more precise, if somewhat antiquated term: see Westermann, "Role," 21.

ity is grounded in God's redemption of Israel from slavery in Egypt, when he heard their groaning, was compassionate toward them, and remembered his covenant with Abraham, Isaac, and Jacob (Exod 2:23-25). The basis of Israel's confidence before God is that he rescues his people when they cry to him because that is who he *is* (Exod 3:14; 6:6-8; Deut 7:7-11).[2]

While the prayer of lament continues to be used by New Testament petitioners (e.g., Mark 14:36; 15:34; 2 Cor 12:7-8; Rev 6:9-11), petitionary prayer material found in that corpus displays three distinctive emphases when compared to that found in the Old Testament. The first distinguishing emphasis of New Testament petitionary prayer is the prayer promise. The prayer promise is a form of prayer instruction, set out in a consistent pattern, in which divine hearing is promised either unconditionally (e.g., Matt 7:7, par. Luke 11:11) or conditionally (e.g., Mark 11:24). The Old Testament and Second Temple literature contain examples of the prayer promise,[3] but the number and similarity of the promises to petition in the New Testament is remarkable by comparison.[4]

A second distinctive emphasis of New Testament prayer instruction is the exhortation to those in the midst of trial and injustice to press on in crying out to God for vindication until the Eschaton, opening the possibility that deliverance may be delayed until that point.[5] The cry of the martyrs in Revelation 6:9-11 provides a good example of this feature. The prayer echoes features of an Old Testament lament: "Sovereign Lord, holy and true, how long will it be before you judge and avenge our blood on the inhabitants of the earth?" (v. 10).[6] The heavenly response is surprising: "They were each given a white robe and told to rest a little longer, until the number would be complete both of their fellow-servants and of their brothers and sisters, who were soon to be killed as they themselves had been killed" (v. 11). The message for the seven churches of Asia Minor is that salvation, while assured, will only be obtained following perseverance through extreme trials.

---

2. See Miller, *They Cried to the Lord*, chapters 2-4, 7-8, for detailed support for this paragraph.

3. For example, Job 22:21-28; Proverbs 15:8, 29; Isaiah 1:15; Sirach 7:10; 17:25; 21:25; 35:16-20.

4. Specifically: Matthew 6:14-15; 7:7-11 (par. Luke 11:9-13); 18:19-20; Mark 9:29; 11:22-25 (par. Matt 21:21-22); John 14:13, 14; 15:7, 16; 16:23, 24, 26-27; Philippians 4:6-7; Hebrews 4:17; James 1:5-8; 4:2-3; 5:13-18; 1 Peter 3:7, 12; 1 John 3:21-23; 5:12-13.

5. Although some Old Testament prayer texts look to God to right wrongs at the judgment (e.g., Pss 1:4-6; 73:16-20), their predominant expectation is salvation or vindication in the present time.

6. Unless otherwise indicated, all Scripture quotations are from the NRSV.

Jesus's parable of the widow and the judge is told with a similar purpose (Luke 18:1–8).

A third distinctive emphasis of lament-type prayer in the New Testament is exhibited in Jesus's prayer in the Garden of Gethsemane. Here Jesus requests that the Father allow the "hour" to pass him by and the "cup" to be taken away from him (Mark 14:36). He then prays, "nevertheless, not what I want but what you want." There are occasional examples of Old Testament laments that seem to go unheard (e.g., Ps 88), but we do not find petitioners ceding their requests and asking that God's will be done rather than their wishes. To give up on making their pleas would suggest the undermining of a rock-solid expectation of deliverance based on God's revealed character. Though the Gethsemane-type prayer is not commonly found in the New Testament,[7] its pattern is laid upon Christians through the third petition of the Lord's Prayer, "your will be done" (Matt 6:10b; 26:42).

A complicating factor in determining the shape and function of New Testament petitionary prayer material, and the prayer of lament in particular, is that its distinctive emphases are not easily reconciled with each other. In particular, contemporary Christian writers and teachers on prayer struggle over whether to stress the promise that God will hear and respond to our cries *or* to emphasize uncertainty regarding divine hearing of prayer because of the condition of the divine will.[8] However, determining a way to maintain *both* teachings—along with the call to persevere in prayer in the context of unrelenting persecution—is what is needed if we are to be faithful to the Scriptures in our praying. In what follows I offer a theological framework that I think allows us to comprehend the New Testament petitionary prayer material with its distinctive emphases and hopefully to pray with greater confidence.

A Theological Framework for New Testament Lament Prayer

My main proposition is that the various distinctive emphases of the New Testament petitionary prayer material, including the prayer of lament, can best be comprehended around two key themes: the "already/not yet" nature of the kingdom of God, inaugurated by Jesus, and the mediation of this kingdom through Jesus to his disciples in the present time. The two themes

---

7. Other examples include Mark 15:34 (par. Matt 27:46); 2 Corinthians 12:7–12; Hebrews 5:7.

8. See the examples in Crump, *Petitionary Prayer*; Cullmann, *Prayer*; Koenig, *Rediscovering*, 53–65; Miller, *They Cried to the Lord*, 321–24.

(God's kingdom and Jesus's mediation) are intertwined, but the framework established by the nature of the kingdom of God is more dominant. I have therefore structured the following discussion around the two simultaneous aspects of God's kingdom: (1) the "already" of God's kingdom and the mediation of blessings through God's Son; and, (2) the "not yet" of God's kingdom and mediation of sufferings through God's Son.

The "Already" of God's Kingdom and the Mediation of Blessings through God's Son

In the Synoptic Gospels, Jesus's teaching about the kingdom of God is presented, firstly, as a time of all-embracing salvation that includes the forgiveness of sins (e.g., Mark 2:8), healing from life-long sickness and disability (e.g., Mark 1:29–31, 40–45), raising of the dead (Mark 5:35–42), expulsion of demons (e.g., Mark 1:23–26), and the taming of creation's chaos (Mark 4:35–41). That is, through Jesus, God is establishing his kingdom, a time when the *causes* of lament are dealt with and joy results. Jesus says that this kingdom has "drawn near" or "appeared" (Mark 1:15, par. Matt 4:17; Luke 11:20, par. Matt 12:28). Jesus's miracles, exorcisms, and teaching are presented as fulfillments of the promise of the new age of God's reign prophesied in Isaiah 35 (see Matt 11:4, par. Luke 7:22) and Isaiah 61 (Luke 4:21; 19:9; also 23:43).

Jesus's prayer promises, which convey confidence to petitioners of being heard and answered by God, are best situated within the context of a kingdom that has already arrived. This kingdom is a rich and generous realm of God's blessing that is being established in the midst of ongoing need. Jesus's conclusion to the prayer promises in Matthew 7:7–11 (par. Luke 11:9–13) stresses God's willingness to give to the helpless and undeserving: "If you, then, who are evil, know how to give good gifts to your children, how much more will your Father in heaven give good things [Luke: 'the Holy Spirit'] to those who ask him!" (Matt 7:11, par. Luke 11:13). In the letter of James, readers needing wisdom are exhorted to "ask God, who gives to all generously and ungrudgingly, and it will be given you" (Jas 1:5). The main point here—and in all of the promises to petition—is not that petitioners can now get whatever they want through petitionary prayer, but that, although they still live in the context of evil (and hence lament), they have a Father in heaven who will generously provide for their needs in ways that they do not expect.

A second, and connected, aspect of New Testament petition is the role of Jesus as the mediator of God's kingdom. In the Synoptic Gospels, Jesus mediates the "already" kingdom in two ways. He dispenses its benefits to others *and* he directs them to believe in the Father who provides (e.g., Mark 2:5, 11–12; 5:34, 36; 7:24–30; 9:22–24). More significantly, Jesus's pre-resurrection mediation of God's kingdom blessings points forward to his ongoing mediation as the crucified and risen Messiah. The book of Hebrews, for example, encourages its readers to approach the "throne of grace" with "boldness" because they "have a great high priest who has passed through the heavens, Jesus, the Son of God" (Heb 4:14–16). In John 14–16, Jesus repeatedly promises his disciples that, because he is "going to the Father," they may ask "anything" from the Father in his "name" knowing that he will do it, "so that the Father may be glorified in the Son" (John 14:13, 14; 15:16; 16:23, 24, 26).

The bountifulness of the already-present kingdom of God, inaugurated through Jesus, thus signals a new era of confidence to come before the Father with open-hearted pleas for help with every expectation of being heard and answered, even in the midst of difficulties.

> Do not worry about anything, but in everything by prayer and supplication with thanksgiving let your requests be made known to God. And the peace of God, which surpasses all understanding, will guard your hearts and your minds *in Christ Jesus*. (Phil 4:6–7; emphasis added)

The "Not Yet" of God's Kingdom and the Mediation of Sufferings through God's Son

Alongside the proclamation of the kingdom of God that has drawn near, Jesus speaks of a kingdom that is yet to be "entered into" (Matt 5:20; 7:21; 18:4; Mark 10:23, 24, 25, par. Matt 19:23, 24). He likens this future kingdom to a feast (e.g., Luke 14:15–24; also Matt 8:11–12, par. Luke 13:28–30), a society filled with righteousness (Matt 5:19; 18:1, 23–35; 20:1–16; 21:43), and a longed for gift or reward (Matt 5:3, 10; 6:33; 19:12, 14; 25:1, 34), which will be revealed when the Son of Man appears in his glory (e.g., Mark 9:1, par. Matt 16:28; Luke 9:37; Matt 20:21, par. Mark 10:37; Mark 14:25, par. Matt 26:29; Luke 22:18).

However, Jesus says that this "not yet" kingdom will only be entered into through persecution: "From the days of John the Baptist until now the kingdom of heaven has suffered violence, and the violent take it by force" (Matt 11:13, par. Luke 16:16; see also Acts 14:22). Jesus is positioned as the mediator of the sufferings attached to God's kingdom: "I came to bring fire upon the earth, and how I wish that it were already kindled! I have a baptism with which to be baptized, and what stress I am under until it is completed" (Luke 12:49–50). Elsewhere Jesus refers to his suffering through the image of the "cup," both at the Last Supper—"this cup is my blood poured out for many" (Mark 14:24, par. Matt 26:28; Luke 22:20)—and in Gethsemane (Mark 14:36, par. Matt 26:39; Luke 22:42). He also applies the same image to the disciples: "the cup that I drink, you will drink; and with the baptism with which I am baptized, you will be baptized" (Mark 10:39, par. Matt 20:23). Those who share the benefits of his suffering will also share his trials (Luke 22:28–32).[9] However, in the "already/not yet" era of God's kingdom, suffering for the "name" of Christ is considered a "blessing" (1 Pet 4:14; Matt 5:10, 12).[10] Indeed, those who "mourn" (i.e., lament) are declared "blessed" (Matt 5:4, par. Luke 6:22b). The reality of severe opposition and the struggle against temptation and Satan's wiles that mark the era of the "not yet" kingdom help us to understand the many New Testament injunctions regarding alertness and supplication until the End (Eph 6:18; Col 4:2–3; 1 Pet 4:7; 5:6–10; Luke 18:1; 21:36). As Jesus agonizes over his own "cup" in the Garden of Gethsemane, he warns the disciples: "Watch and pray that you will not fall into temptation. The spirit is willing, but the flesh is weak" (Mark 14:38 [NIV], par. Matt 26:38; Luke 22:40, 46).

Returning to Gethsemane

We come, finally, to Jesus's Gethsemane prayer and its implications for our own prayers of lament. How does Jesus discontinuing his lament and submissively asking that God's will be done fit into the "already/not yet" framework that is laid out above? We firstly note that Jesus's two requests—that the Father remove the cup, and that God's will be done—concern the same issue: the fulfillment of the divine plan of salvation through the vicarious suffering and death of the Son of Man, Jesus of Nazareth. The "will" that Jesus requests to be "done" is not a hidden decree but what he has stated throughout the Gospel accounts: "The Son of Man did not come to be served but to serve, *and to give his life as a ransom for many*" (Mark 10:45, par. Matt 20:28; emphasis added).[11] In this light, it is interesting to note that there is no implied or explicit criticism of Jesus's first plea, that the cup be

---

9. See 2 Corinthians 1:3–7; Philippians 1:29–30; 3:10–11; Colossians 1:24; 1 Peter 2:23; 3:17–18a; 4:13 (see also 1:6; 2:20; 4:16); Hebrews 12:2 (see also 5:7).

10. See also, Acts 5:41; 1 Peter 1:6–9; 2:20–23; 3:14–17; 4:13–16.

11. Following Stuhlmacher, "Jesus' Readiness," 396–412. See Mark 8:31; 9:12, 31; 10:33, 45; 12:8; 14:21, 36, 41; see also Isaiah 53:10–12.

removed, either in the Gethsemane account or elsewhere in the Synoptic Gospels.[12] It seems we are intended to take *both* Jesus's cry of anguish to the Father ("remove this cup from me") *and* his prayer of submission ("not what I want but what you want") as a whole example for our own lament prayers.[13] That is, we are meant to note the *way* Jesus prays in the midst of extreme distress—how he "entrusted himself to the one who judges justly" (1 Pet 2:23) by pleading with God that he not be required to drink the "cup" *and* by prayerfully submitting to the divine will. In a sense, these two aspects represent the two poles of the "already/not yet" kingdom. Jesus, confessing God's ability to act here and now ("all things are possible with you" [Mark 14:36b]), pleads for release. At the same time, he recognizes that God's salvation plan necessitates his suffering and death to reach fulfillment, and so takes hold of the "cup" through prayer.

The application of the Gethsemane text to our own laments must, of course, take its peculiar factors into account—in particular, that the "cup" that Jesus refers to in Gethsemane is an experience of divine wrath for the sin of others. This work was "laid upon" Jesus alone to complete (Acts 5:30; 2 Cor 5:21; Gal 3:13; see Isa 53:6), and those who now come before the Father do so only through the mediation of the *crucified* and risen Son (Heb 7:25). However, a "cup" remains to be drunk by those who belong to Christ in the "not yet" era. God's will, his plan of salvation, has not yet been fully "done." For this reason, in the Lord's Prayer, we ask the Father both for our physical and spiritual needs *and* for his name to be sanctified, his kingdom to come, and his will to be done. We are to know that it is through our struggle, distress, and cries for help—that is, our lamenting—that God is completing his saving work in the world. Moreover, as Paul reminds us, even as we struggle to know how we ought to pray in this "already/not yet" era, the Spirit "intercedes for us" in ways that we do not comprehend, but which are understood by the Father to whom we cry, "because the Spirit intercedes for the saints according to the will of God" (Rom 8:26–27, 15).

Conclusion

We have seen that situating New Testament petitionary prayer teaching and its prayer of lament within the theological framework of an "already/not

---

12. Jesus's soliloquy in John 12:27–28a does pose a challenge here. See West, "Promises," 214–22, for detailed consideration of this text.

13. This is implied by the way that the Gospel accounts join the two prayers: Mark 14:36 uses ἀλλά, Matthew 26:39 and Luke 22:42 use πλήν, and Matthew 26:42 uses a conditional sentence.

yet" kingdom mediated by Jesus best allows us to comprehend the distinguishing emphases we find there. The promises regarding petition lead us to confidently make our requests before God because his kingdom has already come in and through the person of his Son. The call to persevere in the midst of trials and temptation is necessary because the kingdom revealed in and through Jesus is not complete. Indeed, this kingdom can be seen as a revelation of divine judgment upon sin, ultimately borne by Jesus himself on behalf of "many." The present era is one in which those who belong to him lament and are declared "blessed." Lastly, the challenge raised by Jesus's Gethsemane prayer—where a plea is ceded in submission to the divine will—is best seen as a moment in which the "already/not yet" kingdom of God bears upon Jesus. While this moment has aspects that apply to Jesus alone, it also presents us with a way by which we are now to lament, by crying out to God for release in the midst of trials and the unfolding of God's judgment upon sin *and* asking that his plan of salvation would continue to be accomplished through these very trials. And we may be confident that we are heard in both respects because we have the Son who mediates at the Father's right hand and the Spirit who intercedes for us according to the saving will of God.

Bibliography

Crump, David. *Knocking on Heaven's Door: A New Testament Theology of Petitionary Prayer*. Grand Rapids: Baker, 2006.

Cullmann, Oscar. *Prayer in the New Testament*. Translated by John Bowden. London: SCM, 1995.

Koenig, John. *Rediscovering New Testament Prayer: Boldness and Blessing in the Name of Jesus*. San Francisco: Harper & Row, 1992.

Miller, Patrick D. *They Cried to the Lord: The Form and Theology of Biblical Prayer*. Minneapolis: Fortress, 1994.

Stuhlmacher, Peter. "Jesus' Readiness to Suffer and His Understanding of His Death." In *The Historical Jesus in Recent Research*, edited by James D. G. Dunn and Scot McKnight, Sources for Biblical and Theological Study 10, 392–412. Winona Lake: Eisenbrauns, 2005.

West, Donald S. "Promises to and Limitations upon Petitionary Prayer in the New Testament: A Study of Their Relationship." PhD diss., Edith Cowan University, 2009.

Westermann, Claus. "Role of the Lament in the Theology of the Old Testament." *Interpretation* 28 (1974) 20–38.

9

Man of Sorrows, What a Name!
The Place of Lament in the New Testament

DAVID K. BURGE

THERE SEEMS TO BE a suspicion among Christians, on a popular level at least, that lament is a pre-Christian or sub-Christian activity. As one author states, "Has not every reason for lament been taken from [Christians], are their tears not wiped away by the resurrection of Christ?"[1] Does—or perhaps better, *should*—lament have a place in Christian life and worship?

The New Testament would seem the obvious place to turn to consider this query. Yet, in doing so, further questions arise. If lament is an acceptable activity for Christians, why is it not endorsed more prominently in the New Testament? Can Christians only go to writings that *pre-date* Jesus when struggling with death, depression, or chronic illness? How does the New Testament minister to the lamenting? Is the God of the New Testament as approachable, interested, and helpful as the God of the lament psalms? What does lament in the lives and cries of New Testament saints look like?[2] While we cannot address all of these questions here, many are resolved at least partially when we recognize that the New Testament does not intend to

---

1. Harasta, "Crucified Praise," 208.

2. Following Old Testament tradition, and in light of the contrast with cheerful praise, James 5:13 may well have had psalm-like lament prayers in mind when saying, "Is anyone among you suffering? Let him pray" (Κακοπαθεῖ τις ἐν ὑμῖν, προσευχέσθω), before asking, "Is anyone cheerful? Let him sing praise" (εὐθυμεῖ τις, ψαλλέτω).

match or supplant the lament psalms; rather, the New Testament endorses, enriches, and extends the benefits they offer.

Accordingly, this essay will consider how the New Testament writings affirm the validity of lament by observing its normative presence in the lives and teachings of Jesus and his three most prominent apostles—Peter, Paul, and in a cursory way, John. The sufferings of Jesus and the apostles are recorded in part that we might realize that they, and their good news of hope beyond suffering, welcome the lamenting; we have a high priest who is able "to sympathize with our weaknesses" (Heb 4:15; also 2:9–10).[3] The Christ who suffered for us is supremely approachable, as Christians through the ages have declared:

> I heard the voice of Jesus say,
> Come unto me and rest.
> Lay down, o weary one, lay down,
> Your head upon my breast.
> I came to Jesus as I was,
> weary and worn and sad,
> I found in Him my resting place,
> and He has made me glad.[4]

Lament in the Life and Teachings of Jesus

It is clear from the outset that Jesus was destined for a life of suffering and sorrow. The New Testament draws us straight into the sadness that Isaiah intimated would come with the person of the messiah. Indeed, he is named Jesus (the late Hebrew or Aramaic form of Joshua, meaning "the Lord saves") because "he will save his people from their sins" (Matt 1:21). Jesus was born to die. But worse, he was born to die as one forsaken by his eternal Father, cursed upon a tree, and bearing the world's sin upon his shoulders. Isaiah's Immanuel was born the Messiah of Israel, the Suffering Servant, and Passover Lamb of God. With the passing of years, Jesus no doubt grew to understand the sobering weight of each of these names.[5]

The trials began immediately for the infant Jesus, whose young parents were forced to seek refuge in Egypt to escape the murderous "fury"

---

3. All biblical quotations are taken from ESV unless otherwise stated.
4. From the hymn by Horatius Bonar (1808–1889), "I Heard the Voice of Jesus Say." In the public domain.
5. The prologue to John's Gospel likewise leads us to anticipate struggle for the Son of God; the world he made was the world which rejected him (John 1:11).

(ἐθυμώθη λίαν, Matt 2:16) that his very arrival had "stirred up" (ἐταράχθη) in King Herod (Matt 2:3).[6] At the age of twelve Jesus demonstrated a remarkable grasp of scriptural matters (Luke 2:47), and as he grew in wisdom and stature he also no doubt had a growing, disturbing sense of his *raison d'être*.

By the time of Jesus's public ministry, the Man of Sorrows had thus been forged. With the help of John the Baptizer prior to his beheading, Jesus's formidable task was to help recalcitrant Israel, through graphic and offensive diagnostic teachings, to see what it refused to see—the depth of its plight and its sickness as one in need of a doctor (Mark 2:17; also John 8:39–47). His Sermon on the Mount would be underestimated or snubbed by the self-assured. It is an appeal and a balm from the humble for the humble—Jesus and his message are for those whose song is the song of lament. Only the spiritually down and out will rejoice according to the Beatitudes, which begin with disarming assurance:

> Blessed are the poor in spirit, for theirs is the kingdom of heaven. Blessed are those who mourn, for they shall be comforted. Blessed are the meek, for they shall inherit the earth. Blessed are those who hunger and thirst for righteousness, for they shall be satisfied ... Blessed are you when others revile you and persecute you and utter all kinds of evil against you falsely on my account. (Matt 5:3–6, 11)

The reversals declared by Isaiah are now echoed with authority by Immanuel. "It's okay" in Jesus's world to be poor, mournful, meek, dissatisfied with one's own unrighteousness, reviled, persecuted, and falsely accused (v. 11); more surprising is the declaration that this is not merely acceptable, it is necessary!

Indeed, the kingdom of heaven is *for the poor in spirit*. The coming comfort is for mourners. And it is those who are deeply aware of their sin who shall be satisfied when they receive the righteousness that they presently lament is beyond them. The Beatitudes are for the lowly, and point to a coming time (a time inaugurated with Jesus) when God will forever reverse the fortunes of his struggling people. As the Gospel accounts proceed, the lament and hope of the psalms are wonderfully echoed, embodied even,

---

6. Jesus's birth brought with it the prophesied "weeping and great mourning" for the many parents of Bethlehem and its vicinity whose infants were needlessly massacred by Herod (Matt 2:16–18). It was only when Jesus's father heard that "those who sought the child's life are dead" (Matt 2:20) that he returned to Israel, but despite his youth, Jesus remained an unwelcome citizen in his homeland. Afraid of Herod's son, Archelaus, Joseph's young family "withdrew to the district of Galilee and lived in a town called Nazareth" (Matt 2:22–23)—its insignificance as a hamlet was its chief virtue for a family unjustly in need of refuge.

with Jesus's lowly life and his appalling death, followed by his most pleasing, deserved resurrection.

Thus, the Beatitudes are not exceptional within the Gospels for their lament tone; rather, the Beatitudes are programmatic for the Gospels and for what we might call "Christ-ianity." For Jesus teaches that he is only for those who carry a cross after him (Luke 14:27), and that the life he offers is only for grains of wheat who have fallen into the soil to die (John 12:24), having "hated" their lives in order to gain eternal life (John 12:25). The sin of Jerusalem brought tears of lament to Jesus's eyes (Luke 19:41–44), and so, too, followers of Jesus will be burdened by the sin that is not only around them but also within them. The woman who washed Jesus's feet with her tears and her hair is our model; her lament deepened her gratitude for the one who accepted her as she was. As C. H. Spurgeon says,

> the Christian spirit pants after holiness. He who is born again of incorruptible seed, finds his worst trouble in sin. While he was in his natural state he loved sin, and sought pleasure in it, but now being born of God and made like to God, he hates sin, the mention of it vexes his ears, the sight of it in others causes him deep sorrow, but the presence of it in his own heart is his daily plague and burden.[7]

Spurgeon's point is not that we cannot find any relief from this burden at the cross of Jesus, but that as forgiven children, God's distaste for sin is increasingly ours as we mature in him.[8]

Significantly, Jesus then explicitly endorses the place of lament by praying the words of the lament psalms, which in a prophetic sense were written most specifically about him and for his use.[9] The perfect man laments. Indeed, God laments. Eva Harasta writes:

> The lament of Christ takes place within God himself. It provides a glimpse into God's despair and suffering about the world and about himself. Christ involves the Father and the Spirit in the situation of the godless.[10]

---

7. Spurgeon, "The Glorious Hereafter and Ourselves," 52.

8. Similarly, see the examples of lament in relation to personal sin among the prayers of the Puritans in Bennett, *The Valley of Vision*.

9. E.g., Luke 24:44–47. Christians as early as Augustine have argued that the author of Lamentations, for example, displays a foreknowledge of Christ. See, e.g., Augustine, *City of God*, 18.33. For further discussion, see Brock, "Augustine's Incitement to Lament," 183–95.

10. Harasta, in conversation with the works of Jurgen Moltmann and Dietrich Bonhoeffer, makes some profound theological propositions on this topic, even if at

This is not to equate God's lamenting with ours absolutely, but it does endorse lament as good.

> The lament of believers is not the lament of Christ. His lament is God's lament, the lament of God incarnate. Their lament is the lament of the justified sinner, of the sons and daughters of God.[11]

Both God's lament and ours are deemed entirely appropriate. Before his death, Jesus's lament was borne out of his righteousness—lament through what Gerald Peterman calls his "painful compassion," "grieving anger," his "fear," and even his "discontent."[12] Then, on the cross, the Man of Sorrows bore our griefs and carried our sorrows so that by his stripes we might be ultimately healed.

Self-help books call on readers to lift themselves, but the Gospels show the limits—folly, even—of the self-help approach to life; the person and work of Christ is the balm for those whose weakness is beyond them to overcome. His appeal, perhaps deemed irrelevant to "the strong," is a lifeline to those of us who lament our desperate need of it:

> Come to me, all who labor and are heavy laden, and I will give you rest. Take my yoke upon you, and learn from me, for I am gentle and lowly in heart, and you will find rest for your souls. For my yoke is easy, and my burden is light. (Matt 11:28–30)

Jesus and his gospel assure us that God "hears us." God welcomes his lamenting, prodigal people and promises relief. He swaps yokes, taking upon himself what we find unbearable, and offering his strength as our own. His is not a quick fix; but as we take up a heavy cross and follow him he brings rest, and the promise of rest.

Further, suffering Christians can know that their trials, far from being abnormal, are one indication we are on the right path, a path that ends with peace and rest, banqueting even, in the presence of our Master (Matt 25:23). His "It is finished!" is our "It is finished!" and the resurrection declares his rescue of us a resounding success (1 Cor 15:54–57). Better than anyone, he knows that in this world we will have trouble; but we take heart, because he has overcome the world (John 16:33).

Christian lament is addressed to the crucified one. Christ's death and resurrection has not done away with lament. It is better to say that the "cross reveals God's own acceptance of lament, and the resurrection bears witness

---

times somewhat speculatively. See Harasta, "Crucified Praise," 211.

11. Ibid., 206.

12. Peterman, "A Man of Sorrows," 87–99.

to the transformation of lament in the context of the new, eschatological reality which is brought about by the Spirit 'already.'"[13] The topsy-turvy, wondrous emotions of Good Friday—deep lament and lofty praise—are expressed in the hymn:

> Man of sorrows what a name
> For the Son of God, who came
> Ruined sinners to reclaim:
> Hallelujah, what a Savior![14]

Thus far we have observed, among other things, that our lament is understood by the Man of Sorrows; that lament is a thoroughly Christian activity; that the Gospels foster lament ("blessed are you who weep now, for you will be filled") to a crucified, lamenting Lord; and that lament is to be informed by Christ's death and vindicating resurrection, both of which are ours through our union with him (Rom 6:1–11). Yet it is also important for lamenting people to realize that the risen Jesus continues to hear, welcome, and even endorse lament in the rest of the New Testament and beyond. To consider this further, we turn to the lives and writings of three dominant New Testament apostles—Peter, Paul, and John.

Lament in the Life and Letters of Peter

Peter is also a man of sorrows by the end of the Gospel accounts—grieving a lost friend and struggling with shame. He knew Jesus was the Messiah (Matt 9:20), and worshiped him as God (Matt 14:33). He had assured Jesus of his undying loyalty (Matt 26:35), and rightly so, for Jesus had become the closest of friends to Peter. Jesus was, of course, more worthy of loyalty than any other person in Peter's life. And yet, at Jesus's point of need, Peter slept (Luke 22:40). Worse, when Peter could have stayed with Jesus in his trials (Luke 22:28), three times he deliberately denied that he even knew his abandoned best friend. Luke then records the heart-breaking account of their eye contact as "the Lord turned and looked at Peter. And Peter remembered the saying of the Lord, how he had said to him, 'Before the rooster crows today, you will deny me three times.' And he went out and wept bitterly" (Luke 22:61–62).

If Peter grieved deeply before Christ's death, how much more at the sight of Jesus crucified. He had deserted and lost the man he loved more

---

13. Harasta, "Crucified Praise," 205.
14. From the hymn by Philip P. Bliss (1875), "Man of Sorrows." In the public domain.

than any other (John 21:15). Peter felt things deeply—he was the only one bold enough to step from the safety of the boat to join Jesus upon the water; he was the one who offered to pitch a tent for Moses and Elijah, as though this would be helpful; he was a man who wore his heart on his sleeve, and reacted wholeheartedly to life with Jesus.

In this way, Peter is the perfect foil in God's purposes to portray the wonder of his Son. What others were thinking, Peter expressed through his exuberance (e.g., Matt 14:28–31). How crushed he of all friends must have been after denying Jesus, not once, but three times—worsening the pain of Jesus's death through his abandonment.[15]

It is little wonder Peter was the one who ran to the tomb at the news of Jesus's resurrection (Luke 24:12), and "threw himself into the sea" (ἔβαλεν ἑαυτὸν εἰς τὴν θάλασσαν) at the sight of the resurrected Jesus on the shore, confident he could swim faster than the boat in order to be with him (John 21:7). If ever there was someone who wanted Jesus's death to be reversed, undone, overcome, it was Peter.

John's Gospel records the lovely way the Lord Jesus ministers to his lamenting, ashamed friend. Three times Peter was given the opportunity to "own" Jesus at Jesus's point of need; three times he failed; and three times God orchestrated a cock to crow as an alarming reminder. The use of threes is not redundant, but a powerful intensifier of Peter's experience of lament and restoration. Jesus appears to the disciples three times in John's account, and in a highly charged conversation Jesus kindly allows Peter three opportunities to affirm the sincerity of his love: "Simon son of John, do you love me?" (John 21:15). To repeat the question a second time must have been confronting, but to ask a third time, each time with his personal name "Simon son of John," was more than disarming—"Peter was grieved (ἐλυπήθη) because Jesus asked him a third time, 'Do you love me?'" (John 21:17).

A superficial reunion with Jesus after Peter's denial would not have adequately treated Peter's shame. Instead, a lamenting Peter is provided with an opportunity to assure Jesus of his weak yet undying devotion to him before Jesus departs a final time. Three times, Peter is directed to express his love by caring for Jesus's lambs (vv. 15, 16, 17), meaning that Peter, the rock upon which Jesus would build his church, was graciously restored, affirmed, and re-commissioned to his privileged work. His shame was put wonderfully behind him.

---

15. Harris argues that desertion was taken personally as a betrayal of trust, on the basis of Paul's statement about Demas: "Paul sadly notes that 'Demas, because he has loved this world, has deserted me' . . . Demas's departure was evidence of a desertion that was apparently a betrayal of trust." Harris, *Seven Sayings*, 61–62.

For the poor in spirit who realize just how far we, too, disappoint and fall short of what Jesus deserves from us, this is a deeply restorative encounter. Peter's lament and restoration is written for us! His weakness is recorded for us in our weakness.

Such unforgettable lessons shaped Peter's life, ministry, and letters. Before long, he was imprisoned for Christ (Acts 4:1–3), and towards the end of his life, in the mid-60s AD, Peter assured other persecuted Christians that the One for whom they were suffering is worthy. Jesus understands their suffering (1 Pet 3), provides joy and hope for them to endure it, and assures them that suffering for him will end in glory (1 Pet 1:3, 5, 8–9, 11–13). For though they cannot see Jesus, they are right to share Peter's love for Jesus (1 Pet 1:8), and though they "have had to suffer grief through all kinds of trials," their faith is being proved genuine. A limited time separates them from Jesus's inheritance that can never perish, spoil, or fade (1 Pet 1:3–6).

Peter knew persecution and no doubt lamented the suffering endured by his, and Jesus's, lambs. When Stephen was stoned to death, as one example, we read there was "great lamentation over him" (ἐποίησαν κοπετὸν μέγαν ἐπ' αὐτῷ, Acts 8:2). But things worsened further for God's people, and their suffering for bearing Christ's name was far worse than is perhaps commonly recognized in the Western church today. For if accounts of Nero's pogrom against Christians are chilling reading for us, how much more disturbing must it have been for Peter, their loving shepherd, to experience and witness it firsthand.

Like Jesus, Peter also lived for decades with the knowledge that his life would end as a prisoner and martyr (John 21:18–19), and by AD 67–68 the ominous signs led Peter to say that the putting off of his tent of a body (σκήνωμα) was drawing near (2 Pet 1:13–14). According to Origen, Peter "was crucified with his head downward, having requested of himself to suffer in this way" as one unworthy to die in the same way as his Lord.[16]

Like Jesus, and many saints before and after him, Peter knew what it was to lament. It is against the backdrop of Peter's and the church's "fiery trial" (πύρωσις) that Jesus's grace, power, and promises are more vividly seen and more firmly grasped. In the "now and not yet" of Christ's kingdom, lament, suffering, and grief co-exist with rejoicing (1 Pet 4:13).[17] In this way,

---

16. Eusebius, *Ecclesiastical History*, 3.1. Clement, Dionysius, and Tertullian, among others, mention Peter and Paul's suffering and execution under Nero.

17. Although 1 Peter may not often be deemed one of the more significant New Testament letters by Western Christians, I have heard anecdotally that it is a favorite letter for Christians enduring persecution in Indonesia. Peter assures troubled believers that God hears their cry, that their Lord has suffered ahead of them, and has for fellow "aliens and strangers" (1:1) a future worth living and dying for (4:12–14). Joy

the Beatitudes describe Peter's life and are then reiterated in the themes and vocabulary of his two epistles.[18]

Lament in the Life and Letters of Paul

It might be, and no doubt has been, argued simplistically that the apostle Paul removes the basis for Christian lament. Isn't he the one who commands us to "be joyful always"? Those of us in pastoral ministry may be guilty of subconsciously flattening out depictions of Paul so that we present him as we may, mistakenly, want our churches to be: active, busy, zealous, prayerful, happy, and other such "positive things." Is Paul someone we can hear from in times of lament? Do we sense through his writings that God hears us, and ministers to us in our lament, as I have argued is the case in the lives of Jesus and Peter?

Few would be bold enough to suggest that Paul was anything but a remarkable human being. A typical analysis of Paul's life and achievements may leave us rightly staggered at what God can do through one person.[19] That point cannot and need not be defended here. Sadly, however, Paul's great strengths have led some to deem him as being unloving, arrogant, or at best, intimidating, and not a person we might connect with, particularly in times of lament. Will I not be only more depressed by reading Paul, or worse, by comparing myself with him?

In God's kindness, however, the helpfulness of Paul for lamenting Christians has also been preserved for us in Scripture, even if oft overlooked. He too is a person who hears us and ministers to us as he shares his heart and life with the church. And as with Jesus and Peter, Paul's prescribed path makes lament not only acceptable, but inevitable, as he invites Christians to suffer with him.

It is an understatement to say that Paul endured more than most the trials that come with being God's servant in a fallen world. Indeed, his suffering was part of Jesus's explicit intention and job description for him:

---

is not robbed through suffering and lament; rather, Christians through their persecutions can inwardly rejoice that they participate in their Lord's suffering, and bear his name (4:12, 13, 16).

18. Compare, as one example, Matthew 5:16 and 1 Peter 2:12. For further discussion of the sources of Peter's thought, see Burge, *First-Century Guides*, ch. 9.

19. See, for example, F. F. Bruce's influential work—*Paul: Apostle of the Heart Set Free*, 32–52. See also, Machen, *Origin of Paul's Religion*, 7–8; Reymond, *Paul, Missionary Theologian*, 15–30.

Jesus said, "I will show him how much he must suffer for my name" (Acts 9:16).[20]

Many would concede that Paul suffered physically, but fewer perhaps realize the extent to which Paul struggled emotionally. The texts we shall now consider demonstrate a struggle that cannot be contained to any one dimension of his person; that is, it would be to run against the evidence provided by these texts to argue that Paul's physical suffering took no toll on him emotionally or mentally.

A passage with depths difficult to plumb in this regard is Romans 9–10. The Paul who says, "be joyful always," is the same Paul who can also say (in the sense we saw in the Gospels, where attributes such as joy and rest co-exist with lament) in Romans 9:1–3,

> I am speaking the truth in Christ—I am not lying; my conscience bears me witness in the Holy Spirit—that I have great sorrow and unceasing anguish [λύπη μοί ἐστιν μεγάλη καὶ ἀδιάλειπτος ὀδύνη] in my heart. For I could wish that I myself were accursed [ἀνάθεμα] and cut off from Christ for the sake of my brothers, my kinsmen according to the flesh.

The sincerity of Paul's words is clear—his conscience bears witness, and Paul invokes the name of Christ and the Holy Spirit as those aware that, to paraphrase with the NLT, "his heart is filled with bitter sorrow and unending grief" for the salvation of his own people, the Jews (see also 10:1). So strong is his unmet desire for them that he would be willing to become anathema to Christ, whose love Paul has just celebrated as being inseparable from his people (8:31–39). This was no brief episode of lament, but was presumably endured whenever he observed the Jews' repeated, widespread rejection of their Messiah.

Many Christians who lament the spiritual state of loved ones may find solace not only because Paul expresses in words how they may feel, but also because he works through this struggle towards a doxology *in the very context of his lament*: "Oh, the depth of the riches and wisdom and knowledge of God! How unsearchable are his judgments and how inscrutable his ways!" (Rom 11:33). The doxology does not preclude or nullify Paul's grief and sorrow. Rather, God's unfathomable wisdom and goodness are realities within which Paul expresses and submits his grief.[21]

---

20. See the chapter entitled, "Suffering & the Pauline Mission: The Means of Spreading the Gospel," in Schreiner, *Paul, Apostle of God's Glory in Christ*.

21. Similarly, Jesus submits the hostile rejection of him by his enemies to the will of God when he says, "I praise you, Father, Lord of heaven and earth, that you have hidden these things from the wise and understanding and revealed them to little children;

The limits of this chapter preclude in-depth analysis of Paul's sufferings, but it would be remiss to overlook the condensed summary he provides in 2 Corinthians 11:23–30. He experienced:

> far greater labors, far more imprisonments, with countless beatings, and often near death. Five times I received at the hands of the Jews the forty lashes less one. Three times I was beaten with rods. Once I was stoned. Three times I was shipwrecked; a night and a day I was adrift at sea; on frequent journeys, in danger from rivers, danger from robbers, danger from my own people, danger from Gentiles, danger in the city, danger in the wilderness, danger at sea, danger from false brothers; in toil and hardship, through many a sleepless night, in hunger and thirst, often without food, in cold and exposure. And, apart from other things, there is the daily pressure on me of my anxiety for all the churches. Who is weak, and I am not weak?

The historical Paul, the real Paul, was no stranger to suffering, weakness, and lament. He, like Jesus, would later lament the experience of desertion prior to his execution.[22] Although Paul spoke of the "scars/marks of Jesus" (τὰ στίγματα τοῦ Ἰησοῦ, Gal 6:17) on his body and of his sufferings for Christ, we never sense in Paul a desire for pity. Yet he does urge Christians to "weep with those who weep" (Rom 12:15). Indeed, to avoid Christian lament may require one to avoid the trials or scars of Jesus that come with faithfulness (Gal 1:9–10; Gal 6:12).[23] For "all who desire to live a godly life in Christ Jesus will be persecuted" (2 Tim 3:12; see also 2 Thess 1:4). Thus Paul urges us, as did Jesus and Peter, to be living sacrifices in imitation of our Suffering Servant (Rom 12:1–2; Phil 1:20; 1 Cor 11:1), and to receive the same balm of hope in God's sovereignty and care (Rom 5:1–5; 8:18–39). For Paul is not ultimately broken by his trials, and burdensome though they are, it is extraordinary that he is able to consider them a "light momentary affliction" compared to that which God is doing in us and ahead of us:

> So we do not lose heart. Though our outer self is wasting away, our inner self is being renewed day by day. For this light momentary affliction is preparing for us an eternal weight of glory beyond all comparison, as we look not to the things that are

---

yes, Father, for such was your gracious will" (Matt 11:25; also Luke 10:21).

22. See fn. 15.

23. Such brotherly love and concern, shown through emotional bonds with suffering brethren, distinguished Paul from Stoics like Epictetus who taught adherents to have a strict emotional detachment from the grieving of others. See Burge, *First-Century Guides*, chs. 3 ("Epictetus's Guide to Life") and 11 ("Peter's Guide to Life").

seen but to the things that are unseen. For the things that are seen are transient, but the things that are unseen are eternal. (2 Cor 4:16–18)

Though such texts are not typically considered lament texts comparable to the psalms, they are an excellent tonic for those whose experience of a fallen world is eating away at them.[24]

Conclusion: The Importance of Lament in the New Testament and in the Church

We return to some of the issues raised at the start of this essay. How does the New Testament minister to the lamenting? What comfort does the Triune God offer in the New Testament era and beyond? Is there a place in the life of the church for people who have lost a child, or whose lives are darkened by sin, broken relationships, or depression? Do our churches reflect the open arms of Jesus to a suffering world, where putting on a happy "church face" should neither be needed nor encouraged?

We have argued that Jesus, Peter, and Paul, like the psalmists, endured much suffering and responded in lament. They invite us, urge us even, to demonstrate the same response while living a cruciform life in a hostile and fallen world. As Paul and Peter testify, the Man of Sorrows, our Servant King, offers glory, but only on the other side of suffering.

In this way, the New Testament elucidates and heightens our reason to lament, even as it tells us that we lament with certain hope. As Spirit-filled Christians, we now read as *Christian* literature texts such as Psalms 23:6; 33:16–22; 42:5[6], 11[12], and Isaiah 40:31.[25] On our side of the Messiah's victorious death and resurrection, united with him by his Spirit as a seal and pledge, we have even more certainty than Old Testament saints that he will complete the rescue, vindication, and glorification of his people (Rom 5:9–10; 8:28–39).[26]

---

24. A similar perspective is found in Romans 5:1–11, in which God, through Paul, assures us that even our suffering is used for our good due to its cultivation of hope (ἐλπίς). Romans 8, likewise, makes what we might call an "incomparable comparison" between our present sufferings, longings, frustrations, groaning, and decay and our hope for creation's liberation and the glory that will be revealed in us. Even our groaning is expected, welcomed, and Spirit-led as those whose pain is real, yet whose suffering produces hope in God's ultimate relief (Rom 5:1–5).

25. In the Septuagint, ἐλπίς ("hope") is used in these texts to translate בטח (*bṭḥ* "to trust"), חסה (*ḥsh* "to flee for refuge"), and יחל (*yḥl* "to wait, to hope").

26. Second Peter 1:19 speaks of the "made-more-sure prophetic word" (βεβαιότερον

Christian joy and peace are gifts of Christ to help us endure what must be recognized as a truly painful period between promise and relief, between the first and second comings of Jesus. Words of lament are also a gift. Our churches are weakened to the extent our leaders deny or avoid the need for such words; indeed, for the sake of the hurting, for the sake of the entire body, and for Christ's sake, we must embrace lament and rightly weep with those who weep.

On this side of the cross and resurrection, and with the blessings brought by the Spirit, Christians enjoy a more advanced "now" than that of the psalmists, while still awaiting that which is still, painfully, "not yet." The extent to which the New Testament sheds further light upon God and his goodness (e.g., John 1:14, 18; Heb 1:1–3) is the extent to which it extends the lament psalms' reason for hope and joy amid trials. When we read the lament psalms as people who know the Messiah, their gravitas and usefulness are magnified. In this way, the New Testament helps us to appreciate the Old. Conversely, the lament psalms aid our reading of the New Testament—they heighten our appreciation for what the Man of Sorrows endured, and why.[27]

Having given our attention to Jesus, Peter, and Paul in order to survey the New Testament through the eyes of its most prominent figures, it seems fitting to conclude with at least a cursory recognition of the apostle John, who brings the canon to a close from his exile in Patmos. The tearful hope and patient endurance of Christ's precious people under the cruelty of Rome will finally and forever cease when the old order of things has passed away (Rev 21:4). God assures his waiting, lamenting people, "It is done" (Rev 21:6); "Surely I am coming soon." And his people reply, "Amen. Come, Lord Jesus!" (Rev 22:20).

Bibliography

Augustine, *The City of God*. Translated by Markus Dods. Edinburgh: T. & T. Clark, 1949.

τὸν προφητικὸν λόγον) on the basis that the spectacular prophecies in the Old Testament have proven true with the miraculous Christ-events to which Peter was an eyewitness.

27. Harris (*Seven Sayings*, 60), for example, observes, "Like the psalmist, Jesus feels abandoned by God—a God whom he has always trusted but now seems distant and silent, unaffected by his servant's dire distress in the face of death. But unlike the psalmist, Jesus is enduring actual abandonment by God and experiences no rescue through divine intervention."

Bennett, Arthur, ed. *The Valley of Vision: A Collection of Puritan Prayers & Devotions.* Edinburgh: Banner of Truth, 1975.

Brock, Brian. "Augustine's Incitement to Lament, from the *Enerrationes in Psalmos*." In *Evoking Lament: A Theological Discussion,* edited by Eva Harasta and Brian Brock, 183–203. London: T. & T. Clark, 2009.

Bruce, F. F. *Paul: Apostle of the Heart Set Free.* Carlisle: Paternoster, 1977.

Burge, David K. *First-Century Guides to Life and Death: A Comparative Study of Epictetus, Philo and Peter.* Milton Keynes: Paternoster, 2017.

Droge, Arthur J., and James D. Tabor. *A Noble Death: Suicide and Martyrdom among Christians and Jews in Antiquity.* New York: HarperSanFrancisco, 1992.

Eusebius. *Ecclesiastical History.* Loeb Classical Library 153. Translated by Kirsopp Lake. Cambridge: Harvard University Press, 1980.

Harasta, Eva. "Crucified Praise and Resurrected Lament." In *Evoking Lament: A Theological Discussion,* edited by Eva Harasta and Brian Brock, 204–17. London: T. & T. Clark, 2009.

Harris, Murray J. *The Seven Sayings of Jesus on the Cross: Their Circumstances and Meaning.* Eugene, OR: Cascade, 2016.

Machen, J. Gresham. *The Origin of Paul's Religion.* New York: Macmillan & Co., 1923.

Peterman, Gerald W. "A Man of Sorrows: Emotions and the Suffering of Jesus." In *Between Pain and Grace: A Biblical Theology of Suffering,* edited by Andrew J. Schmutzer and Gerald W. Peterman, 83–101. Chicago: Moody, 2016.

Reymond, Robert. *Paul, Missionary Theologian: A Survey of his Missionary Labours and Theology.* Fearn: Christian Focus, 2000.

Schreiner, Thomas R. *Paul, Apostle of God's Glory in Christ: A Pauline Theology.* Downers Grove: IVP, 2001.

Spurgeon, C. H. "The Glorious Hereafter and Ourselves." In *The Metropolitan Tabernacle Pulpit: Sermons Preached and Revised by C. H. Spurgeon During the Year 1870,* vol. XVI, 49–60. London: Passmore & Alabaster, 1871.

Part III

The Exegesis of Lament

10

The Role of Lament in the Shape of the Psalter

Dan Wu

When he opened the fifth seal, I saw under the altar the souls of those who had been slain because of the word of God and the testimony they had maintained. They called out in a loud voice, "How long, Sovereign Lord, holy and true, until you judge the inhabitants of the earth and avenge our blood?" (Rev 6:9–10)[1]

And I heard a loud voice from the throne saying, "Look! God's dwelling place is now among the people, and he will dwell with them. They will be his people, and God himself will be with them and be their God. He will wipe every tear from their eyes. There will be no more death or mourning or crying or pain, for the old order of things has passed away." (Rev 22:1–5)

How long, O Lord? (Pss 6:3; 13:1, 2; 35:17; 74:10; 79:5; 80:4; 89:46; 90:13; 94:3)

Praise the Lord! (Ps 150:6)

THIS CHAPTER SEEKS TO explore how recent studies that focus on the editorial shaping of the Psalter might benefit our reading, teaching, and living of the book. My thesis can be stated as follows: Even if there is a resolved

---

1. Unless otherwise indicated, all biblical references are taken from the NIV.

"story" in the editorial shaping of the Psalter, it is one in which lament continues to play an integral part to the end. More fully, recent studies have majored on the question of whether there is an intentional "shape" to the order and arrangement of the individual psalms.[2] In particular, discussion has revolved around the notion of the book following a "story," of either the history of Israel's relationship with Yahweh, and/or an analogy of the life of faith in general. My suggestion is that if this is the case, then the significant presence of lament in the later parts of the book implies the ongoing legitimacy and importance of the genre to the overall message of the book, and thus to Christian life in the overlap of the ages, even in light of the victory of Christ.[3]

However, before embarking on the main part of the study, it is helpful to make note of exactly which psalms we are talking about. As noted previously in this volume, modern Psalms study, including the classification of the lament form, springs from the work of Hermann Gunkel's form criticism.[4] Within a broader spread of four main genres and six minor ones within the Psalter,[5] Gunkel identified two "types" of lament—communal and individual—and listed them as follows:[6]

Communal laments: Psalms 44; 58; 74; 79; 80; 83; 105; 125

Individual laments: Psalms 3; 5; 6; 7; 13; 17; 22; 25; 26; 27:7–14; 28; 31; 35; 38; 42; 43; 51; 54; 55; 56; 57; 59; 61; 63; 64; 69; 70; 71; 86; 88; 102; 109; 120; 130; 140; 141; 142; 143

I will return to this list later in the chapter. For now, I will make two brief comments about it. First, the above list represents only those psalms that fully fit the template of the genres, in Gunkel's assessment. His complete lists also included several other "mixed genre" psalms that feature laments, or

---

2. For recent surveys of this discussion, see the collected essays in McCann, *Shaping of the Psalter*; deClaissé-Walford, *Shaping of the Book of Psalms*.

3. By "overlap of the ages," I mean what is otherwise called "the now-not-yet tension," or inaugurated eschatology. For exploration of the role of lament in light of the New Testament, see chapters 7–9 in this volume.

4. See Harper, "Lament and the Sovereignty of God" (chapter 6 in this volume). See further Gunkel and Begrich, *Introduction*, 1–21; Sweeney, "Form Criticism," 227–41; Broyles, "Lament, Psalms of," 384–99. For critiques of form criticism, see, e.g., Hely Hutchinson, "Psalms and Praise," 93–95; Wilson, *Editing of the Psalter*, 1–5.

5. Gunkel's other main genres were the (communal) hymn and the (individual) thanksgiving. The six minor genres were blessing and curse sayings, pilgrimage songs, victory songs, thanksgiving songs, legends, and Torah psalms (Gunkel and Begrich, *Introduction*, v).

6. Ibid., 82, 121.

lament fragments, within them.⁷ Second, it should thus be clear that lament is a dominant theme in the book, with forty-seven full psalms in the genre (as classified by Gunkel), and many others containing elements of lament within them.

Psalms Study since 1985: The "Shape" of the Psalter

Gerald Wilson

While form criticism has been, and continues to be, the foundation of modern Psalms criticism, a second major stream of research has emerged in recent times, catalyzed by Gerald Wilson's landmark 1985 study, *The Editing of the Hebrew Psalter*.⁸ Building on the insights of Brevard Childs, Wilson noted the tendency of form criticism towards fragmentation of the Psalter, favoring interpretation of individual psalms in genres, but without much regard to their placement within the book as a whole.⁹ Wilson proposed instead that the Psalter displayed a purposeful, editorial "shape," modeled on the story of Israel's relationship with God, from the Davidic covenant to the hope of the diaspora in Yahweh's kingship alone. In particular, he highlighted the use of royal psalms at the "seams" of each of the collections (or "books") within the Psalter as waypoints for this story.¹⁰

While some have expressed significant points of reservation with details of Wilson's work (e.g., his suggestion that the Davidic kingship fades into obsolescence in Books IV–V),¹¹ the general consensus in Psalms studies is that "his basic directions and conclusions are convincing."¹² Moreover, it has generated a new stream of Psalms study that offers fruitful new dimensions in understanding both the whole book, and the individual lament psalms within it.¹³ I will outline two of the recent contributions on this front, from Claus Westermann and Walter Brueggemann, before offering my own suggestions and conclusion.

---

7. E.g., most of Psalm 119 is included as individual lament.
8. Wilson, *Editing of the Psalter*.
9. Childs, *Old Testament as Scripture*.
10. For a fuller description of Wilson's work, see Harper, "Silence of the Lambs" (chapter 11 in this volume).
11. E.g., Hely Hutchinson, "Psalter as a Book," 38–41.
12. McCann, "Changing Our Way of Being Wrong," 24.
13. For a worked example of this (on Ps 8), see Harper, "Silence of the Lambs."

Claus Westermann

Prior to Wilson, Westermann had already condensed Gunkel's spread of psalm genres to just two: praise and lament.[14] However, this was not simply a matter of clearing up redundant categories. Rather, Westermann analyzed the distribution of the two genres within the Psalter, and concluded that (individual) laments were concentrated in the first half of the book, while larger groups of praise psalms were only found in the second half of the book. As such, the Psalter demonstrates a sweeping move *from lament to praise*.[15]

Westermann's analysis can be seen as consistent with Wilson's work, and provides a strikingly simple, yet remarkably accurate, reading of the shift in the Psalter's overall emotional tone. Perhaps an analogy to certain sermon preparation methods is apposite here: if Westermann provides the "big idea" statement of the Psalter ("from lament to praise"), Wilson gives us the five "points from the passage" that support it.[16] In any case, Westermann's analysis is very helpful in encapsulating the overall message of the Psalter, although I will return to it in due course to add more nuance to its broad sweep.

Walter Brueggemann

Brueggemann has published extensively on the Psalter, but has done so with a focus on the *social function* of the psalms, both in ancient Israel, and in contemporary Christian settings. In essence, Brueggemann suggests that the psalms are particularly expressive of "when the most elemental and raw issues [of human life] are at play."[17] In other words, the psalms present the extremes of human existence, when all coping mechanisms and defenses—ancient or modern—have been stripped away. As such, their cries are as appropriate for contemporary Christians to take on their lips as they were for ancient Israelites: "We may anticipate a *commonality of function* even when other matters diverge."[18]

---

14. Westermann, *Praise and Lament*, 252–58.

15. Ibid., 33, 75, 257.

16. These taglines are drawn from Haddon Robinson's popular preaching method, as featured in his *Biblical Preaching*; see also Chapman, *Setting Hearts on Fire*; Cook, "A Method of Preparation."

17. Brueggemann, "Psalms and the Life of Faith," 6.

18. Ibid. (emphasis original). Brueggemann derives these classifications especially from the work of Paul Ricoeur.

In line with his emphasis on the experiential aspect of the psalms, Brueggemann's distinctive classification of psalm types is the famous triad: *Psalms of Orientation, Psalms of Disorientation,* and *Psalms of Reorientation*.[19] These categories go on to provide Brueggemann's interpretative grid for analysis of individual psalms.

The Psalms of Orientation present a simple (or, perhaps better, simplistic) worldview, characterized by orderliness, goodness, and, most significantly, a lack of tension to solve. Brueggemann included creation psalms (e.g., Ps 104) and some of the Deuteronomistic/Proverbial wisdom psalms (e.g., Ps 37) in this category.

The lament psalms belong to the Psalms of Disorientation category. Here, the naïvely idyllic view presented in the Psalms of Orientation has been displaced or shattered by an experience of suffering or distress at the seeming failure of God's promises. These psalms variously present the stages of denial and acceptance, but in the main they involve the critical turn from yearning for the old order, to accepting that it is gone, and now being ready for a new orientation.

The Psalms of Reorientation present that new circumstance, which breaks free of the (actually) inhibiting old order. It is instead characterized by newness, surprise, and gift, all of which ought to be celebrated. However, this celebration is different to that of the Psalms of Orientation, for it is truer and no longer naïve; it is a hope "after the pit." Thus the hymns and thanksgiving songs belong to this category.

It is important to note at this point that, for Brueggemann, the Psalms of Disorientation (i.e., lament psalms) are the binding force and hermeneutical key to the entire Psalter. They encapsulate the journey of the book, with its whole sweep of emotions, within the particulars of the genre. The plea section looks backward, yearning for the old order and grieving its loss, while the praise section strains forward, looking to the hope of the new.[20]

Brueggemann has developed this schema further into the macro structure of the whole book, arguing that the beginning, middle, and end of the Psalter are indicative of this move.[21] For Brueggemann, Psalm 1, a Torah Psalm of Orientation, was intentionally placed there by the Psalter's editors to establish *obedience* as key to life at the beginning of the book. Its Deuteronomistic terms present life in a simple (simplistic?) deed-consequence pattern, in which obedience is blessed, and disobedience is cursed.

---

19. Ibid., 9–15.
20. Ibid., 24.
21. Brueggemann, "Obedience and Praise."

This obviously stands in contrast with much of the rest of the Psalter, but Brueggemann argues that this is precisely its canonical function.²²

Brueggemann then moves to Psalm 150, whose placement is equally intentional. What is especially striking about this closing psalm is the absence of reasons for praise. It is "determined, enthusiastic, uninterrupted, relentless ... [and] unrelieved" in its praise. This is because by now, Israel has learned, through the course of the book, all the reasons for praise. Thus there is no need to restate them. All that remains is a glad abandonment and focus on God himself.²³ Brueggemann thus concludes that the Psalter moves *from obedience to praise*, or "from willing duty to utter delight."²⁴

At the heart of this move from obedience to praise—in fact, what enables it—is *"candor about suffering* and *gratitude about hope"* in the face of the crisis resulting from the apparent failure of Yahweh's faithfulness to his promises (i.e., his חֶסֶד, *ḥesed*—"faithful love" or "covenant loyalty").²⁵ The main bulk of the Psalter, then, wrestles with the gap between the expectation of Yahweh's חֶסֶד (*ḥesed*, "faithful love"), and the suffering that casts such striking doubt on its reality. Accordingly, Brueggemann sees Psalm 73 as the pivotal psalm in the book. Drawing on Wilson's work, Brueggemann observes that Psalm 72, a "royal seam psalm," closes the second Book of the Psalter with reference to Solomon, whose failure to exercise righteous kingship eventually led to the dissolution of the kingdom. Psalm 73, then, responds to this utter crisis of faith, and wrestles with the seeming incongruity of the promises of God in the old order (Ps 73:1 *qua* Ps 1), and the present experience of the oppressive flourishing of the wicked (Ps 73:2–12).²⁶

Brueggemann sees the decisive turning point in the psalm as v. 17, which he takes as the psalmist's encounter with God in the sanctuary, "mov[ing him] from calculating conduct to trustful communion as ... [he] discerns that face to face engagement with God is finally what matters."²⁷ This, claims Brueggemann, moves the Psalter beyond the claims of Psalm 1 to focus in on communion with God as the key to true life. This move

22. Ibid., 66.

23. Ibid., 67–68.

24. Ibid., 71. It is important to note that Brueggemann does not view obedience and praise as mutually exclusive, but as intimately connected: "Only the obedient can praise God." However, the movement is only one way: "obedience has been overcome, transcended and superseded in the unfettered yielding of Psalm 150." Ibid., 69–70.

25. Ibid., 72 (emphasis original). For further reflection on the centrality of this theme in the psalms, see Wu, "The Psalms and Perplexity," 243–46.

26. Brueggemann, "Obedience and Praise," 82–88. See also Brueggemann and Miller, "Psalm 73 as a Canonical Marker."

27. Brueggemann, "Obedience and Praise," 85–86.

prepares the way for Psalm 150's self-abandoned praise: "The speaker has traversed, as Israel regularly traverses, the path from obedience to praise, by way of protest, candor and communion."[28]

Brueggemann thus views Psalms 1 and 150—obedience and praise—as the boundaries of the life of faith, held in supportive tension by the crisis of Psalm 73 at the theological mid-point. The rest of the psalms then lurch between these poles, again and again, doing the hard work of the daily life of faith, but all the while drawing closer to the unhindered praise of Psalm 150. As Brueggemann concludes: "Israel's life of faith consists in an abrasive, buoyant conversation about God's ḥesed which fails and then reappears with power . . . the literature of the Psalms [thus] articulates the shape, not only of a biblical book, but of Israel's faith and of Israel's life."[29]

An Evangelical Appropriation of the Role of Lament in the Shaping of the Psalter

While I do not agree completely with any of the above analyses, recent work on the shape of the Psalter can prove immensely beneficial for our understanding of the book as a whole, and thus the role of the lament psalms within it.[30] As such, I will give a brief outline of the message of the book, seeking to appropriate relevant insights, and then examine the place and role of the lament psalms and genre within it.

---

28. Ibid.

29. Ibid., 91.

30. For brief critiques of some of Brueggemann's interpretative points see, for example, Hely Hutchinson, "Psalms and Praise," 91–92; Wu, "Psalms and Perplexity," 245–46. Particularly problematic is Brueggemann's reliance on Psalm 1 being expressive of a simplistic Deuteronomistic view of obedience and blessing, and the "trajectory" relationship he sees between obedience and praise. This is especially the case in light of some works that re-examine the nature of both Deuteronomistic theology and wisdom literature, e.g., Hubbard, "Wisdom Movement," esp. 17–20. Against Brueggemann's suggestion is the sustained presence of Psalm 1-like Deuteronomistic theology in the final parts of the Psalter (e.g., Ps 119), including Book IV, the "new hope," beginning with a psalm of Moses (the Lawgiver), and the final "Hallelujah" psalms also featuring Torah psalms (e.g., Pss 145; 146). If these psalms were reflective of a naïve version of faith, which must give way to something more mature, it seems incongruous for the editors to include them this late in the piece. Perhaps the disjunction between obedience and praise, and between so-called Psalms of Orientation, Disorientation, and Reorientation, is not as pronounced as Brueggemann's model suggests.

The Shape and Message of the Psalter

My own suggestion for the message of the Psalter, derived from its canonical shape, can be expressed as follows:

> *We find blessing in God's righteous king, which leads to a life of praise.*[31]

As already observed, scholars have noted the importance of the opening and closing psalms for the framing of the book.[32] Specifically, Psalms 1 and 2 stand as the introduction to the Psalter, bracketed by the term "blessed/happy,"[33] while Psalms 146–150, the "hallelujah" psalms, form its conclusion. Thus Psalm 1 establishes the key subject of the book: "Who is the righteous, Torah-keeping man, who wins God's blessing?" Psalm 2 then gives the basic answer to this question: "The (Davidic) Messiah of Yahweh, who also shares his blessing with those who take refuge in him."[34]

The first of the psalms "of David," Psalm 3, beginning the Psalter proper, introduces an immediate surprise. For the David we meet there does not seem to be the conquering, victorious Messiah of Psalm 2; instead, he is the persecuted sufferer. The rest of the psalms in Books I (Pss 1–41) and II (Pss 42–72), with their concentration of Davidic ascriptions, then variously reflect aspects of the experience of this David in his (and perhaps also his descendants') kingship of Israel as well as the experience of the nation under his rule. In summary, while legitimate high points do feature (e.g., Ps 19), the main tone of Books I and II, as commonly observed, is that this "Davidic Psalter" is characterized by the lament of the suffering servant, and David's continued failure to be the righteous king God's people need (e.g., Ps 51). As noted above, Book II concludes with Psalm 72, "Of Solomon," thus ending "The prayers of David, the son of Jesse" (Ps 72:20) on an ominous note, seemingly on the doorstep of the utter failure of the Davidic kingship to bring in the promised kingdom of Psalm 2.

Book III (Pss 73–89), unfortunately, brings no relief. Instead, it is dominated by the persistent presence of lament. Indeed, the mood seems to become darker as the book progresses. In addition, the focus expands from (mainly) individual psalms to (mainly) communal. Increasingly, in

---

31. By "we," I mean the perspective of the faith community who comprise the hearers/readers of the book.

32. Besides Wilson and Brueggemann, see Hely Hutchinson, "Psalms as a Book," 25; Howard, *Structure of Psalms 93–100*, 200–207; Taylor, "Psalms 1 and 2."

33. Hebrew אַשְׁרֵי, *'ašərê* (Pss 1:1; 2:12).

34. See Hely Hutchinson, "Psalter as a Book," 25. The strong echoes of 2 Samuel 7 in Psalm 2 reinforce the likelihood that the Messiah here is the Davidic king.

this book, the psalms have to do with Israel and its place among the nations, and not simply the sin of the Davidic rulers, but also of the entire nation.[35] These themes come to their despairing climax in Psalm 89, which cries out in agony over what appears to be a loss of all hope: the absolute failure of the Davidic promises, the destruction of the kingdom, and the scattering of the exile.

In the face of such disaster, Book IV (Pss 90–106) begins on the striking note of Psalm 90, "A Prayer of Moses the Man of God." Reaching back before the monarchy, Israel in exile is drawn back to Yahweh's fundamental covenant promises at Sinai.[36] Though there is an acknowledgment of the continuing distress of the exile, and of the sin that precipitated it, nonetheless the psalm ends with a note of renewed hope in Yahweh's favor and deliverance. The Book as a whole demonstrates a remarkable, continued confidence in Yahweh, and his power to save, rule, and bring judgment on the nations. Indeed, Book IV stresses Yahweh's ultimate kingship (featured most prominently in the יְהוָה מָלָךְ, *Yhwh mālak* ["Yahweh reigns"] psalms), and concludes with a "mini hallelujah chorus" (Pss 103–106), perhaps in anticipation of the final victory note at the end of the Psalter. What is also interesting, however, is that Psalm 90's hearkening back to Moses (and thus the Torah) appears also to recall the Psalter's own introductory psalms (i.e., Pss 1 and 2). Perhaps then, Psalm 89 was not Yahweh's final word on the Davidic kingship.[37]

Book V (Pss 107–150) completes the Psalter's story. Yahweh's people are regathered from exile (e.g., Ps 107:2–3), and are graciously forgiven and restored. His promises to his people drive towards unshakeable fulfillment, and thus (as Westermann observed), the tone of the Psalter shifts towards praise. In view of this, the Psalter fittingly ends with a series of rising, communal "Hallelujah!" choruses (Pss 146–150). Both the enemies of God's people and their sin, having been dealt with, fade from view, culminating in the final victory of Psalm 150, where all that is left to say, again and again, is "praise Yahweh!"[38]

---

35. See McCann, "Books I–III," 95–100, who notes that Book III is dominated by communal psalms and, particularly, communal lament psalms.

36. For Wilson, this move is indicative of the passing of Davidic kingship in favor of Yahweh's kingship alone, which is the main thrust of Book V and the final answer to Psalm 1 (Wilson, *Editing of the Psalter*, 215–28). Others, however, have argued against Wilson's almost complete subordination of the Davidic kingship to Yahweh's alone. For more detail, see the references in Howard, "Psalms in Current Study," 26–27.

37. *Pace* Wilson.

38. So Brueggemann, but cf. Hely Hutchinson's caveat that Psalm 150:2 *does* in fact give a rationale for praise ("Psalms and Praise," 92).

The "Story" of the Psalms

BOOK 1 (1-41)	BOOK 2 (42-72)	BOOK 3 (73-89)	BOOK 4 (90-106)	BOOK 5 (107-150)
INTRO (Ps 1 & 2): Blessing in life under the Son THE PSALMS OF DAVID: God's suffering King?	FROM DAVID TO SOLOMON: Is this the Son you're looking for?	FROM SOLOMON TO EXILE: The Great problem in Israel's history	BACK TO MOSES & GOD'S LAW PLEA FOR GOD TO REIGN: Yahweh Reigns Psalms	GOD WILL ACT TO DELIVER & REIGN & DAVID REAPPEARS... PRAISE THE LORD!

Figure 10.1 Overview of the five books of the Psalter

However, it is also intriguing to note that immediately prior to this conclusion sits a cluster of Davidic psalms (Pss 139–144). Read in light of Psalms 1–3, it would seem that *here*, finally, is the David of Psalm 2 we have been looking for. Only once he is re-established as Yahweh's vice-regent can the promised blessings flow unhindered to his people such that they can respond accordingly with unadulterated praise.[39]

Perhaps we may extend this further to account for both the particular focus on the individual (David) and the communal (his people). That is, it is only by binding their lives to this suffering, vindicated, and finally victorious David—sharing something of his experience, and coming under his kingship—that will finally lead God's people to the life of blessing and praise forecast in Psalm 1.[40] Thus the final message arising from the shape of the Psalter, as stated previously, may be summarized as:

> *We find blessing in God's righteous king, which leads to a life of praise.*

---

39. Note the answering echo of Psalm 2:3 in Psalm 149:8—the rebellious kings have been subdued by this Messiah, finally fulfilling the prospect envisioned at the opening of the Psalter.

40. It is interesting to note not only the mix of individual and communal laments in the Psalter, but also, say, in the key example of Psalm 73, the intertwining of the experience of the individual lamenter, and their effect on the community (e.g., Ps 73:13–15). See further Wu, "Psalms and Perplexity," 244.

THE THEOLOGICAL MESSAGE OF THE PSALMS

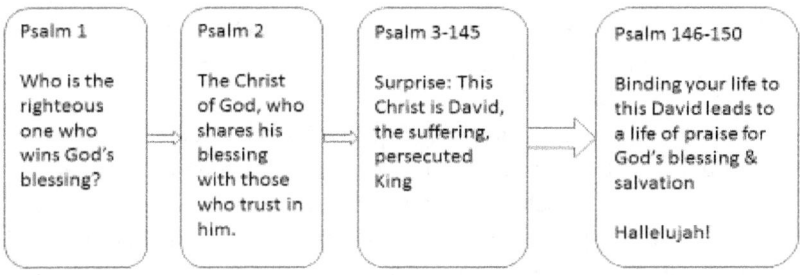

Figure 10.2 Overview of the theological message of the Psalter

The Place and Role of Lament in the Shape of the Psalter

It should be clear to the reader that such a reading of the Psalter's editorial shape derives from a strong biblical theological reading, which sees the fulfillment of the Old Testament Scriptures in Jesus's death on the cross, resurrection, and final return. There is, of course, much more to be said to adequately substantiate and explore the implications of such a reading for Christian appropriation and application of the psalms of lament. For that, the reader is referred to the rest of the essays in this volume. If my reading of the Psalter may be held as plausible for now, though, what I wish to reflect on is the place and role of the lament psalms within this structure.

Earlier, I gave a list of psalms classified by Gunkel as laments. Here is the same list, except this time, arranged in canonical order:

Book I (Pss 1–41)	3; 5; 6; 7; 13; 17; 22; 25; 26; 27:7–14; 28; 31; 35; 38
Book II (Pss 42–72)	42; 43; 44; 51; 54; 55; 56; 57; 58; 59; 61; 63; 64; 69; 70; 71
Book III (Pss 73–89)	74; 79; 80; 83; 86; 88
Book IV (Pss 90–106)	102; 105
Book V (Pss 107–150)	109; 120; 125; 130; 140; 141; 142; 143

Table 10.1 Lament psalms in canonical order

What is of note here is that, as much as the Psalter displays a move from lament to praise (so Westermann), and as much as Book V envisions the inexorable march towards final victory of Yahweh, *lament remains a prominent feature of the Psalter to the end*. Indeed, when Gunkel's psalms of mixed genre that include lament are added to this list—many of which come in

Books IV and V—the impression is only reinforced. Especially striking is that four of the six final Davidic psalms (Pss 139–144) are laments![41] The point is clear: even if one accepts an editorial "story" behind the shaping of the Psalter, which drives towards the victory of Yahweh and his people over all, it is one that must include a place for suffering and lament, up to the last word.

Before I conclude, I will make one brief statement about the implications of this for Christian life. While not agreeing with much of Brueggemann's reading of the Psalter, he *is* correct in seeing an analogy in its story to the life of faith, especially in the light of Christ's union with his people.[42] As such, if the Psalter forms something of a "script" for the experience of God's people in this world, which ends in their blessing and eternal praise of God, then it is a script which will include lament, even in the light of assured victory, until that final day.

The biblical citations at the beginning of this essay reflect just this perspective. The day *is* coming, when frustration, mourning, and pain will pass away, and the only tears left will be ones of joy. This truth remains a sure anchor for our souls, no matter what our experience, even unto death. But until Christ returns to usher in the new creation, we will still find occasion where the Scriptures not only allow, but expect, that we will cry out in tune with the psalms of lament: "How long, O Lord?" Understanding the place of lament in the shape of the Psalter thus gives us a powerful and liberating warrant to cry out our pain and vulnerability even while being sure that, one day, these cries will grow into shouts of unhindered praise!

Conclusion

I will sum up with a reflection on the canonical shaping of the Psalms. One of the main reasons why editorial shaping of the Psalter has proven so attractive and fruitful for evangelicals is because it is so easily appropriated into a framework of Biblical Theology. It provides a consistent, theological trajectory to the book, which meshes fairly seamlessly with evangelical convictions (encapsulated, say, in the Five *Solas* of the Reformation). This in turn legitimates an interpretative metanarrative to each individual psalm (at least in principle) that drives towards the gospel. Thus, this branch of Psalms study can be a tremendously helpful development in critical scholarship for evangelicals to benefit from.

---

41. I.e., Psalms 140; 141; 142; 143.
42. For further reflection on this, see ibid., 250–51.

On the other hand, as Hely Hutchinson also warns, there is a danger in making too much of this "macro" approach to the Psalter if it polarizes us against taking individual psalms as having their own integrity. Hely Hutchinson makes three observations in this regard: first, that the New Testament authors demonstrate little explicit interest in the contexts of the psalms they cite; second, that the individual psalm numbering is original to the text; third, that Wilson's likening the Psalter to a symphony actually lends itself to taking one part or theme on its own terms, without having necessarily to refer to the rest.[43]

To this we can add a further, related danger, that the "story" becomes such a dominant hermeneutical script that one feels an overwhelming pressure to be able to specifically squeeze the order and minute detail of every psalm into this ghostly metanarrative lurking in the background, no matter how unnatural it may seem to the psalm itself.[44] The reality is that, while there does seem to be a discernible story to the Psalter, it is not the same as a linear narrative from psalm to psalm. Rather—and somewhat in line with Brueggemann's suggestion—as one reads through the book, individual psalms seem to oscillate in their focus on the various aspects of God's plans and purposes for his people, and their king. The result is a thick, rich statement of the experience of God's Messiah, and the people who have bound themselves to him, as they walk the hard, glorious road to the cry of victory: "Hallelujah!"

As such, Hely Hutchinson concludes that "we enjoy the freedom and flexibility to benefit from both the macro and the micro approaches . . . micro psalm exegesis needs to remain firmly on the agenda . . . at the same time, sensitivity to the macro psalter shape yields a particular appreciation of its clear gospel message."[45] My hope is that an examination of the role of lament in the shape of the Psalter has provided one such avenue for exactly that.

Bibliography

Broyles, Craig C. "Lament, Psalms of." In *Dictionary of the Old Testament: Wisdom, Poetry and Writings*, edited by Tremper Longman III and Peter Enns, 384–99. Downers Grove: IVP, 2008.

---

43. Hely Hutchinson, "Psalms as a Book," 43–44.

44. Indeed, some works in the area suggest such complex and intricate reasons for the arrangement of the psalms; they give the impression that every ancient Israelite would have needed a doctorate in higher literary criticism to understand *any* psalm!

45. Ibid., 43, 45.

Brueggemann, Walter. "Bounded by Obedience and Praise: The Psalms as Canon." JSOT 50 (1991) 63–92.

———. "The Psalms and the Life of Faith: A Suggested Typology of Faith." JSOT 17 (1980) 3–32. Reprint, *The Psalms and the Life of Faith*, edited by Patrick D. Miller, 3–32. Minneapolis: Fortress, 1995.

Brueggemann, Walter and Patrick D. Miller. "Psalm 73 as a Canonical Marker." JSOT 72 (1996) 45–56.

Chapman, John C. *Setting Hearts on Fire: A Guide to Giving Evangelistic Talks*. Kingsford: St Matthias, 1999.

Childs, Brevard S. *Introduction to the Old Testament as Scripture*. Philadelphia: Fortress, 1979.

Cook, David. "A Method of Preparation." In *How to Prepare a Bible Talk*, edited by Sarah Buckle-Dykes, 16–24. Croydon: SMBC Press, 2003.

deClaissé-Walford, Nancy L., ed. *The Shape and Shaping of the Book of Psalms: The Current State of Scholarship*. Ancient Israel and Its Literature 20. Atlanta: SBL, 2014.

Gunkel, Hermann and Joachim Begrich. *Introduction to Psalms: The Genres of Israel's Religious Lyric*. Translated by John D. Nogalski. Mercer Library of Biblical Studies. Macon: Mercer University Press, 1998 [orig. 1933].

Hely Hutchinson, James. "The Psalms and Praise." In *Interpreting the Psalms: Issues and Approaches*, edited by Philip S. Johnston and David G. Firth, 85–100. Downers Grove: IVP, 2005.

———. "The Psalter as a Book." In *Stirred by a Noble Theme: The Book of Psalms in the Life of the Church*, edited by Andrew G. Shead, 23–45. Nottingham: Apollos, 2013.

Howard, David M. "The Psalms and Current Study." In *Interpreting the Psalms: Issues and Approaches*, edited by Philip S. Johnston and David G. Firth, 23–40. Downers Grove: IVP, 2005.

———. *The Structure of Psalms 93–100*. Biblical and Judaic Studies 5. Winona Lake: Eisenbrauns, 1997.

Hubbard, David A. "The Wisdom Movement and Israel's Covenant Faith." *Tyndale Bulletin* 17 (1966) 3–33.

McCann, J. Clinton. "Books I–III and the Editorial Purpose of the Hebrew Psalter." In *The Shape and Shaping of the Psalter*, edited by J. Clinton McCann, 93–107. JSOTSup 159. Sheffield: Sheffield Academic, 1993.

———. "Changing Our Way of Being Wrong." In *The Shape and Shaping of the Book of Psalms: The Current State of Scholarship*, edited by Nancy L. deClaissé-Walford, 21–25. Ancient Israel and Its Literature 20. Atlanta: SBL, 2014.

———, ed. *The Shape and Shaping of the Psalter*. JSOTSup 159. Sheffield: Sheffield Academic, 1993.

Sweeney, Marvin A. "Form Criticism." In *Dictionary of the Old Testament: Wisdom, Poetry and Writings*, edited by Tremper Longman III and Peter Enns, 227–41. Downers Grove: IVP, 2008.

Robinson, Haddon W. *Biblical Preaching: The Development and Delivery of Expository Messages*. Grand Rapids: Baker, 2001.

Taylor, J. Glen. "Psalms 1 and 2: A Gateway into the Psalter and Messianic Images of Restoration for David's Dynasty." In *Interpreting the Psalms for Preaching and Teaching*, edited by Herbert W. Bateman and D. Brent Sandy, 47–62. St. Louis: Chalice, 2010.

Westermann, Claus. *Praise and Lament in the Psalms*. Translated by Keith R. Crim and Richard N. Soulen. Atlanta: Westminster John Knox, 1981.

Wilson, Gerald H. *The Editing of the Hebrew Psalter*. Society of Biblical Literature Dissertation Series 76. Chico: SBL, 1985.

Wu, Dan. "The Psalms and Perplexity." In *Stirred by a Noble Theme: The Book of Psalms in the Life of the Church*, edited by Andrew G. Shead, 230–51. Nottingham: Apollos, 2013.

11

Silence of the Lambs
A Lost Cry of Lament in Psalm 8

G. Geoffrey Harper

PSALM 8 IS THE first praise psalm in the Psalter. Its words are addressed entirely to Yahweh, the extolling of whose name forms a frame around the whole (vv. 1, 9). Due to being quoted or alluded to many times in the New Testament, perhaps most strikingly in the book of Hebrews (e.g., Heb 2:6–9), Psalm 8 is one of the better-known psalms.[1] Its central verse, "What is man that you are mindful of him, and the son of man that you care for him?" (8:4 ESV) is widely recognized. In fact, v. 2's "Out of the mouth of babes and infants" has passed into popular expression as a catchphrase for acknowledging profundity. Yet, in spite of such seeming familiarity, my contention in this essay is that the voice of Psalm 8's "little lambs" has all but been silenced. Indeed, the generally positive take on what the children of v. 2 are doing may have unwittingly robbed them of their very purpose in the psalm. To substantiate this claim, I first of all chart some of the recent developments that have been made in regard to the canonical arrangement of the Psalter in order to elucidate the implications this has for interpretation of individual psalms. Then, having clarified the exegetical problems posed

---

1. For other citations of Psalm 8 in the New Testament, see the listing in NA28; see also Vesco, *Le Psautier*. Unfortunately, the utility of Vesco's excellent work is hampered by the lack of a comprehensive indexing system.

by the "babes and infants" of Psalm 8, I suggest an alternate reading which seeks to better attend to their cries.

The Arrangement of the Psalter

Since the publishing of Gerald Wilson's doctoral thesis in 1985 there has been a veritable explosion of studies devoted to the subject of the Psalter's structure (or lack thereof). Wilson's central premise, based on comparison with similar anthologies of poetic texts from the ancient Near East, is that the ordering of individual psalms within the Psalter is not random. Rather, deliberate editorial strategies may be discerned in the compilation's final arrangement. These strategies, argues Wilson, extend beyond the five-book division to include the function of Psalms 1 and 150 as introduction and conclusion respectively.[2] Furthermore, instances of editorial activity converge to emphasize particular themes across the collection. Books I–III focus attention on the Davidic covenant. Within this material, Wilson suggests that a progression of thought may be discerned by looking at the so-called "seam" psalms: Psalm 2 introduces the idea of the Davidic covenant; Psalm 41 highlights Yahweh's protection of the king; Psalm 72 looks beyond David as it petitions for his heir(s). Psalm 89, however, placed at the end of Book III, laments the seeming failure of the covenant, and with it the seeming failure of the God who made it.[3] Book IV (Pss 90–106) in Wilson's scheme constitutes the "editorial center" of the collection in that it provides a response to the questions raised by Psalm 89 through its sustained focus on *Yahweh's* kingship.[4] The Psalter's final section—Book V—pictures restoration for the diaspora, contains a renewed focus on David, and concludes the collection with sustained praise of Yahweh (Pss 146–150).

In the three decades since *The Editing of the Hebrew Psalter*, Wilson's ground-breaking work has been followed by a multitude of studies which have variously sought to affirm, deny, or further develop his proposals. Summarizing the now vast body of literature devoted to the subject is well beyond the limits of what I can hope to accomplish here. Interested readers will benefit from the surveys published elsewhere.[5] What this current essay

2. For the conclusions reached, see Wilson, *Editing*, 199–228.

3. Ibid., 209–14.

4. Psalms 93, 95–99 are frequently referred to as the *Yhwh mālak* psalms due to the presence of a repeated phrase: יהוה מָלָךְ "Yahweh reigns" (93:1; 95:3; 96:10; 97:1; 99:1; also 98:6). For a helpful discussion of the role of this theme in the Psalter, see Mays, *The Lord Reigns*, 12–22.

5. See Wu, "The Role of Lament in the Shape of the Psalter" (chapter 10 in this

is directly concerned with, however, is articulating the *implications* of this recent research.

Although many aspects of the psalms' canonical ordering are, and probably will continue to be, debated, Wilson's primary insight is widely held to be valid: the Psalter is not a random collection of Israelite poems; rather, it displays editorial purpose in the arrangement of the final-form text. Where the exegetical rubber hits the road is in relation to the interpretation of individual psalms. Although much contemporary appropriation, sermons included, continues to echo the approach of form criticism with its treatment of psalms solely as standalone pieces, this is not really tenable in light of the recent scholarly work noted above. Instead, it has become increasingly apparent that psalms ought to be approached and interpreted as *interrelated* units. This is not to deny that the Psalter is a collection of unique poems written by numerous individuals separated by time and space, which of course it is. Rather, it recognizes that being brought together to form a wider whole has implications for the parts. At the very least, the placement of psalms in proximity with one another invites comparison of similar themes and the resolution of seeming theological conflict. Thus, in order to more fully understand a given psalm, the exegete must attend to the various levels of literary context that may be imposed upon it by, for example, the psalms which immediately adjoin it, inclusion in a "mini-collection" (e.g., the Psalms of Ascent [Pss 120–132]), the Book it has been placed in, its relationship to the Psalter's introduction, conclusion, and major themes, and so on.

What exactly this might look like in practice, as well as ways in which attention paid to canonical placement can aid the interpreter, will become apparent below. Before being able to appreciate the helpfulness of these recent insights with respect to Psalm 8, however, it is first of all necessary to clarify the problems raised by the "babes and infants" of v. 2.

Problems in Psalm 8:2a

Although well known, Psalm 8 is surprisingly problematic. The issues are complex; thus, some technical discussion is unavoidable. That said, the benefits (as I hope to demonstrate) make such a foray worthwhile. With that positive end in mind, let us take a closer look at Psalm 8:2. The ESV renders the first two verses of the psalm as follows:

---

volume), for a helpful introduction to the topic. For more detailed discussion, see the recent collection of essays in deClaissé-Walford, *Shaping of the Book of Psalms*.

> *To the choirmaster: according to The Gittith. A Psalm of David.*
> 1 O Lord, our Lord,
>   how majestic is your name in all the earth!
> You have set your glory above the heavens.
>   2 Out of the mouth of babes and infants,
> you have established strength because of your foes,
>   to still the enemy and the avenger.

This translation, like any other, makes interpretative decisions, which invariably smooth over a number of underlying issues. Those raised by v. 2, however, are especially formidable. In fact, seasoned psalms exegete Peter Craigie suggests that "the ... translation of vv 2-3 should be considered as tentative."[6] Yet it is precisely here that I think reading Psalm 8 as an *interrelated* unit can serve to ease at least some of the difficulties. In order to validate this claim, I will first of all unpack v. 2a more fully in order to clarify the nature of the difficulties it presents. Then, in the section which follows, I will suggest (albeit tentatively) a way forward that takes into account data stemming from consideration of Psalm 8's canonical placement and, in particular, its relation to nearby lament psalms.

While at first glance v. 2a seems rather benign, two prominent, and related, problems lie just below the surface. The first concerns translation. The ESV quoted above, like any version, reads smoothly. When placed against the NIV[1984], however, an immediate issue comes to the fore.

> Out of the mouth of babes and infants,
> you have established strength because of your foes (ESV)

> From the lips of children and infants you have ordained praise
> because of your enemies (NIV[1984])[7]

Verse 1 makes it clear that the addressee of the psalm is Yahweh. Thus the "you" in v. 2a, in context, denotes Yahweh as the subject of the verb that follows. However, what Yahweh is said to have done is markedly different in each version. In the ESV Yahweh has "established strength," yet in the NIV[1984] he has "ordained praise." How do we account for (and resolve) this difference in translation that goes far beyond the variance we find, say, for example, between "babes and infants" (ESV) and "children and infants" (NIV[1984]), or between "foes" (ESV) and "enemies" (NIV[1984])?

One can of course appeal to the underlying Hebrew. There we find that the word rendered respectively as "strength" or "praise" is עֹז, *'ōz*. HALOT indicates that עֹז (*'ōz*) as a noun means "strength, might," or derivatively as

---

6. Craigie, *Psalms 1–50*, 105.
7. For discussion of the changes made by NIV, see fn. 28 below.

an adjective, "fortified, strong, well founded."[8] A homonym,[9] עֹז (II), has the obviously related sense of "refuge, protection" (hence NRSV's "bulwark") and is found elsewhere in the Psalter (Ps 28:8, for example).[10] So then, we arrive at a simple solution: the ESV is correct; the NIV[1984] is mistaken.

However, the matter becomes more complex when we consider the Old Greek (OG) translation of Psalm 8.[11] The Greek text of v. 2a reads, "Out of the mouth of infants and nurslings you furnished praise" (NETS).[12] The translator(s) responsible for Psalm 8 have chosen the noun αἶνος—which unambiguously means "praise"—to render the Hebrew word.[13] While this initially seems odd, Wilson suggests that עֹז ('ōz) can on rare occasions have this sense, but when it does, it is always accompanied by a verb of giving, which is patently not the case here.[14] So, once more, we seem to have arrived at a solution, albeit a slightly more complex one than before: the ESV is correct; the NIV[1984], seemingly following the OG, is incorrect.

But once again v. 2a reveals another layer of complexity, because in Matthew 21:16 Jesus quotes this verse. Responding to the indignation of the chief priests and scribes at hearing children proclaiming "Hosanna to the Son of David," Jesus recites Psalm 8:2a verbatim *from the OG*: "Out of the mouth of infants and nurslings you furnished praise."[15] Here Jesus (or at least Matthew) cites the Greek Old Testament, not the Hebrew, perhaps because it better fitted the context of children singing his praise. Thus we come to an interesting dilemma: the presence of two different versions of the same verse, both of which are canonical—the Hebrew with its focus on Yahweh establishing might or power, and the Greek (Old Testament and New Testament) which has Yahweh eliciting praise from the lips of infants. At least this solves the variance between the ESV and NIV[1984] that I noted above. The ESV follows the Hebrew of Psalm 8:2a whereas the NIV[1984] (possibly due to the influence of Matt 21) follows the text of the OG. The resulting

---

8. *HALOT* 2:805.

9. A homonym is a word that sounds like another, maybe even being spelled the same way, yet which has a different meaning.

10. See *HALOT* 2:806.

11. The term "Septuagint" (LXX) technically only applies to the Pentateuch.

12. ἐκ στόματος νηπίων καὶ θηλαζόντων κατηρτίσω αἶνον.

13. Although αἶνος originally meant "tale, story," it only appears in the OG Bible in the later translated books (2 Chron and Pss), and always with the meaning "praise" (see LEH 1:11).

14. Wilson, *Psalms*, 202. Furthermore, Vesco observes that the OG's rendering of יסד (*ysd*, "establish, found") with the verb καταρτίζω ("prepare") is unique to this verse (Vesco, *Le Psautier*, 359).

15. Ἐκ στόματος νηπίων καὶ θηλαζόντων κατηρτίσω αἶνον.

questions that this raises in relation to inspiration and which text we ought to consider as authoritative (i.e., the Greek Old Testament or the Hebrew Old Testament) are intriguing, but lie well beyond what I can address here.

For the purposes of the remainder of this essay I will use the Hebrew text of v. 2a. The primary reason for this decision is that Hebrew was the original language of composition; the OG is derivative. Furthermore, the OG is not simply a translation. As Randall Gauthier helpfully makes clear, the Greek Old Testament is better understood as a text in its own right.[16] Thus, while at times the Greek may follow the original Hebrew closely, at other times the translators have seen fit to make changes. Sometimes deviations from the Hebrew are simply errors, due to not understanding or misreading the underlying text. But on other occasions, changes seem to be motivated by theological or literary reasons.[17] The OG of Psalm 8:2a is certainly different from the Hebrew; less clear are the reasons for why it is. On this occasion the change may well be deliberate. What might have motivated a different reading will become apparent in the next section.

Translation, involving lexical, grammatical, and structural decisions, cannot in the end be separated from meaning. This brings us to a second, related, problem: what does v. 2 mean? Moreover, how does this verse fit with the rest of Psalm 8? In short, what do crying babies have to do with anything? The answer has not been forthcoming, as even a cursory survey of the commentaries indicates.[18]

Popular understanding frequently runs along the lines of Wilson's take on the verse: "the rough, unschooled babblings of very young children can be an unexpected source of praise to their creator."[19] Or as C. H. Spurgeon in exemplary nineteenth-century style puts it: "How doth their simple prattle refute those learned fools who deny the being of God!"[20] Yet, as discussed above, understanding Psalm 8:2 (MT) to refer to the *praise* of infants is problematic from a grammatical point of view.[21] Moreover, even if granted, an additional problem remains. If such "unschooled babblings" are, in fact, elicited by Yahweh in order to "refute ... learned fools"—presumably the

16. Gauthier, "Psalm 54," 166.

17. For an example of what this looks like in relation to Psalm 54, see ibid., 175–79. It also possible that variances are due to an OG Vorlage that differed from what later became the MT.

18. The recently published NICOT commentary ignores the matter entirely. See deClaissé-Walford et al., *Book of Psalms*, ad. loc.

19. Wilson, *Psalms*, 202.

20. Spurgeon, *Treasury of David*, 1:80.

21. It is perhaps worth noting that Wilson's commentary is in the *NIV* Application Commentary series.

foes, enemy, and avenger mentioned in v. 2—then how is this accomplished? The babblings of babies might be interpreted by their omniscient Creator as praise, but this would unlikely be the case for *human* adversaries. Thus it is difficult to see how such "praise" would refute anyone.

Robert Alter, reading עֹז (*ʿōz*) as "strength," takes a different tack. He suggests, "Perhaps the innocence of infants is imagined as a source of strength."[22] But what he means by this is not entirely clear. Nor is it apparent how "innocence" would cause the enemy and avenger to cease (8:2b). Indeed such an idea would seem to have very little traction in the real world, a world in which, then as now, the innocent frequently suffer at the hands of the powerful. Thus Alter's solution seems to raise as many questions as it answers.

In his commentary on the Psalms, John Goldingay suggests reading v. 2a with v. 1c, which, with his translation, gives the following: "One who put your majesty above the heavens / at the word of babies and sucklings."[23] Goldingay understands v. 1c to be a declaration of Yahweh's sovereignty made over the cosmos at the beginning of creation. He explains the relationship to v. 2a as follows. "Yhwh's might and majesty were asserted and/or acknowledged at the Beginning in anticipatory recognition that this would be important for the vulnerable [i.e., for (suffering) babies]."[24] Yet Goldingay doesn't explain how Yahweh's majesty was asserted *at the word of* babies and sucklings, all the more so if this was something done at the beginning of creation. Once again, a proposed solution raises as many questions as it answers.

Coming at v. 2 from a completely different angle, Mark Smith and Klaus Seybold posit much darker readings. Smith understands the reference to יֹנְקִים (*yōnəqîm*, "nursing babies") as representing all-devouring cosmic foes.[25] Seybold argues that the word pair originally read "criminals" and "violent ones."[26] For both scholars, then, v. 2a establishes the threat for which a stronghold is needed. While I think Smith and Seybold may be on to something in their understanding of a causal connection between the "mouth of babies" and the "stronghold" or "refuge" which Yahweh establishes, I think there is a better way to construe that causality. I will return to the point shortly.

---

22. Alter, *Psalms*, 22.

23. Goldingay, *Psalms 1–41*, 155.

24. Ibid., 156.

25. Smith, "Psalm 8:2b–3," 639. Smith bases his reading on the Ugaritic cognate *ynqm*.

26. Seybold, *Die Psalmen*, 49–50.

In summary, working out the meaning of v. 2a is far from straightforward. Alter's assessment perhaps sums up the general sentiment: "it is far from clear what these infants are doing in our poem, and the relevance to the context of the following line about foes and avengers is equally obscure."[27] Yet all is not lost. In the following section I want to propose an alternate solution, one that takes into account the implications of recent developments in Psalms scholarship that I charted earlier.

An Alternative Reading of Psalm 8:2

In order to substantiate an alternative reading of Psalm 8:2, I will first need to marshal some extra data. Having done so, I will then be able bring the various pieces together to offer an interpretation of the verse that I hope may shed light on Psalm 8's crying babies.

Translating v. 2

First, there are a couple of translation-related points to make. One of these has already been discussed above, so I will simply summarize here. In relation to what Yahweh is said to have established in v. 2a, I argued that it is better not to read the Hebrew word עֹז (ʿōz) as "praise." Rather, the noun ought to be understood with its usual sense of "strength" or "might." More precisely, I think the related homonym עֹז (II) gives the best sense in context. The abstract idea of "strength" or "might" thus becomes the more concrete image of "a refuge" or "bulwark" (NRSV): a strong, well-founded place of protection.

A second translation issue relates to the preposition מִן (min) found at the start of v. 2 which, in this case, is attached to the noun פֶּה (peh, "mouth"). Like most prepositions, מִן (min) has a wide range of possible meanings depending on use. Accordingly, the versions render the preposition-noun unit differently. A majority understand מִן (min) as denoting source. Thus, v.2 is translated, "*From* the mouth(s) of . . . " (NASB, CEB, NET, JPS), or "*Out of* the mouth of . . . " (KJV, ASV, NRSV, ESV). Other versions read מִן (min) as indicting agency. Accordingly, RSV renders the phrase, "*by* the mouth of . . ."; NJB, similarly, has "even *through* the mouths of . . . "[28] While all of the

---

27. Alter, *Biblical Poetry*, 148.

28. NIV also reads מִן (min) as "through" but inexplicably renders the word for "mouth" as "praise." Verse 2a is thus translated as follows: "Through the praise of children and infants you have established a stronghold against your enemies."

above are valid translations of the preposition, I think another nuance fits better here. מִן (min) can also have a *causal* sense—that is, the preposition can be used to show the reason or rationale behind an action (e.g., Deut 7:7).[29] In English, this sense is best captured with the word "because," or perhaps "for." Hence, I translate the preposition-noun unit at the beginning of v. 2 as "*Because of* the mouth of . . ." As noted beforehand, both Smith and Seybold understand the clause similarly. The reasons for why I think this gives a better reading will become clear below. Before I proceed further, however, here is my translation of the Hebrew text of v. 2:

> Because of the mouth of infants and nursing babies you have established a refuge, on account of those hostile to you, to cause the enemy and the avenger to cease.

Infants and Nursing Babies

A second datum to consider is what is conveyed by the phrase "infants and nursing babies."[30] The word "infant" (עוֹלֵל, *'ôlēl*) appears twenty times in the Old Testament, usually, as in Psalm 8:2, in the plural. It can be used to portray very young children, like in Job 3:16 where the word is found in parallel with נֵפֶל (*nēpel*, "miscarriage"). Throughout the Old Testament the fate of these "infants" is generally not good. They want for food in Lamentations (2:11, 19; 4:4); they are stillborn (Job 3:16) or are killed (1 Sam 15:13; 22:19); they become objects of wrath (Jer 6:11), exile (Jer 44:7; Lam 1:5), and death (Jer 9:20); they are even eaten by their own mothers (Lam 2:10). More frequently than any other fate, these "infants" find themselves dashed upon rocks (2 Kgs 8:12; Ps 137:9; Isa 13:16; Hos 13:16[14:1]; Nah 3:10). On only two occasions is "infant" used in either a neutral (Joel 2:16) or positive manner (Ps 17:14).

The phrase "nursing babies" translates the noun יוֹנֵק (*yônēq*), derived from the participle of יָנַק (*ynq*, "to suck"). The suitability of the noun (lit. "sucking one") for describing babies is immediately apparent. Thus again, very young children are in view. As with "infants," the lot of these "nursing babies" is not a happy one. Six of the ten occurrences of the noun outside Psalm 8:2 are found in strongly unfavorable contexts.[31]

---

29. See Arnold and Choi, *Biblical Hebrew Syntax*, 117, for further examples.

30. Cf. the discussion of the phrase by Goldingay (*Psalms 1–41*, 156).

31. The noun יוֹנֵק (*yônēq*) also appears in Isaiah 53:2 where it is translated as "shoot" or "young plant" rather than "nursing baby."

When "infant" and "nursing baby" are used in conjunction, however, the inference is almost universally negative.[32] In 1 Samuel 15:3 "infants and nursing babies" are to be devoted to destruction; likewise, 1 Samuel 22:19 records that they have been put to death with the sword. In Jeremiah 44:7 these young children are cut off from before Yahweh due to his wrath against the wickedness of his people. Twice in Lamentations "infants" and "nursing babies" are the victims of scarcity and famine (2:11; 4:4). They cry out in vain to their mothers for food (2:12) but instead their tongues stick to the roofs of their mouths (4:4). Thus the phrase "infants and nursing babies" in the Old Testament does not convey the quiet cooing of newborns, nor even the babbling of toddlers. Rather, the cry of these children is primarily one of distress and great anxiety; as such it occupies the same conceptual space as lament.

The Canonical Placement of Psalm 8

A third factor to consider in the interpretation of Psalm 8 is its canonical placement. As I argued earlier in this essay, recent developments in scholarship have highlighted the importance of reading psalms as *interrelated* units. Important, therefore, are connections between Psalm 8 and adjacent psalms.

Psalm 7 concludes with the words, "I will sing praise to the name of Yahweh, the Most High" (v. 7:17 ESV [adapted]). This stated intention to praise "the name of Yahweh" is enacted by the words of Psalm 8, which opens with the declaration, "O Yahweh our Lord, how majestic is your name in all of the earth." Thus, in its canonical position, Psalm 8 becomes an example of how one might go about praising Yahweh's name.[33] Moreover, the lament of Psalm 7, linked by its superscription to an episode in David's life, suggests that Psalms 7 and 8 are to be understood as his righteous responses to situations of adversity.[34]

The motif of praising Yahweh's name is also found in the opening words of Psalm 9: "I will be glad and exult in you; I will sing praise to your name, O Most High" (v. 2 ESV). The reasons for singing such praise follow in vv. 3–10. In language reminiscent of Psalm 2, Yahweh is said to sit upon his throne, judging righteously (vv. 4, 7–8); from there he rebukes and destroys the wicked (v. 5). And yet there is frank acknowledgment that

---

32. Joel 2:16 is the sole exception.
33. See Tate, "Exposition," 343–47.
34. For discussion on whether the superscriptions in the psalms are canonical or authoritative, see VanGemeren and Stanghelle, "Psalm Titles."

this reality is not fully experienced. Thus Yahweh is also praised for being "a stronghold for the oppressed, a stronghold in times of trouble" (v. 9 ESV). The righteous response is to adopt a position of trust: "those who know your name put their trust in you, for you, O Lord, have not forsaken those who seek you" (v. 10 ESV).

The wider movement evident in Psalms 1–8 is also important. Psalms 1 and 2 function as a double introduction to the Psalter.[35] Yet the lofty claims made therein regarding the blessedness of the one who meditates on torah (1:1–2) and the unassailable rule of Yahweh and his anointed king (2:4–6) are quickly brought into question by the lament psalms which follow. In Psalms 3–7, David (see the superscriptions) cries out to God because of his many foes (3:1), enemies who want to rend him like lions (7:2); he is distressed and subject to shame (4:1–2); he faces divine rebuke and anger (6:1); his subsequent weeping is endless (6:6). Against this succession of laments, Psalm 8's "hymn of praise" breaks the flow by presenting readers with the Psalter's first psalm of praise, despite the collection's traditional title *tehillim* ("praises").[36] Therefore, using Walter Brueggemann's terminology, Psalm 8 functions in its current setting to reorient readers following the disorientation of Psalms 3–7.[37]

Putting the Pieces Together

So then, in light of the above, is it possible to gain any clarity with regards to what the babies in Psalm 8:2 are doing and how they are connected to the following line about stopping enemies? I think it is.

In 8:2a, Yahweh is said to have established "a refuge." The reason given is twofold. First, it is "because of the mouth of infants and nursing babies." As outlined above, in the Old Testament the image conveyed by the cries ("mouth") of "infants and nursing babies" is not positive. Rather, their protestation is educed by situations of distress and desperate need; it is a cry of lament. Yet *because* of these cries, Yahweh has set up a refuge—a strong, well-founded place of protection. Second, and relatedly, the psalmist declares that Yahweh has done so, "on account of those hostile to you." In other words, it is those who are hostile to Yahweh who are responsible for the suffering of the "infants and nursing babies." Accordingly, Yahweh acts on their behalf "to cause the enemy and the avenger to cease" (8:2b).

---

35. See further Hely Hutchinson, "Psalter," 25–28; Cole, "Psalms 1 and 2," 183–95.

36. For discussion on the genre of Psalm 8, see Craigie, *Psalms 1–50*, 106; Weiser, *Psalms*, 140.

37. Cf. Brueggemann, *Praying the Psalms*, 13–21.

But Yahweh's intervention is more than just general altruism on behalf of the vulnerable. In the context of Psalms 1-8, cries of lament have primarily come from the mouth of David. Although he is the king whom Yahweh has installed in Zion (cf. 2:6), the rulers of the earth who take their stand against Yahweh have also taken their stand against Yahweh's Anointed (2:2). Thus David exclaims, "O Yahweh, how many are my foes" (3:1). He implores Yahweh: "save and deliver me from all who pursue me, or they will tear me apart like a lion and rip me to pieces with no one to rescue me" (7:1a-2 NIV). Yet, sprinkled through the laments of Psalms 3-7 are references to Yahweh's protection in the midst of adversity: he has been a "shield" (3:3; 7:10) and a source of refuge and safety (4:8; 5:11; 7:1). Accordingly, in Psalm 8 Yahweh is rightly praised for having established a refuge because of the bitter cries of defenseless "infants,"— that is, for responding to his anointed but lamenting king, persecuted and suffering at the hands of enemies, and powerless to effect self-salvation.

This reading of Psalm 8:2 gives the psalm a reason for praise, an expected element that Goldingay notes is missing here.[38] It also adds definition to the psalm's central verse. The psalmist's question regarding why Yahweh is mindful of "man" and cares for the "son of man" is not just an abstract query, but rather is asked in the context of experienced deliverance. Yahweh has been, and will continue to be, a necessary refuge for his Anointed and for all who follow his righteous lead,[39] until the complete subjugation of enemies envisaged by Psalms 2 and 8 is realized.

Conclusion

The crying babies of Psalm 8 have puzzled interpreters for generations. Yet developments in recent scholarship, particularly the focus on the editorial shaping of the psalms, serve to open new avenues of investigation. The embedding of Psalm 8 in wider Psalter and Old Testament contexts has a distinct bearing on its interpretation. Additional layers now impose upon the meaning of this psalm and must be taken into account. Moreover, as I have attempted to demonstrate in this essay, attention paid to the Psalter's *intra*-textuality coupled with sensitivity to a given psalm's canonical placement has the potential to provide new angles on well-known cruxes. Thus, to gain

---

38. Goldingay, *Psalms 1-41*, 154.

39. Gordon Wenham posits that the crowning of generic humanity in v. 5 has significant hermeneutical implications for reading the psalms. By suggesting that every human is "crowned," the righteous sufferer in the Psalter is not just the king but anyone who lives by torah; Wenham, *The Psalter Reclaimed*, 64-65.

a thicker understanding of these ancient Israelite poems in preparation for preaching, teaching, singing, and praying their words, understanding how each part relates to the wider whole proves essential.

Bibliography

Alter, Robert. *The Art of Biblical Poetry*. Rev. ed. New York: Basic Books, 2011 [orig. 1985].

———. *The Book of Psalms: A Translation with Commentary*. New York: W.W. Norton & Company, 2007.

Arnold, Bill T. and John H. Choi. *A Guide to Biblical Hebrew Syntax*. Cambridge: Cambridge University Press, 2003.

Brueggemann, Walter. *Praying the Psalms*. Winona: Saint Mary's Press, 1993.

Cole, Robert L. "Psalms 1 and 2: The Psalter's Introduction." In *The Psalms: Language for All Seasons of the Soul*, edited by Andrew J. Schmutzer and David M. Howard, 183–95. Chicago: Moody, 2013.

Craigie, Peter C. *Psalms 1–50*. Word Biblical Commentary 19. Waco: Word, 1983.

deClaissé-Walford, Nancy L., ed. *The Shape and Shaping of the Book of Psalms: The Current State of Scholarship*. Society of Biblical Literature Ancient Israel and Its Literature 20. Atlanta: SBL, 2014.

deClaissé-Walford, Nancy L., Rolf A. Jacobson, and Beth LaNeel Tanner. *The Book of Psalms*. NICOT. Grand Rapids: Eerdmans, 2014.

Gauthier, Randall X. "Psalm 54 (The Septuagint): He Who Saves from Discouragement and Tempest." In *The Psalms: Language for All Seasons of the Soul*, edited by Andrew J. Schmutzer and David M. Howard, 165–79. Chicago: Moody, 2013.

Goldingay, John. *Psalms: Volume 1: Psalms 1–41*. Baker Commentary on the Old Testament Wisdom and Psalms. Grand Rapids: Baker, 2006.

Hely Hutchinson, James. "The Psalter as a Book." In *Stirred by a Noble Theme: The Book of Psalms in the Life of the Church*, edited by Andrew. G. Shead, 23–45. Nottingham: Apollos, 2013.

Mays, James L. *The Lord Reigns: A Theological Handbook to the Psalms*. Louisville: Westminster John Knox, 1994.

Seybold, Klaus. *Die Psalmen*. Handbuch zum Alten Testament 1/15. Tübingen: Mohr Siebeck, 1996.

Smith, Mark S. "Psalm 8:2b-3: New Proposals for Old Problems." *Catholic Biblical Quarterly* 59 (1997) 637–41.

Spurgeon, C. H. *The Treasury of David: Containing an Original Exposition of the Book of Psalms*. 3 vols. Peabody: Hendrickson, n.d. [orig. 1875].

Tate, Marvin E. "An Exposition of Psalm 8." *Perspectives in Religious Studies* 28 (2001) 343–59.

VanGemeren, Willem and Jason Stanghelle. "A Critical-Realistic Reading of the Psalm Titles." In *Do Historical Matters Matter to Faith?: A Critical Appraisal of Modern and Postmodern Approaches to Scripture*, edited by James K. Hoffmeier and Dennis R. Magary, 281–301. Wheaton: Crossway, 2012.

Vesco, Jean-Luc. *Le Psautier de Jésus: Les citations des Psaumes dans le Nouveau Testament*. Lectio divina. Paris: Les Éditions du Cerf, 2012.

Weiser, Artur. *The Psalms: A Commentary*. Old Testament Library. London: SCM, 1962.

Wenham, Gordon J. *The Psalter Reclaimed: Praying and Praising with the Psalms.* Wheaton: Crossway, 2013.

Wilson, Gerald H. *The Editing of the Hebrew Psalter.* Society of Biblical Literature Dissertation Series 76. Chico: Scholars Press, 1985.

———. *Psalms. Volume 1.* New International Version Application Commentary. Grand Rapids: Zondervan, 2002.

12

Weeping with the Afflicted
The Self-Involving Language of the Laments

ANDREW SLOANE

THE PSALMS, IF NOT precisely unique, are at least unusual in biblical literature inasmuch as they adopt an almost exclusively first person stance. This has a number of effects: literary, psychological, communal, and theological. One of the most interesting is the phenomenon of self-involvement. It is on this that I wish to focus, both from a literary-existential and a theological point of view (if they can be clearly distinguished, which I think they cannot).

There is nothing new about seeing the psalms as self-involving. Their incorporation into the canon of Scripture and their (related) use in the spiritual life of individuals and communities of Jewish and Christian faith presupposes it. Indeed, the characteristic first person language of the psalms (I give you thanks; we praise you) encourages us to use these words as our words in addressing God. This chapter will explore this phenomenon in light of speech act theory and its contribution to both philosophy of language and theological interpretation.

I will begin by pointing out some of the features of lament psalms that necessitate the use of the category of self-involvement, before moving on to a brief outline of the philosophy of language that has illuminated the phenomenon. I will close by returning to lament, and considering some of the ways that these notions can both complicate and enrich our understanding and use of psalms of lament.

Engaging with a Dark World: Self-Involving Features of Lament

What happens when we take the words of a lament on our lips? Let's look briefly at a short lament of classical form. Psalm 13 opens with one of the typical questions of lament—"How long, Yahweh?" and closes with equally typical words of praise—"I will sing to Yahweh, for he has requited (or dealt [kindly] with) me." Form-critical analysis notes that this is just what we might expect with a psalm of this kind. And that, of course, is true. I do not intend to repeat that form-critical analysis, or to rehearse the exegetical, canonical, and theological questions that rightly inform interpretation of a text such as this.[1] Rather, presupposing that work, I would like to draw attention to the function of the *first person* language that this psalm employs (as do most other psalms).

The way we use the psalms in the first person is, as has often been noted, in clear contrast to most other biblical literature.[2] There the language is second person—"you"—whether singular or plural, as is the case in commandments, prophetic speeches, New Testament letters, and the like; or it is third person—"he/she/they"—words telling us about the actions of others, such as in the narratives found in the Torah and the "historical" books, the Gospels, and so on. Furthermore, the first person quality of the psalms is different to that found in, say, first person reports such as found in Ezekiel 1 and Revelation 1, or in the letters of Paul, for the psalms are texts designed for first person *use*. While all Scripture is given to us for our use (2 Tim 3:16, yet again), the function of the first person language in, say, Ezekiel, is quite different to that of the Psalter. In Ezekiel it functions as part of the rhetoric of a book that is, broadly speaking, in the third person; it less invites us into the experience of the prophet than it gives us the perspective that shapes the prophet's experience and hence the viewpoint of the book.[3] In contrast, the book of Psalms, while opening with a third (or perhaps, by implication, second) person blessing on the righteous and closing with a second person

---

1. Useful treatments of these matters can be found in Broyles, *Psalms*, 85-87; Craigie, *Psalms 1-50*, 139-43; Goldingay, *Psalms 1-41*, 203-9; Longman, *Psalms*, 95-97; Mays, *Psalms*, 76-80; McCann, "Psalms," 725-28; deClaissé-Walford et al., *Psalms*, 158-63; Weiser, *Psalms*, 161-63; Wilson, *Psalms, Vol. 1*, 277-85.

2. See, for instance, Athanasius, "Letter to Marcellinus."

3. See Renz, *Rhetorical Function of Ezekiel*, esp. 57-68.

invitation to join in the universal praise of Yahweh, is predominately *first person* (singular—"I," or plural—"we"); and the laments are universally first person. Furthermore, whatever their origins,[4] psalms seem designed for personal and communal use as prayers and praises; that is certainly how they have been used throughout the known history of Jews and Christians. The intention of the collection seems to be, among other things, that users of the Psalter take these words as their own when they address God.

That is certainly how Psalm 13 works. It opens addressing Yahweh, asking how long he will forget *me*; it closes with "*I* will sing to Yahweh for he has requited *me*," and everything in between presupposes that first person stance: it is *my* life/soul, *my* heart, *my* enemies and foes, *my* eyes; *I* will trust, rejoice, sing. This remorselessly first person perspective means that in using this lament I don't just recount or remember or rehearse another's lament. In using this lament, *I* lament. This language is *self-involving*: using it rightly requires that we appropriate its perspective; it entails the adoption of stances and attitudes that fit the words we have taken to be our own.

Such a stance can easily lapse into uncritical pietistic use, or be reduced to a simplistic identification with the imagined or presumed circumstances of "David" or the (often unnamed) psalmist and superficial empathy with their emotional state. This is not to say that the psalms should not shape our piety, or that imagination and empathetic engagement with the world of the psalms is illegitimate. But to limit our "I" stance to such perspectives is to rob the psalms of much of their existential and theological function. It is a temptation to be resisted. But to understand how and why that is a temptation rather than an appropriate response, and to know how to effectively resist that temptation, we need to explore, however briefly, what has been called "the logic of self-involvement."[5]

The Nature of Self-Involving Language

There is no need for me to rehearse the history of speech act theory or its central concepts. That has been done effectively by others.[6] Here I simply want us to think about a class of utterances which is such that, in using

---

4. This history is rehearsed in all major commentaries and introductions to the Psalms. See, for instance, Lucas, *Exploring the OT*, 1–34; Howard, "The Psalms and Current Study."

5. Evans, *Logic of Self-Involvement*. See also the brief introduction to the issues in Briggs, "Getting Involved."

6. See Kit Barker's essays in this volume. See also, Ward, *Word and Supplement*; Wolterstorff, *Divine Discourse*.

them, I involve myself in certain stances, commitments, relationships, and so on. Now, in one way, all speech does that. For instance, if I assert something (claim that, for instance, God is good), I make a claim about reality using the shared medium of language.[7] And I do so for a reason, with particular intentional force—say, with the intent of persuading my hearers to believe the claim, or to reinforce their belief. Because language is an interpersonal phenomenon aimed at communicating, there is no meaningful use of language that is not self-involving in this (philosophically) trivial way. The stronger sense of self-involvement that I want to explore occurs in contexts in which the relational elements of language use are more prominent, or more central to what people are doing with their words.

Here I would like to turn briefly to the work of Donald Evans.[8] While there are important conceptual problems in his work,[9] and his taxonomy of self-involving discourse has not been generally adopted,[10] he rightly points out that some uses of language entail our involvement in the matters of which we speak in particular and unique ways. He sees this kind of self-involvement as inherent in the logic of behabitives (words that adopt particular attitudes in relational-behavioral contexts—such as, "I thank") and commissives (words that commit one in some way in relational contexts—such as, "I promise").[11] Leaving aside his specific terminology, it is worth examining these kinds of speech in order to understand this notion of self-involving discourse.

The first thing to notice is that, while these are classes of speech acts, they are inherently personal and particular. I don't thank *in general*, just as I can't love *in general*. I thank (or love) particular people, and do so for particular reasons—although those reasons might be general or specific. I might thank my wife for years of tolerant, faithful love, or for a particularly thoughtful random gift of appreciation. I might thank a colleague for her trustworthiness as a colleague, or for her assistance in proofreading a manuscript. A number of things are going on here. First, there are some entailments (things that must be true in order for the words to work at all). It must be the case that my wife has been tolerant, faithful, and loving, or

---

7. To put it a little more technically, asserting something involves me adopting a stance in the shared social space of language, by way of particular words, towards purported features of the world, and doing so with particular intentional force (to persuade others to believe a particular propositional claim, or whatever).

8. Evans, *Logic of Self-Involvement*.

9. For instance, his rejection of the language of illocution and perlocution in favor of *performative* and *causal*, respectively, is misguided (see ibid., 68–74).

10. Briggs, "Getting Involved."

11. Evans, *Logic of Self-Involvement*, 35–36.

that she has given me a gift. It must be true that my colleague is trustworthy, or that she proofread my manuscript. And, what's more, they must have conferred real benefits on me. These are "public facts," and unless they are true, then something goes wrong with my thanks, whether I realize it or not. If, for instance, my colleague is a terrible proofreader who introduced innumerable errors into an otherwise pristine document, then there's something wrong about thanking her, is there not (other than as an exercise in irony)? Furthermore, there are "private" facts (Evans calls them "autobiographical") that must also be true. I must actually either feel a sense, or acknowledge a debt, of gratitude, and be expressing that sense or acknowledging that debt in the words I use. And normally that thanks must be directed to that particular person. It might be done publically (such as in the acknowledgments of a book, or an anecdote in an article, or a speech on a more-or-less formal occasion); but unless they receive the thanks they have not, in fact, been thanked. It's amazing how complex perfectly ordinary uses of words can be.

It is instructive here to consider how thanking is both similar to, and differs from, *praising*.[12] While I cannot thank someone who has not benefited me in some way, I can praise someone who has never done me good. As far as I am aware, I have never benefited from John Harrower's work as Anglican Bishop of Tasmania. But, knowing what I do about his integrity and costly actions in confronting and effectively dealing with the horrors of clerical child sexual abuse in his diocese, I can praise him for it (and, of course, hereby do). And, indeed, I can praise someone from whom I have benefited without thanking them. For instance, I have benefited greatly from John Austin's work in speech act theory, and hereby praise him for that work.[13] But I have not ever *thanked* him (and cannot do so, given he is dead). Even so, once again there are certain facts entailed in the act of praising someone. Some are public facts: the person must be worthy of praise, and in that particular respect. Some are private facts about my attitudes: I must see the traits for which I praise someone as desirable traits and as being worthy of praise, and believe that the person I'm praising exemplifies them (and to such an extent that they are worthy of that praise).[14]

The point, of course, is that we do different things in *thanking* someone than in *praising* them. And one of the key differences is the way that thanks

---

12. For an insightful discussion of some of these matters, and one which stimulated my own thinking on the subject, see Brümmer, *What Are We Doing When We Pray?*, 86–98. However, he neither adequately distinguishes between the (relational) logic of thanks and praise, nor accounts for the phenomenon of lament.

13. Austin, *How To Do Things with Words*.

14. For interesting explorations of these elements of praise with respect to God as creator, see Evans, *Logic of Self-Involvement*, 145–268.

and praise involve us differently in both the public world of shared language and in our relationships with other people. They are both self-involving speech acts, and entail the adopting of certain beliefs, attitudes, even behaviors, and the expressing of certain feelings, and so on; but they do different things in relationship. They are self-involving in different ways. And this, let me note in passing, is reflected in the Psalter: praise is normally third person (e.g., Ps 113, "Praise Yahweh"), whereas thanks is second person (either directly—"I thank you Yahweh," as in Ps 9—or we are exhorted to engage in such thanks—"Give thanks to Yahweh for he is good," as in Ps 136).

So, then, how does this relate to the phenomenon of lament? Granted it *is* self-involving, what kind of self-involving discourse is it? Is it more like praise (self-involving speech *about* God) or thanks (self-involving speech *directed to* God)?

Re-Engaging the Text: The Logic of Self-Involvement in Lament

The first thing to note is that lament is more like thanks than praise. That is, it is a directly personal and relational phenomenon, and so involves us in its discourse in particular ways. It is, inherently, an expression of relationship, even (indeed, precisely when) that relationship seems strained, broken, non-existent, or malformed.[15] One of the things that characterizes lament as faithful psalmic speech (in contrast to grumbling) is that it directly addresses God in prayer, however angry, agonized, even despairing that prayer may be. That is clear throughout Psalm 13, for instance, and as far as I can see, is a *universal* and necessary feature of lament. If I may digress for a moment, it is this first person stance in which God is addressed in the second person that is lacking in Psalm 73. While Psalm 73 addresses problems and concerns typical of lament, the psalmist complains, even grumbles, about these phenomena, casting doubt on the validity of the whole faith enterprise, rather than addressing God with those questions and complaints. It is not until the "turn" in v.15, that "you" language is used—the very point at which the psalmist recognizes that his previous speech constituted a betrayal of God's people. From then on the psalm is almost entirely first person, addressing God in the second person. In thanks and trust and praise, it is true. But I would suggest that the key turn in Psalm 73, the one that signals a turn *to* fidelity, is not the turn from doubt to faith—after all, in lament the doubts, and questions, and pain are expressions *of* faith, not alternatives to it. The

---

15. I explore these ideas from the perspective of epistemology and "theodicy" in Sloane, "Lament and the Journey of Doubt."

key turn is towards God in addressing God as relational counterpart. The key is that the language becomes self-involving, and so evokes a relationship with God (and one of a particular kind).[16] But let me return to lament.

Addressing God directly has a number of entailments, key theological truths, if you like.[17] For lament to work as a speech act, some things need to be both true about the world and believed by the psalmist. Let me note some. Lament presupposes that God exists—and a God of a particular kind. For lament to work at all, there must be a God who rewards those who earnestly seek him; and this God must be the God of the psalmist, both the one the psalmist trusts, and the one rightly identified as the God who is in faithful covenant relationship with those who fear him (and so, with the psalmist). And so, in turn, lament presupposes that Yahweh our God is the one, true, and living God. And it presupposes that God both desires and is able to respond in relationship to God's people. These features of lament are, of course, deeply paradoxical, for it is the questions arising out of the psalmist's circumstances, such as whether God is able or willing to act, which prompt lament in the first place. However, if God is the sovereign judge—as is presupposed by the prayers of lament—then how can the psalmist call God to account, request or even require that God respond to the psalmist's pleas? But that is fundamental to the logic of lament.[18] Unless God is good, and sovereign, and merciful, and judge, and the one who responds to prayer, there is no point in praying. But they are precisely the things under question. Crucial as all of that is, however, addressing God in lament involves *us* in relationship with God in particular ways, ways commensurate with those beliefs held by the psalmist and expressed in the psalm, and which are presumed to be facts of the matter.

So, in lamenting we adopt the stance of one who is in distress, for whatever reason. It may be a result of violent oppression (Ps 10) or personal sin (Ps 51) or, as in Psalm 13, the reason may not be clear. The distress, however, is clear, as is the power of the words used to describe it (Ps 22:1,

16. For insightful comments on Psalm 73 and its dynamics, see Broyles, *Psalms*, 299–305; Longman, *Psalms*, 274–78; McCann, "Psalms," 966–70; Mays, *Psalms*, 240–44; deClaissé-Walford et al., *Psalms*, 584–93; Tate, *Psalms 51–100*, 226–39.

17. Fløysvik, *When God Becomes My Enemy*, esp. ch.7, "Theological Assumptions and Implications," 135–76.

18. For a contrary view, see Waltke et al., *Psalms as Christian Lament*. They explicitly reject Walter Brueggemann's influential work on lament in favor of what they see as the "classical" view, which deems lament as inappropriate for Christians in light of the hope we have in the gospel (for which see xi–xv). Justification of the pastoral and theological appropriateness of lament is dealt with in Brueggemann, "The Costly Loss of Lament"; Cohen, *Why O Lord?*; Lee, *Lyrics of Lament*; Sloane, "Lament and the Journey of Doubt"; Villanueva, "Preaching Lament."

for instance). Using words such as these involves us in them, inviting or compelling us into a world of darkness, and insecurity, and distress. They force us to see the world as a place where friends may be enemies, and enemies are all around, where nature turns against us—even our own bodies fail us—and delight is replaced with distress, and feasting with tears and ashes. In pleading for God's mercy, we confess that God is merciful—but not now, not to me. And we throw ourselves on the mercy of God—an act of vertiginous trust given the yawning chasm of God's absence and inaction that the psalm expresses. That element of trust is, in fact, at the heart of the self-involving nature of lament, and helps us to see why there are so many prayers of this kind in the Psalter, and why they have been so important for so many people of faith for so long. For the stance we adopt is one of suffering fidelity, of questioning faith, of trusting doubt. The stance we adopt is one in which we neither ignore our questions, and pain, and doubt, nor abandon the faith that contributes to them; a stance of trusting the one who seems to have abandoned us, trusting that, as most of these psalms demonstrate, God will prove to be trustworthy.

This speech is, of course, *appropriated discourse.* These are not, in the first instance, *my* words: we are, to borrow Rolf Jacobson's memorable phrase, "burning our lamps with borrowed oil."[19] They are the words of the psalmist—and of the church, the faith community of which I am a part and into whose patterns of belief and behavior I have been inducted. But by using them first-personally I make them my own. These words—their words, our words—become my words. I appropriate them for this time and this use, and in so doing endorse the stance/s reflected in them. A number of things are worth addressing in passing. Let me note two: this act of appropriation gives words to people who might otherwise be silent; and it disciplines the words of those whose words might transgress the limits of fidelity. There are many horrible aspects to unremitting distress. One is the way that such experiences may rob us of words—words that we need both to understand ourselves and what we're going through, and to communicate that to others. Appropriating the discourse of lament breaks the silence, and invites us back into the shared world of language. But it also shapes that involvement in particular ways—if we appropriate these words, they become the forms we use to articulate our experience and they come to shape the way we approach God. For suffering can prompt us to turn from God or to overstep the bounds of creaturely propriety. Appropriating the language of lament requires that we address God, and do so from a stance of faith, and within the limits of that faith. Admittedly, little seems to be "off the table" in lament.

---

19. Jacobson, "Burning Our Lamps with Borrowed Oil."

Complaint, accusation, plea, even demand all seem to be warranted speech we can appropriate in, well, the appropriate circumstances. Even so, lament disciplines our language as the language of trust.

This has implications for our *use* of lament in both public worship and private devotion. Let us first consider the obvious users of such texts: those who are themselves lamenting. For them, the very phenomenon of addressing God as my God—and our God—*in prayer* entails a personal stance of trust, one in which God is understood to both hear and respond to prayer, and in which God's own commitment to justice, and to acting on behalf of the poor and downtrodden, can be called upon. It both requires and develops a robust faith in which God can be questioned and called to account and to action on the basis of what is known to be true about God and what is experienced to be true about the world, and the disparity between them. It also fosters alignment between the pray-ers' interests and commitments and God's, both challenging and endorsing patterns of prayer (do our concerns line up with God's? Are we lamenting *for the right things*?). Praying for justice for ourselves or our community helps us to discern God's own commitment to justice; but it also requires that we "surrender retribution to the Lord," remembering that justice is integral to God's agenda in the world, and is ultimately a divine responsibility.[20] This necessarily shapes both piety and theology in interesting ways.

But others, also, ought to use these texts: the Psalter functions both as a "menu" from which we can choose texts appropriate to our circumstances, and a discipline through which we need to work, regardless of our current experience.[21] For those who do not find themselves lamenting, the very phenomenon of praying such prayers individually and/or communally entails solidarity with, and growing understanding of, those whose prayers they naturally are. It also calls for solidarity with, and commitment to, the God whom they (we) so address, and requires that we adopt a broader view of our own personal story than myopic attention to the particular slice of time in which we currently find ourselves. That is to say, it requires that we involve ourselves in the concerns of both suffering people and the God who cares for them. Individually, it requires that I expand my comfortable horizons to recognize others' brokenness when I am comfortable—and even to wonder whether my comfort comes at their expense (am I, perhaps, among the powerful who oppress or neglect the poor and vulnerable?

---

20. For which see Barker, "Divine Illocutions in Psalm 137"; Barker, *Imprecation as Divine Discourse*; Day, *Crying for Justice*; Firth, *Surrendering Retribution*. Contra Cottrill, *Lament*, 92–94, 146–50.

21. Peterson, *Answering God*; Wenham, *Psalms as Torah*.

Am I, perhaps, on the wrong side of this prayer?). Communally, it requires sympathetic acknowledgment of the brokenness that exists within our communities (some, at least, of my gathered community find themselves in circumstances of lament when I do not—and praying this way prompts me to recognize that); and acknowledgment of the larger context of brokenness beyond my community (if ours is a suffering or persecuted community, it helps us understand that in this we are not alone, and that there are other forms of brokenness in the world than the ones we are enduring; if it is not, it requires that we appreciate the distress in which others find themselves in the world, and join with them in praying that God might act to bring them relief).

Such "out of phase" use also requires that we expand our understanding of our own story. For while lament may not be our native tongue *now*, perhaps it once was, and it is certain that at some point it will be. For death will come to us all, as either visitor in another's face or resident in our own. That is to say, people we love and whose wellbeing we wish for will suffer fatal accident or ailment. In their faces of suffering and death, death will visit us. And all of us will die. For some of us, death will signal its coming with the pain of cancer, or the slow decay of age and looming dementia. And in such circumstances lament might become our native tongue. Using these words now allows us to learn the language we one day will need to speak. Involving ourselves in lament is one way we in the West, with our pathetic and often frantic cultural amnesia about the reality of finitude and death, might learn the wisdom of the *ars moriendi*.

So, this "unnatural" mode of self-involvement in lament expands our affections and broadens our horizons, prompting us both to see and hear those who weep and to weep along with them, and to become aware of our own finitude. It also entails the adoption of the values implicit in the lament, and of the God who is rightly addressed with these words. Praying these prayers with right intent requires that we care about—and for—those who suffer; it requires that we care about—and engage in—justice for the oppressed. But it also prompts us to remember the larger historical horizons in which these prayers are rightly used. These are prayers that have been prayed by the faithful people of God for millennia. The circumstances that prompt such prayer persist in the face of it and require that we persist in lament in this broken world as long as it is still broken, anticipating that somehow God will act to fix it—a somehow that is both anticipated in, and guaranteed by, the work of Christ and the Spirit. Indeed, in lament we join in prayer with Christ and the Spirit: for inasmuch as Jesus, our faithful representative, used lament in his own suffering identification with us (Mark 15:34), we identify with him when we lament; and inasmuch as the Spirit groans with the groaning anticipation of a suffering world (Rom 8:26), our groans are expressions of the fellowship of the Holy Spirit.[22] Clearly, the self-involving language of lament entails a stance of yearning faith in God, and hope for the final vindication of God and God's purposes and God's people in Christ and the eschaton. Lament, then, involves us in the lives of others, and in God's grand purposes in the world. Lament as self-involving prayer disturbs and disrupts our comfortable experience and perception of the world, and reconfigures our theology and engagement in the world. The proper exercise of lament, far from being a distortion of Christian faith, is a deeply faithful act by which God continues the work of forming us in the image of Jesus, the one who joined in the company of lamenters.

Conclusion

The psalms of lament, then, invite us to use these words as our words. Given the prevalence of "I" language in lament, using them as our words engages us in self-involving discourse. It requires that we take up the stances adopted in the psalm, with all that is entailed in them, and address ourselves to God in ways shaped by their words, our words. As such it gives voice to that which might otherwise silence us, and provides patterns for faithful engagement with God. It requires that we acknowledge the reality of suffering—present or past or future—and be schooled in bringing that to God. It requires the recognition of our own finitude, and the learning of patterns of trust on which some day we must depend. It demands that we look around our communities and our world, and find the people for whom lament is native speech and engage with them and for them in sympathetic prayer and faithful action. But above all, lament involves us in a relationship with God. One in which, along with Jesus, we can honestly tell God of the world as we experience it and, in so doing, find God to be faithful. Of course, little of what I've said is radically new. However, I believe that framing the discussion in terms of speech act theory and the logic of self-involvement brings clarity and some cohesion to our understanding of (some of) the functions of lament in individual and corporate prayer and worship.

Bibliography

Athanasius. "Letter to Marcellinus on the Interpretation of the Psalms." http://www.athanasius.com/psalms/aletterm.htm.

Austin, J. L. *How To Do Things with Words*. Cambridge: Harvard University Press, 1975.

---

22. Sloane, "Lament and the Journey of Doubt."

Barker, Kit. "Divine Illocutions in Psalm 137: A Critique of Nicholas Wolterstorff's 'Second Hermeneutic.'" *Tyndale Bulletin* 60 (2009) 1–14.

———. *Imprecation as Divine Discourse: Speech Act Theory, Dual Authorship and Theological Interpretation.* JTISup 16. Winona Lake: Eisenbrauns, 2016.

Briggs, Richard S. "Getting Involved: Speech Acts and Biblical Interpretation." *Anvil* 20, (2003) 25–34.

Broyles, Craig G. *Psalms.* Peabody: Hendrickson, 1999.

Brueggemann, Walter. "The Costly Loss of Lament." In *The Poetical Books: A Sheffield Reader*, edited by David J. A. Clines, 85–97. Sheffield: Sheffield Academic Press, 1997.

Brümmer, Vincent. *What Are We Doing When We Pray? A Philosophical Inquiry.* London: SCM, 1984.

Cohen, David J. *Why O Lord? Praying Our Sorrows.* Milton Keynes: Paternoster, 2013.

Cottrill, Amy C. *Language, Power, and Identity in the Lament Psalms of the Individual.* Library of Hebrew Bible/Old Testament Studies 493. New York: T. & T. Clark, 2008.

Craigie, Peter C. *Psalms 1–50.* Waco: Word, 1983.

Day, John. *Crying for Justice: What the Psalms Teach Us about Mercy and Vengeance in an Age of Terrorism.* Grand Rapids: Kregel, 2005.

deClaissé-Walford, Nancy L., et al. *The Book of Psalms.* NICOT. Grand Rapids: Eerdmans, 2014.

Evans, Donald D. *The Logic of Self-Involvement: A Philosophical Study of Everyday Language with Special Reference to the Christian Use of Language about God as Creator.* Library of Philosophy and Theology. London: SCM, 1963.

Firth, David G. *Surrendering Retribution in the Psalms: Responses to Violence in Individual Complaints.* Paternoster Biblical Monographs. Milton Keynes: Paternoster, 2005.

Fløysvik, Ingvar. *When God Becomes My Enemy: The Theology of the Complaint Psalms.* St. Louis: Concordia, 1997.

Goldingay, John. *Psalms 1–41.* Grand Rapids: Baker, 2006.

Howard, David M. Jr. "The Psalms and Current Study." In *Interpreting the Psalms: Issues and Approaches*, edited by Philip S. Johnston and David G. Firth, 23–40. Leicester: Apollos, 2005.

Jacobson, Rolf A. "Burning Our Lamps with Borrowed Oil: The Liturgical Use of the Psalms and the Life of Faith." In *Psalms and Practice: Worship, Virtue, and Authority*, edited by Stephen Breck Reid, 90–98. Collegeville: Liturgical Press, 2001.

Lee, Nancy C. *Lyrics of Lament: From Tragedy to Transformation.* Minneapolis: Fortress, 2010.

Longman, Tremper, III. *Psalms: An Introduction and Commentary.* Tyndale Old Testament Commentaries. Nottingham: IVP, 2014.

Lucas, Ernest. *Exploring the Old Testament, Vol. 3: The Psalms and Wisdom Literature.* London: SPCK, 2003.

Mays, James L. *Psalms.* Louisville: Westminster John Knox, 1994.

McCann, James C. "Psalms." In *NIB*, 4:639–1280.

Peterson, Eugene H. *Answering God: The Psalms As Tools for Prayer.* San Francisco: HarperCollins, 1989.

Renz, Thomas. *The Rhetorical Function of the Book of Ezekiel.* Boston: Brill, 2002.

Sloane, Andrew. "Lament and the Journey of Doubt." *Christian Scholar's Review* 29 (1999) 113–27.

Tate, Marvin E. *Psalms 51–100*. Dallas: Word, 1990.

Villanueva, Frederico G. "Preaching lament." In *"He Began with Moses . . .": Preaching the Old Testament Today*, edited by Grenville J. R. Kent et al., 64–84. Nottingham: IVP, 2010.

Waltke, Bruce K., James M. Houston, and Erika Moore. *The Psalms as Christian Lament: A Historical Commentary*. Grand Rapids: Eerdmans, 2014.

Ward, Timothy. *Word and Supplement: Speech Acts, Biblical Texts, and the Sufficiency of Scripture*. Oxford: Oxford University Press, 2002.

Weiser, Artur. *The Psalms*. Translated by Herbert Hartwell. London: SCM, 1962.

Wenham, Gordon J. *Psalms as Torah: Reading Biblical Song Ethically*. Grand Rapids: Baker, 2012.

Wilson, Gerald H. *Psalms, Vol. 1*. New International Version Application Commentary. Grand Rapids: Zondervan, 2002.

Wolterstorff, Nicholas. *Divine Discourse: Philosophical Reflections on the Claim That God Speaks*. Cambridge: Cambridge University Press, 1995.

13

Baking the Bread of Tears
A Recipe for Translating Psalm 80

Andrew G. Shead

Psalm 80 is part of a collection of communal laments whose superscriptions connect them to formal liturgical worship in the temple during a troubled period of Israel's history. Its tune suggests that care has been taken to achieve a beautiful result. There is nothing impromptu about it.

Like Israel, the Western church has a strong identity and history, but our God often seems slow to act. Should we not, like Israel, take time to craft beautiful laments?

The aim of this chapter is to offer a method for translating psalms, with the ultimate goal of translating the laments of ancient Israel into the life of our churches. I shall do this by presenting a new translation of Psalm 80 and commenting on the process involved in creating it, including its exegesis. My hope is not so much to advance scholarship as to encourage preachers to try their hand at translation—indeed, to make translation the heart of the preaching task. For the sake of non-Hebraists, I have minimized technicalities and provided the occasional definition, enough to give access to some of the riches of this great literature and to spur every reader to apply their full powers of imagination to the reading of Psalms.

Goal and Method

The goal of the present translation is to go beyond formal or functional equivalence and achieve some level of aesthetic equivalence.[1] This does not mean replicating Hebrew rhymes and rhythms, which would equate to transliteration. Forms must be created that make the poem feel like a poem in English, in a manner analogous to its feel as a poem in Hebrew. This begs the question of what an English poem "feels like," to which there is no single answer. As always, a translation style must suit its audience and purpose. For this occasion I made a translation with a strong sense of meter—something uncommon in contemporary poetry, but which codes a text as poetry for those of us who last "did" poetry at school. However, rather than domesticate the text into a neat ballad or song lyric, the English meter changes regularly to reflect the changing dynamics of the poem, a technique that imitates the fluidity of Hebrew poetic meter.[2] The language is formal and the style somewhat elevated. This is not an intimate outpouring of grief, but the formal, albeit passionate, complaint of a gathered community.

The result does not sound much like a contemporary English poem, or even a contemporary translated poem. It has stuck too close to the original words to allow the breathing space for poetic novelty. The aim instead has been for the result to count as Scripture, rather than a new poem inspired by Scripture.

The translation is the end result of an iterative process:

1. Beginning with sounds, rhythms, and echoes within the text, a word-by-word rendering is given some aesthetic equivalence, one strophe[3] at a time.

2. The whole must then interact with the parts. This involves revising the stichometry, so that the balance of individual lines serves the balance of the whole, and searching for consistency of poetic technique (e.g., meter) and language (especially tone or voice). Inevitably this will drive one back to the first step.

3. The translation should be set aside for a while if possible, and offered up to others for criticism. This helps to expose infelicities and idiosyncrasies, allowing decisions to be re-examined in the light of day.

---

1. Shead, "Theology in Poetry," 134–43.
2. Alonso Schökel, *Hebrew Poetics*, 34–44.
3. A strophe is a group of juxtaposed lines, usually a two-line bicolon, sometimes a three-line tricolon.

4. Detailed exegesis of the text, with a view to (a) context within the Psalter and ancient Near Eastern culture, (b) the emotional journey of the psalm, and (c) its unfolding argument, generates further modification, especially to structure.

5. The emerging theological message of the psalm provides a last input into the translation, by indicating choices that best reflect its final meaning.

The bulk of the present chapter consists of a verse-by-verse illustration of steps 1 and 2, plus a brief exegesis that extends the initial poetic reflections along the lines of steps 4 and 5. The translation below is the end result of the whole process.

The omission of historical context merits comment. The assaults against the Northern Kingdom in the eighth century make a convincing backdrop to the psalm.[4] Yet the connection with Asaph suggests the Jerusalem temple. Was the psalm brought south by refugees after Samaria's fall? Or re-used a century later when the South faced its own destruction, or in a time of exile, when the call to "bring us back" meant literal return? Each historical possibility can be supported by some detail of the text—and this is the genius of the Psalter, that poems from specific occasions have been molded to suit every generation of God's people. The context Scripture gives for this psalm is not a historical context, but a reading context, namely, the block of eleven Asaph psalms that opens Book III, with their focus on God as judge of the nations, and Israel as oppressed by the nations.[5]

The Translation[6]

For the director: to "the lilies of the covenant." An Asaph Psalm.

I

¹You who shepherd Israel, lend your ear,
    you who muster Joseph like a flock.
You who mount the Cherub throne, blaze bright
    ²in front of Ephraim, Benjamin, Manasseh.
Stir up your strength!
    Come, be our salvation!

4. The LXX tradition adds "over the Assyrian" to the superscription, and though the words are probably a secondary addition to the Greek text (see Rahlfs, *Psalmi*) they reveal ancient beliefs about the psalm's occasion.

5. Brown, *Psalms*, 94.

6. English verse numbering is used throughout.

³*Bring us back, O God, and make*
　　　your face to shine for our salvation's sake.

　　　　　　II

⁴Lord, God of Armies, how long
　　　have you smoldered at your people's plea?
⁵You've made them eat the bread of tears,
　　　and filled them bowls of tears to drink.
⁶You heap our neighbors' scorn on us;
　　　our foes deride in mockery.
⁷*God of Armies, bring us back and make*
　　　your face to shine for our salvation's sake.

　　　　　　III

⁸A vine from Egypt you uprooted once.
　　　You drove out nations and you planted her,
⁹clearing ground around her so her roots
　　　rooted down and then she filled the earth.
¹⁰Mountains by her shadow were eclipsed,
　　　and by her boughs the lofty cedar trees;
¹¹her branches stretched themselves to reach the Sea,
　　　and to the celestial River her tendrils twined.
¹²Why have you burst her walls apart—
　　　that all may pluck her as they pass,
¹³wild boars trample over her,
　　　swarming insects feed on her?
¹⁴*God of Armies, return!*
　　　Look down from heaven and see!
　　　Take notice of this vine!

　　　　　　IV

¹⁵Her seedling, which your right hand planted,
　　　you raised for yourself to shade a son.
¹⁶Burned with fire, cut to pieces,
　　　at your frowning face they die.
¹⁷Rest your hand on your right hand man,
　　　the son of man you raised for yourself,
¹⁸and we will not turn back from you.
　　　Return us to life, and we'll shout your name.
¹⁹*Lord, God of Armies, bring us back and make*
　　　your face to shine for our salvation's sake.

Towards an Initial Translation

Verse 1. In the first stages, a text layout such as the one below has been used. Hebrew words requiring further investigation are underlined; meter and distinctive sounds are noted. Literal translation equivalents are given in italics, with alternative possibilities placed below them. To avoid tedium, only v. 1 is laid out in this way.

v. 1 [2]	רֹעֵה יִשְׂרָאֵל הַאֲזִינָה o-eh ... i-ah	*Shepherd of Israel, hear/give ear/listen up!/!* You who shepherd Israel, pay us heed! | lend your ear!
	נֹהֵג כַּצֹּאן יוֹסֵף o-eh ... o-eh	*herdsman/drover/leader, like the flock, of Joseph,* You who guide | direct | gather | round up | muster Joseph like a flock,
3+3+3	יֹשֵׁב הַכְּרוּבִים הוֹפִיעָה: o-eh ... i-ah	*dweller on the Cherubim: shine!* You who mount the Cherub throne, blaze bright! | shine forth! | flame! | flare!

Table 13.1 Exegetical workings (Ps 80:1)

Each three-beat line of v.1 begins with an attribute of God—"shepherd," "herdsman," "sitter" (יֹשֵׁב, נֹהֵג, רֹעֵה—*rōʿēh, nōhēg, yōšēb*)—like a threefold invocation; and my choice of a threefold "you who" plus a regular four-beat meter is designed to achieve a similar effect. The cost of creating a regular English meter is an extra word here and there: "lend your ear" for "listen"; "blaze bright" for "shine." Word choices are governed by rhythmical considerations. "Drive" is more natural than "muster" but lacks the scansion.[7] "Throne" creates rhythm, and though an addition, it is an accurate one (see 1 Sam 4:4). "Mount" makes for a more poetic line than "dwell on," and as a descriptor of God is not as different from "dwell" as it would be in a verbal clause. It is reminiscent of Psalm 18:10, the only other time cherubim appear in the psalms.

Verse 2. There is no one way to set v. 2a, which artfully connects to the lines on either side. Choosing how to lay out the text is the same as deciding on one particular performance. With most English versions, I have attached it to v. 1. Admittedly, this dilutes the effect of the threefold "you who"; however, the imagery of v. 1c alludes to Deuteronomy 33:2, describing God's shining presence with the Israelites in the wilderness, and this implies a connection with the tribes in v. 2a. It also allows the imperatives of v. 2bc their due prominence at the head of two short, sharp lines. These lines are dominated in Hebrew by the vowel *ah* (וּלְכָה לִישֻׁעָתָה לָּנוּ, *ûləkâ lîšuʿātâ lānû*);

---

7. Scansion refers to the appropriate location of stressed and unstressed syllables in the line.

the translation grabs attention with alliteration and short lines rather than by assonance.

Verse 3. To give the refrain suitable prominence, so that the repetitions will feel memorable, the translation introduces a rhyme and enjambs[8] the lines. For the sake of the rhythm the noun "salvation" stands for the verb "save."

Verse 4. "How long," a rhetorical question expressing despair, is usually followed by a *yiqtol* conjugation (see Ps 82:2, "how much longer will you judge unjustly?"). By contrast, the *qatal* used here suggests an established state of past and present troubles: "how long have you been smoldering?" (see Exod 10:3, 7). To smolder is to be surrounded by smoke, as God was on Sinai (Exod 19:18), or will be in bringing covenant curses on his people (Deut 29:20). It rightly suggests wordless anger in English.

Verse 6. The term "mock," also used in Psalm 2:8, is imitative of foreign speech (see also Greek "barbarian"). The word's venom is conveyed by a double translation. The perspective shifts constantly from "them" (v. 5) to "us" (v. 6a) and back again. These uneasy shifts create a sense of agitation, like a camera constantly cutting from subject to subject.

Verses 8–9. The change of pace from complaint to narration has been conveyed in translation by lengthening the lines from four to five beats. "Once" (v. 8) adds a syllable, and establishes the narrative mode of the stanza. In this narrative context (note the *wayyiqtols* in vv. 9a, 10a) the difference between *yiqtol* in v. 8 and *qatal* in v. 9 is probably aspectual: God's successive acts of uprooting, driving out, and planting amount to a state of prepared ground. The distinction is tenuous, however; the poet may simply have chosen *qatal* because of its assonance in the line (פִּנִּיתָ לְפָנֶיהָ, *pinnîtā ləpānêhā*). The translation was able to reflect this assonance with "ground around," as well as the root-play(!)[9] of "her roots rooted" (וַתַּשְׁרֵשׁ שָׁרָשֶׁיהָ, *wattašrēš šārāšêhā*).

Verses 10–11. The Hebrew lines lend themselves to a shorter English meter: "Eclipsed were mountains by her shadow, / by her boughs the lofty cedars; / her branches stretched and reached the Sea, / and to the celestial River her tendrils." To stretch this out, "themselves" and "twined" were added. Because the language is elevated, distant from the psalmist's immediate reality, some Hebrew word-order inversions are retained for their archaizing effect.

---

8. Enjambment is the continuation of a clause across a line break.

9. Root play is the combination of different words derived from the same word root.

Many commentators take "sea" and "river" to be the Mediterranean and Euphrates respectively,[10] but the extravagant hyperbole feels more cosmological than mundane—not least because "lofty" translates the divine term אֵל (ʾēl). I therefore take these as referring to the cosmic waters (see Ps 93:3).

Verses 12–13. With the return of agitated complaint the meter of the translation returns to four beats per line. Again, words have been rearranged and trimmed to achieve this, while staying as close as possible to direct equivalence. It is difficult to match the agonized "why" plus fivefold *ah* of v. 12 (לָמָּה פָּרַצְתָּ גְדֵרֶיהָ, *lāmmâ pārastâ gədērêhā*). "Broken through her walls" would have been more precise for v. 12a, but the more violent and plosive wording was chosen, along with alliteration in v. 12b, as an alternate vehicle for intensity.

Verses 14–15 are the most difficult of the psalm, compounded by some difficult Hebrew.[11] Because the "seedling" of v. 15a refers back to the vine, many versions attach it syntactically to v. 14, which could generate the following: "God of Armies, pray return! / Look downwards from the heavens and see. // Take notice of this vine, whose shoot / your right hand planted. Over a son / you raised her for yourself." However, the Masoretic reading tradition groups the three imperatives of v. 14, and this strengthens the poem by creating a strong parallel to v. 2b. Just as the refrain lengthens each time, so the plea of v. 2 is now longer, and as the only tricolon of the poem there is a natural climax. This leaves v. 15 to open a final stanza bound together by playing on the idea of God's right hand raising up his vine/son.

Verses 17–18 accomplish an elegant turn to end the poem. The vine of the right hand (v. 15) becomes the man of the right hand (v. 17), and

---

10. E.g., Kraus, *Psalms*, 142; Hossfeld and Zenger, *Psalms 2*, 315. However, see Keel, *Symbolism*, 21.

11. The opening word of v. 17, תְּהִי־יָדְךָ, (*təhî-yādəkā*) might be a noun plus possessive ("her shoot/trunk"), or an imperative: "establish!" A noun seems more likely here. The second colon is usually translated the same way as v. 17b, giving "Establish what your right hand planted, / [and for] the son you grew strong for yourself." However, v. 17b is an unreliable guide to v. 15b. Where the governing verb in v. 17a makes good sense of the next line's preposition: "Let your hand be . . . / upon the son of man," the same preposition in v. 15b does not have such a ready antecedent. It must be taken to mean "for the sake of," and made into a relative clause: "which your right hand planted, / and [which] for a son's sake you grew strong." Either we have a line that does not belong, that was lifted from v. 17b and added into the shorter verse by a scribe for balance (some English versions delete v. 15b accordingly); or we have a line whose meaning differs from v. 17, on which it will play in due course. I judge the verb most likely refers to the vine, not the son. This is a more natural reading, albeit one featuring "defamiliarized" syntax (Lunn, *Word-Order*, 95–120), and it keeps the focus resolutely on the vine.

the vine God "raised" (v. 15) becomes the man God "raised." Verse 18b is usually rendered "call upon your name," but the inversion of the normal word order for this phrase changes its meaning to "proclaim your name" (see Exod 33:19; Ps 116:13).[12] This yields the expected "vow to praise" with which so many laments conclude.

Towards a Final Translation

The stanza divisions, especially the layout of vv. 12–14, were only settled through exegesis, as were many other adjustments. The method of approach with each stanza is to consider literary, and sometimes cultural, context, give concise expression to the unfolding emotional and propositional story, and point towards theological implications.

Stanza I

The opening invocation is a way of naming God for who he is. The divine shepherd who, according to Psalm 78:52, musters his sheep through the wilderness has abandoned them in our psalm. He alone was their protection, guidance, wisdom, and purpose. But unlike any human ruler, Israel's shepherd is lifted high above the earth, whence he blazes like the sun. He is their light; without him they are alone in the dark. The word translated "blaze" in v. 2 is used of the God who blazes from Zion with myriads of holy ones (Deut 33:2), and God who blazes in judgment on all humanity (Ps 94:1–2). Psalm 50 associates this blazing presence with the sun's journey across the earth:[13]

> The Mighty One, God, the Lord,
>   speaks and summons the earth
>   from the rising of the sun to where it sets.
> From Zion, perfect in beauty,
>   God shines [*blazes*] forth. (Ps 50:1–2 NIV)

This dramatic shift from pastoral to celestial, immanent to transcendent, evokes the divine shepherd who, as a pillar of fire, led Israel safely

---

12. Kraus, *Psalms*, 143.

13. A personal seal of Hezekiah found in 2009 includes a winged sun icon (Hebrew University, "Royal Seal," n.p.). While it would be wrong to conclude from this that Hezekiah was a sun worshiper, the sun was undoubtedly a powerful symbol for Israelites of their Creator's character. On God's solar presence see Brown, *Seeing the Psalms*, 84–89.

through the wilderness: a God at once near and inaccessible, safe and dangerous, merciful and just. By this melding of metaphors a vision is constructed not only of God but of ourselves, defined in relation to him. To be God's human is to depend, to pray, to trust, to fear, and yet to hope. And to name these relationships, to place a claim upon our God, is to exercise our proper role; it is righteous behavior. The urgency is honest—it is who we are in our desperation, and to respond in acts of rescue is who God is as ruler. God is being invoked (doxology) in the form of vivid but careful theological statements, and to name God in this way exerts a powerful moral force in both directions.[14] In this context the urgent imperatives of v. 2 are a call to "be who you are."

The image of God's radiance becomes the *Leitmotif* of this psalm in v. 3. Like "blaze," "shine" is a solar word, but occurs in contexts of blessing that comes when God illumines his people with his protection (Exod 13:21) or grace (Num 6:25) or glory (Isa 60:19). Rather than a fire it is a face that shines here, and this effectively incorporates the pastoral image into the celestial. The shining face of God brings together the same contrasting attributes of mercy and splendor that featured in vv. 1–2, and turns them into the theological core of the psalm.

Modern Bibles begin v. 3 with "restore," but exegesis supported the more common meaning "bring back." The call to "bring us back" is enigmatic at this stage, begging the question "Back from where?" It sets us searching for the answer as we read on. As for the question, "Back to what?" an answer is already in the air. This is a call for God to bring us back to himself.

Stanza II

This stanza moves systematically through the dimensions of the "socially embedded self," whereby every aspect of a person's being, from their relationship with God (v. 4) to their self-identity (v. 5) to their interaction with the world (v. 6) contributes to an integrated anthropology.[15] Wholeness in any of these relational dimensions equates to life; a decrease in any of them is an encroachment by death.

Death is not too strong a word. God is not just an absent light, but a dark presence, red and menacing as he withholds himself. "What is a human that you are mindful of him?" asks Psalm 8. It is only in God's presence

---

14. Speech is powerful, but these are prayers rather than magical "self-acting words of power" such as the pagans used; Mowinckel, *Psalms*, 146.

15. Di Vito, "Anthropology," 225; Janowski, *Arguing with God*, 42. See also Cohen, "'Why O Lord?'" (chapter 5 in this volume).

that humans can know themselves as human;[16] our humanity dies in his absence. No sin is confessed, but it hovers in the background here as a horrible suspicion that this living death is no more than they deserve.

As opposed to the individual God-self-enemy lament of Psalm 13:1–2, the lament here is corporate. Everything that gives the community its richness and texture has been swallowed up in grief. Sorrow fills their stomachs and throats, leaving no room for contentment or even basic living. There are no children or parents, teachers or servants or farmers or priests, just nameless bodies eating and drinking death. The self that is dying in this verse is the social self, whose individuality emerges within a network of social relationships.

The shifts in person across vv. 5–6 already hint at this dissolution of identity, but the mockery of enemies makes it explicit. In the Psalms as a whole, it is the figure of the enemy that typically has the power to dissolve the social self.[17] It is hard for those of us who have not grown up in an honor/shame culture to appreciate the diminution of self, the existential shrinking into nothingness, that mockery such as this can work.

The root cause of all this dying is God, and the tension this generates cannot be dispelled simply by suggesting they deserve it. Indeed, it compounds the problems of God's absence in Stanza I. This is not a prayer of repentance, but of pain at the withholding of forgiveness irrespective of repentance. At each repetition the refrain gains a divine descriptor. God's brute power, currently their undoing, could equally prove their salvation, if only he would turn his face towards them.

Stanza III

As with many laments, the people move from presenting their pain to reliving their past. The grief and desperation of the opening stanzas have given way here to sadness and a shared remembrance of paradise lost. The metaphor of the vine evokes the eighth-century prophets (Hos 10:1; Joel 1:12; cf. Isa 5:1–7), and Ezekiel re-used it after 597 (Ezek 19:10–14). All these texts highlight Israel's sin and God's consequent wrath and grief, but Psalm 80 presents the perspective of the traumatized people, adding in allusions to the exodus. The people are reliving an idyllic history, using the same metaphor God used to condemn that history. How are they giving those words back to God—as an act of regret? pleading? complaint?

---

16. Kraus, *Theology*, 148.
17. Janowski, *Arguing with God*, 106–7.

The net effect of this device is to create a poignant narrative of a lost past, focused somewhat pointedly on God's care and devotion in bringing Israel into being. In an echo of Stanza I's dynamic, images of the vine move from pastoral to celestial. The imagery evokes a mythical world tree, but its referent is thoroughly historical and this-worldly. Israel's founding was an act of divine creation with cosmic significance. Among the nations, looming over them, a source of life grew and flourished, its rich wine ready to fill the earth with joy. The end of the story should have been a universal pilgrimage, as in Isaiah 2. This is who God is, or at least was: when he reaches down to take us in hand we burst with life. Life flows from God's fingertips; a dusty patch of weeds becomes a cool and verdant garden, heavy with fragrance, humming with life. This was what it was like when God was our God.

Shared memory prompts a renewed appeal, now reframed by historical awareness into something altogether bigger. No longer is this simply a community apparently abandoned by their God; it is a matter of God's wanton destruction of his masterpiece. The allegory is trashed. The vine now is confined within walls, laid bare by God to the casual depredations of travelers and the mindless befoulment of unclean animals. The language of v. 12 sounds like a rape. We are filled with dismay and horror at the injustice of Israel's predicament and the tarnishing of God's glory that flows from what God has done. This is not a confession; it is a theodicy.

The appeal that follows in v. 14 is the emotional climax of the poem: a powerful, even unique, fourfold summons. First, God is urged to approach, followed by three verbs of seeing, all focused on *"this* vine," locating the community among the wreckage. What is the psalmist counting on: the pathetic spectacle, or the presence within it of penitent worshipers? The final stanza will reveal that it is neither of these, but rather God's own prior commitment to them.

Stanza IV

After the emotional climax of Stanza III the final stanza turns in a new direction by introducing a son. Initially (v. 15) he was protected by the vine, and was in fact the reason God divinely strengthened the vine. Elsewhere the Davidic king is called a "son" only in Psalms 2:7 and 72:1. The link to the king of Psalm 2 is inescapable, through whose rule God exerts power to crush his enemies. Yet that kingdom is no more: in v. 16 the metaphor of a burned vine (feminine singular) resolves into the reality of dying people (masculine plural). The shining face turned away in abandonment (Stanza I) has become the frowning—literally, "rebuking"—face turned towards Israel in judgment.[18] This is the logical endpoint of the psalm's meditation on the face of God, and it is no accident that it is now, when the son enters the picture, that the theme of the people's culpability first becomes explicit. Yet the third-person verb "they die" places the speakers among the survivors, bereft of a glorious kingdom, but with the son still among them, sharing their sufferings and their hope.

Verse 17 may appear to have given up on the hope that God would take notice of his vine, but the re-use of language suggests otherwise. God's right hand, which planted the vine, now strengthens the son (Ps 110:1); the world-spanning presence of the vine is now transferred to the son (Ps 2:8–9). The nation has been burned to the ground by the blazing wrath of their shepherd, but in the person of the son their hope stays alive. This is the only time in the Psalter the king's ordinary humanity is foregrounded with the parallel term "son of man" (only used here and in Pss 8:4; 144:3; 146:3).

The vow to praise in v. 18 is no facile promise to reward God for blessing them; it is closely connected to the son's future, an assertion, in effect, that his restoration will enable them to turn and praise. The parallel line illuminates this dynamic with the language of resurrection. In its first stages the translation had "revive us" here (Pss 22:29; 41:2), but in view of the way death pervades this psalm it became clear that the meaning "bring us back to life" was the right one (Pss 30:3; 71:20). God's people are experiencing a living death; the son is their hope of life. Enemies will be crushed as God exerts his power through the son. Society will re-form around his rule, each individual taking up his or her proper place and identity within it. And as God turns towards the son in remembrance, his subjects will be bathed in the light of God's shining face and live.

In the final verse God's covenant name, Yahweh, is mentioned for the first and last time, evoking his faithfulness despite Israel's sin, a faithfulness that reflects his deepest nature. Psalm 80 grapples with the theological crisis generated by the failure of God's people to flourish. Along the way this crisis is addressed in a number of ways, but in the end the question and the answer lie together, in the character of God.

Conclusion

Thoughtful translations of biblical lament do not only provide words to say together; they tutor us in the careful theological statements that lament

---

18. "Rebuke" often describes God's destruction of his enemies, and many commentators take this as a wish for Israel's enemies to die, but there is no indication from context of a new subject here.

demands if it is to avoid falling into sentimentality, self-pity or protest against enemies.[19] The next translational step should be the crafting of a new Psalm 80 for Christ's church to sing today. What vision must that song project?

Psalm 80 projects a vision of God that soars from earth to heaven, from intimacy to transcendence, but the world remains dark. Not that God is ever truly absent. He is there behind the darkness, silent while we are unmade. By coming together to tell him our pain we engage in one of the few activities of life that grief permits us. Our Life has left us, but we cling to him regardless, not just out of a refusal to give up, but because we know that Life, not Death, is who he is. How do we know? We remember last time he shone: we were so filled with life that like God himself our life soared from earth to fill the heavens. If that was God, how can this be God? He is not just hurting us, but himself.

It is in the Son that we see the extent of God's self-involvement with his people. Whatever we have done to earn this darkness, we know the depth of God's love for his Son, and we pin our hopes on him, trusting that when God raises his Son above the heavens we will be raised to life with the life that comes from the Son, God's new human being, our true king.

Lamenting together is not about wresting blessing from God, or even simply about speaking our pain. It is a fundamental act of solidarity with the Son, into whose broken body we are joined by faith. The bread of tears we eat, he ate before us, and the disappointments we suffer as an untriumphant, beleaguered church, he suffered before us. Lamenting these troubles together before God, and not remaining silent, is how we express who we are. It is how we follow faithfully in his steps, who "offered up prayers and petitions with fervent cries and tears to the one who could save him from death" (Heb 5:7).

Bibliography

Alonso Schökel, Luis. *A Manual of Hebrew Poetics*. Subsidia Biblica 11. Rome: Pontificio Istituto Biblico, 1988.

Brown, William P. *Psalms*. Interpreting Biblical Texts. Nashville: Abingdon, 2010.

———. *Seeing the Psalms: A Theology of Metaphor*. Louisville: Westminster John Knox, 2002.

Di Vito, Robert A. "Old Testament Anthropology and the Construction of Personal Identity." *Catholic Biblical Quarterly* 61 (1999) 217–38.

---

19. See Janowski, *Arguing with God*, 39.

Hebrew University of Jerusalem. "Impression of King Hezekiah's Royal Seal Discovered in Ophel Excavations South of Temple Mount in Jerusalem." http://new.huji.ac.il/en/article/28173.

Hossfeld, Frank-Lothar and Erich Zenger. *Psalms 2: A Commentary on Psalms 51–100.* Translated by Linda M. Maloney. Hermeneia. Minneapolis: Fortress, 2005.

Janowski, Bernd. *Arguing with God: A Theological Anthropology of the Psalms.* Translated by Armin Siedlecki. Louisville: Westminster John Knox, 2009.

Keel, Othmar. *The Symbolism of the Biblical World: Ancient Near Eastern Iconography and the Book of Psalms.* Translated by Timothy J. Hallett. New York: Seabury, 1978.

Kraus, Hans-Joachim. *Psalms 60–150.* Translated by Hilton C. Oswald. A Continental Commentary. Minneapolis: Fortress, 1993.

———. *Theology of the Psalms.* Translated by Kenneth Crim. A Continental Commentary. Minneapolis: Fortress, 1992.

Lunn, Nicholas P. *Word-Order Variation in Biblical Hebrew Poetry: Differentiating Pragmatics and Poetics.* Paternoster Biblical Monographs. Milton Keynes: Paternoster, 2006.

Mowinckel, Sigmund. *The Psalms in Israel's Worship, Volume 2.* Translated by D. R. Ap-Thomas. Oxford: Basil Blackwell, 1962.

Rahlfs, Alfred. *Psalmi cum Odis.* Septuaginta Vetus Testamentum Graecum 10. 2nd ed. Göttingen: Vandenhoeck & Ruprecht, 1967.

Shead, Andrew G. "Theology in Poetry: The Challenge of Translating the Psalms." In *Stirred by a Noble Theme: The Book of Psalms in the Life of the Church*, edited by Andrew G. Shead, 133–57. Leicester: Apollos, 2013.

Part IV

The Practice of Lament

14

Preaching Lament

Peter J. Davis

THE WESTERN WORLD HAS lost the language of lament, particularly in the contemporary church. In many churches, a focus on the positive dominates, with preachers struggling to know how to speak to the daily realities of human pain. In this chapter, I will look at the practicalities of preaching lament from a number of perspectives: Purpose, Content, Language, Form, and Delivery.[1] These categories enable preachers to think in practical terms about the why, what, how, and when of faithful preaching in times of crisis.

Of course, not all cultures have lost this ability. When calamities unfold, some cultures have a deeply ingrained capacity for lament. This is especially so in cultures where people live daily with extremes of poverty, violence, and exploitation. In such cultures, lament has a remarkably consoling effect. It is also very much alive within some subcultures in the Western world. The African-American church still shows signs of a capacity to lament due to its history of slavery, discrimination, and marginalization. A generation ago, Henry Mitchell identified and helped the wider church appreciate the place of celebration within the African-American preaching tradition.[2] Luke Powery's recent work has examined the interconnection of lament and celebration in two publications, one outlining a homiletic of lament and the

---

1. These categories are an adaption and extension of those employed by Lucy Atkinson Rose, *Sharing the Word*.

2 Mitchell, *Celebration and Experience*.

other examining African-American spirituals as a resource for exploring the homiletical interface of death and hope.[3] Powery's premise is that outward signs of the Spirit's presence are vital to African-American experience and are manifest in five ways: through lament, celebration, grace, unity, and fellowship.[4] These manifestations of the Spirit are important aspects of African-American experience because they are signs of the presence of God both with and for people. Even though lament is strongly grounded in the African-American experience, Powery observes that the African-American church is also frightened of lament, noting that even his own tradition has lost the sense that "the Spirit also manifests itself through laments and not solely through celebrations."[5]

I write as an Anglo-Australian pastor and educator who works with mainstream congregations in an urban context. I have worked with churches who want to grow, innovate, be biblically grounded, be spiritually healthy, and serve their local communities in the name of Christ. In those contexts, the focus is on the relevance of what we preach, on engaging communication, and on effectiveness in ministry. Pastors work hard at shaping worship services that are appealing, preaching sermons that empower people, and leading programs that connect local communities with the gospel of Christ. Where does lament fit into that?

Yet it is clear that the Bible is full of the language of lament. We experience lament on the personal level (Job, the Psalms), national level (Lamentations), and also the covenantal level (the Prophets). We also see lament embodied in the life of Christ, particularly in the passion narratives. Lament is present throughout the Scriptures as a normal part of the life of faith.

When tragedy looms large—be it on the local, national, or global level—preachers have both the opportunity and the responsibility to speak to the situation. Recent events, both domestic and abroad, have demonstrated the need for lament in the face of human tragedy. In times of great grief, there is a communal outpouring as people search for ways to express their emotion and find consolation. Preachers have a role to play in such times. A well-spoken and timely word has the power to help people by calming their fears and refocusing on what matters most: trust in the faithfulness of God, a reminder of who we are, and the invitation to embody the character of Christ in daily life.

---

3 Powery, *Spirit Speech*; Powery, *Dem Dry Bones*.
4 Powery, *Spirit Speech*, loc. 190.
5 Ibid., loc. 144.

Fear of Lament

There is evidence that the Western church has not only lost the language of lament but is frightened of lament. There are a number of possible reasons for this.[6] Firstly, many Anglo-Australian congregations have conflicting responses to emotion. By nature we are emotional creatures, but we are cautious of emotionalism. We want sermons to have emotional resonance but are cautious about overt public displays of emotion. Secondly, we want to distance ourselves from suffering. We are used to being in control of our environments or, at least, like to think that we are in control of our lives. So when sickness or tragedy intrudes, we struggle to know how to respond. Reading psalms can be overwhelming for the modern reader. The cries of the psalmists are fine in small doses, but the repeated cries for deliverance in the face of enemies and trouble can be exhausting. Western readers do not feel that embattled and the biblical witness feels too much. That is not the case for people from other cultures. Thirdly, we are not used to approaching God so directly. David Jacobsen regards lament as a profound expression of faith in the promises of God in which the supplicant is willing to work it through with God in the presence of others.[7] Contemporary Christians are less than comfortable in approaching God in this way. Fourthly, for many people in the Western world there is a fear of ambiguity. We prefer a faith that is certain and sure, based on unshakeable foundations. So when we encounter life experiences that are less than sure, it not easy for us or the people that we lead. Finally, we are obsessed with that which is positive, life affirming, practical, and effective. We want sermons that help us become stronger people and allow our churches to be vital places.

If that is the case, how does lament fit in to the modern Western landscape? In what ways can and should the sermon be a form of lament? Ian Hussey notes that Australian congregations value sermons that relate in practical ways to their lives, and that effective preachers are able to find the balance between practical helpfulness and biblical exegesis.[8] His study observes that helpful sermons are humorous, passionate, bold, structured well, not "dumbed-down," well prepared, and allow engagement through multimedia and interaction. Some of these factors are well suited to lament, particularly passion and boldness. But other factors pull the preacher in the opposite direction. Preachers feel pressure to simultaneously be truth-

---

6. For further discussion, see Ciano, "Lament Psalms in the Church" (chapter 1 in this volume).

7. Jacobsen, "Augustine," 224.

8. Hussey, "The Other Side," 16.

ful, engaging, passionate, profound, and practical. They look for ways to be relevant to their congregations and are frightened to be too serious too often. So the practicalities of effective preaching and the importance of lament do not sit together easily. How does the faithful preacher preach lament in this landscape?

Preaching Lament

Purpose

At its most basic level, the purpose of preaching lament is simple. Lament is a natural response to human suffering and tragedy. When suffering occurs, there is an automatic response that longs for a word of comfort, reassurance, and hope. This is true at the political level, the religious level, and the social level. André LaCocque notes that "life is lived between the two poles of lamentation and praise . . . It is clear that the suppliant is caught up in a struggle with himself between these two conflicting feelings."[9] It is a personal struggle, a struggle within oneself, a struggle with God, a struggle with circumstances and external enemies. Consequently, lament is a normal response to human suffering. It is normal for us to call out to God in the light of these circumstances, to seek comfort and meaning, to pray for ourselves and for others, and to seek assurance of the faithfulness of God. Paul Ricoeur notes that the "Psalms of Lamentations are there to recall that the individual is fragile, exposed to illness and death, vulnerable to the attacks of others."[10] In contrast, Thomas Troeger observes that Western culture views praise and lament as polar opposites; this is the reason why congregations want sermons and services that are upbeat.[11] The focus on the upbeat has become big business in contemporary preaching. Powery labels this "candy" theology: it tastes good but it is based on the conviction that consumption can "fill spiritual emptiness and quiet the longing in a hurting people."[12] Rather than viewing praise and lament as opposites, Jacobsen argues that they are actually flip sides of the same reality, the promises of God.[13]

When tragic events occur, congregations look to their ministers to address these realities in worship and preaching. Preachers do their congregations a disservice if they fail to respond appropriately. Readers will recall

9 Cited in Ricoeur, "Lamentation as Prayer," 219.
10 Ricoeur, "Lamentation as Prayer," 226.
11 Troeger, "House of Prayer," 1248.
12 Powery, *Dem Dry Bones*, 4.
13. Jacobsen, "Augustine," 224.

their own experience in light of September 11. What was preached in the following weeks? As people spoke in worship services, prayer meetings, and the public square, what did the preacher say and what impact did his or her message have upon the hearers? When tragedy or human suffering happens, the preacher should minister to people with honesty and candor by bringing the Scriptures to bear on their experience. Preaching lament is a holistic response that addresses the disjuncture between the compassion of God and the injustices of the present situation. This involves interpreting the situation, giving voice to an assortment of human emotions, and acting in response to the situation.

It is not always the case that preachers respond to such calamities effectively. William Willimon tells of his experience of church on the Sunday following the assassination of Dr Martin Luther King Jr.[14] He was a student at Yale Divinity School at the time and went home to South Carolina that weekend, heartbroken (as was the whole country). The preacher that Sunday spoke on the theme "God says, 'I want you to be my valentine.'" Needless to say, he was devastated. When tragedy strikes, it is important for the preacher to offer a biblical word that will minister to people in their distress, even if this means putting the planned message aside.

An important aspect of preaching lament, therefore, is helping our listeners to think and act through the Scriptures. Lament is the cry of the human heart as it struggles with the disjuncture between experience and its own worldview and assumptions. It is a prayer asking why there is an apparent contradiction between the promises of God on the one hand and the injustices of the present on the other. It is an attempt to make sense of the disjuncture. In short, it is an attempt to think and act Christianly. Walter Brueggemann notes that preaching endeavors to state in the boldest, most extreme ways the contrast between how people in our society generally think and what it would mean to think life or to act life through the gospel.[15] The purpose of preaching lament, therefore, is to bring normal human responses to suffering to God so that we might be enabled to respond in distinctive ways that exhibit deep faith in the promises of God and reflect the character of Christ. In the face of injustice, people naturally find themselves angered, feeling the desire for revenge, and being overwhelmed by grief or filled with despair. Lament brings these responses to God corporately, asking God to hear the prayer of his people and intervene. As Geoff New notes, the biblical laments demonstrate a bold faith where people can shake their fist at God

---

14. Personal conversation with the author.
15. Cited in Davis, *Preaching*, 54.

and yet trust him.[16] Rather than get caught up in sentimentality, political ideology, or therapeutic language, the Scriptures hold out an alternate way of responding characterized by deep engagement with the character of God, the life of Christ, and the pattern of faithful discipleship.

Content

In this chapter, I argue that the biblical text is the primary vehicle for lament. As already noted in previous chapters, the psalms in particular are patterns of prayer which God offers as righteous responses to human suffering.[17] Biblical laments are gifts from God that will hold people in times of distress and give voice to their grief. The preacher's role, therefore, is to hold that space, allowing Scripture to be the content that nurtures people in their need. The preacher does well to make the biblical text, not the situation, the primary content of their sermon. The text is a repository of godly responses to a variety of human experiences. In preaching lament it is important that we are Scripture-centered, not focusing on human subjectivity (whether individual or communal), but focusing on what the Scriptures have to say about the character and the promises of God.

For the Christian preacher, the Scriptures are ancient resources that speak timelessly in the present. In his analysis of Psalm 22, Ricoeur speaks of the poetry of the text preserving "enough indications to keep the lament within the horizon of an individual experience and . . . to raise the suffering to the rank of a paradigm."[18] Paradigms hold together the general and the particular. The psalms, in particular, are a timeless source of inspiration. Kit Barker notes that the psalms originally functioned as divinely sanctioned responses to commensurate situations.[19] For this reason, when preachers are searching for a text that speaks significantly into a human experience, it is often the psalms to which they turn. Whether it be a funeral, bedside ministry, or responding to a global, national, or local crisis, the poetry of the psalms allows the reader to "transform the 'I' into an empty space capable of being occupied in each case anew by a different reader."[20] The Scriptures therefore provide words when human insights and responses escape us. The role of the preacher is to exercise spiritual discernment so that the situation of a group or congregation might be located within an appropriate para-

---

16. New, "The Voice," 38.
17. See Barker, "Lament as Divine Discourse" (chapter 4 in this volume).
18. Ricouer, "Lamentation as Prayer," 215.
19. Barker, "Divine Illocutions," 13.
20. Ricouer, "Lamentation as Prayer," 216.

digm, one that is a good fit between the situation of the text and the particularities of the present. Although there may be benefit in preachers being prepared in advance by having resources available to use at short notice, nothing diminishes the need for the astute linking of text and context.

Biblical preaching takes place at the interface between the text, preacher, and congregation. As rhetorical theory reminds us, effective preaching is a three-fold strand that weaves together the content of the message, the character of the speaker, and emotional resonance with both theme and context. One important question is what constitutes appropriate self-disclosure on the part of the preacher. Is it appropriate for the preacher's emotions and experience to be part of the content of the sermon? Some preachers never include personal sharing in their sermons, but I believe that preachers should value the place of personal sharing, provided that it serves the main idea of the sermon and is treated with caution until the preacher has perspective on his or her situation. Personal sharing should never dominate a text, but rather complement or enhance it. There is danger when preachers respond emotionally to situations when they still lack perspective. This is particularly difficult when traumatic events occur immediately before worship events. At the same time, there are situations where preachers should and must respond quickly.[21] However preachers respond, it should be personal, honest, and helpful. The preacher needs to make judgment calls on how to hold these elements together.

One way preachers can help their congregations respond to tragedy and suffering is to preach systematically across the whole canon of Scripture. Every sermon can contribute to the unvoiced concerns carried by individuals or communities. To do this faithfully means preaching from all the genres of Scripture so that our regular preaching programs build opportunities for people to think through questions of lament. There are passages that we might typically ignore or skip over, but by taking people to those places regularly, it helps people prepare for those moments when tragedy strikes. It is good practice for preachers to conduct periodic audits of both their own preaching and the preaching programs in their congregations. Over a period of five years, how often does the preacher touch on passages to do with lament, and does this reflect their frequency in Scripture? Are there parts of Scripture that are neglected and other parts that are favored? The weekly preaching program of a congregation functions like plant litter

---

21. For an example of a quick and effective pastoral response, see the sermon by Howard-John Wesley, which was preached the morning after a Florida jury found George Zimmerman not guilty of Trayvon Martin's death. http://swampland.time.com/2013/07/18/the-best-sermon-about-trayvon-that-you-will-hear.

on a rainforest floor: it provides the nutrients required for mature and godly responses to diverse life experiences.

Language

The preacher is encouraged to be honest with congregations in every sense and should reflect this in their use of language. Powery notes that the language of lament is direct and imperatival.[22] Consequently, preachers should speak directly with their hearers in a way that reflects the seriousness of the situation and their response to it. Preachers should not try to be clever or overly analytical; rather, they should be honest in every sense of the word: emotionally, intellectually, and spiritually.

In times of lament, preachers should speak openly to their hearers. They should be honest about their fears and doubts without laboring them. Central to all that, there should be a deep trust in God that locates him in the center of human anguish.

Biblical texts cover the whole range of human experiences: fear, shame, guilt, vulnerability. These texts are extremely honest in their dealings with distressing situations and sometimes preachers baulk at their raw honesty. It needs to be recognized that the language of lament will frequently be raw. Yet, rather than recoil from the rawness of the Scriptures, the preacher is encouraged to embrace it. Psalm 137, for instance, is disturbing, concluding in a way that confronts readers and preachers alike.[23] The temptation for the preacher is to bracket out this part of the psalm by truncating the psalm at v. 6, remembering homeland and pledging to remain faithful and hopeful even in the midst of oppression. Brad Braxton notes that preachers are right to denounce the violence of these passages, but by failing to engage with these troubling verses, preachers may forfeit an opportunity to examine the dynamics of pain and oppression.[24] Rather than be daunted by the intensity of these texts, preachers are encouraged to trust the Scriptures. These passages have a way of ministering to the deepest places of our lives and preachers can trust them to hold, comfort, and reassure their listeners. As Barker points out, the cry of this psalm is not simply inciting hatred, but is a call for God to be faithful to his covenant.[25] By trusting the psalm to do its work, preachers will find that they help their congregations to trust in God's covenantal faithfulness and to embody the life of Christ in their own

---

22 Powery, *Spirit Speech*, loc. 764.

23. See Barker, "How Could We Sing?" (chapter 20 in this volume).

24. Braxton, "African American Lectionary," Ps 137.

25. Barker, "Divine Illocutions," 13; Barker, "Psalms of the Powerless," 225–29.

discipleship. Preachers don't have to shy away from the rawness of the text, but trust the agency of the text to speak into people's lives. Just as an effective counselor holds the therapeutic space so that their clients can process their experiences, effective preachers hold people in the biblical text trusting the words of Scripture to provide comfort, reassurance, and clarity. As Barker emphasizes, psalms such as this are appropriate responses to extreme violence, and readers are invited to pray like this when faced with similar situations.[26] The rawness of the text is a gift to us—we preachers can trust the Scriptures to hold us, to lead us through, and not feel like we have to sanitize it or explain it away.

Form

In preaching lament, the preacher does not need to be creative, articulate, or clever, but rather faithful to the message, mood, and motivation of the Scriptures. As the Scriptures provide paradigms for contemporary circumstances, the preacher is encouraged to allow the movement of the text to shape the movement of the sermon. As Geoff Harper emphasizes earlier in this volume, the psalms invite readers to take up these words and use them to articulate their own response to God.[27]

David Lose observes that, in the New Homiletic, experience trumps both form and content; in their desire to "create a profound, even transformative experience the New Homileticians risk sacrificing a genuinely Christian experience."[28] Preachers should resist the temptation to produce profound experiences for their hearers by focusing instead on helping their listeners to encounter the truth of the Scriptures and by being attentive to the movement of the text. Dennis Cahill notes that one of the important insights of recent homiletical scholarship has been the relationship between the genre of the text and the form of the sermon; in fact, the form of the text is part of the meaning of the text.[29] It is good practice for preachers to pay close attention to the particular shape of biblical lament and to allow that to shape the specific contours of their sermon. Each biblical lament has its own sense of movement, both a movement of ideas and an emotional progression. Paying careful attention to this progression is an important part of building a connection between the biblical text and the situation of contemporary readers.

26. Ibid., 14.
27. Harper, "Lament and the Sovereignty of God" (chapter 6 in this volume).
28. Lose, "Whither Hence," 263.
29. Cahill, *The Shape of Preaching*, 59.

Adapting Claus Westermann's work, Harper lists the elements which are typical of lament in an earlier chapter in this volume: an appeal to God for help, reference to God's past deliverance, the lament proper, confession of trust, petition for God's intervention, assurance of being heard, and a vow of praise.[30] Powery also draws on Westermann and highlights the following as the distinctive movement within the psalms of lament:[31]

1. The address is to God, indicating divine-human relationship
2. A description of the situation of trouble, whether that be sickness, loneliness/abandonment, danger before enemies, shame or death
3. Asking God to act decisively
4. Giving reasons for why God should right the wrong
5. An assertion that the speaker will give or pay something as an offering in response to deliverance
6. A shift from plea to praise.

Powery focuses on the essence of this movement by noting that lament "begins with the realization that something is not right but moves in faith toward a God who can make things right. . . . It begins in hurt, rage, need, indignation, isolation, and abandonment. The proper setting of praise is a lament resolved."[32] Consequently, anticipation of resolution lies at the heart of lament, but resolution is neither easy nor formulaic. Lament is voiced in trust and in expectation that God will both hear and answer the supplicant's prayer. As Judith McDaniel notes, lament is always voiced with the expectation of satisfaction.[33]

Consequently, there are a multitude of forms in the psalms and the preacher does well to attend to the movement of the selected text, allowing their hearers to follow a similar journey. If praise and lament are flipsides of divine promise, then the tension between the two is pivotal. Because psalms of lament reflect the life of faith lived in real situations, the interplay between these two dimensions is never neat or orderly. It is rarely the case that there is a linear movement, so Federico Villanueva suggests that preachers should pay close attention to the particular movement in lament psalms and identify what experiences of suffering are being depicted in the movement.[34] Vil-

---

30. Harper, "Lament and the Sovereignty of God."
31. Powery, *Spirit Speech*, loc. 797.
32. Ibid., loc. 785.
33. McDaniel, "Interpreter of Dreams," 1232.
34. Villanueva, "Preaching Lament," 81.

lanueva identifies a number of patterns: the most common is the movement from lament to praise (God answers and delivers), but there is also alternation between lament and praise (restoration is a process), return to lament after praise (ambiguity and tension remain even with divine response), the reverse movement from praise to lament (faith is not all about answers), and the absence of movement (faith does not always resolve life).[35] Villanueva stresses the importance of these diverse forms because they recognize that faith does not always lead to neat outcomes. Careful attention to the movement of Scripture enables preachers to outline the diverse responses that represent mature responses to pain and suffering in its various forms.

Delivery

Preachers are encouraged to speak simply, clearly, and directly to their hearers. Preaching lament is not the time for eloquence. It is a time for preachers to name some of the feelings that they and their hearers are feeling, bringing these before God with honesty and candor. It is not a time to make judgments, particularly when the details may only be partially known. It is preferable to make observations without arriving at premature conclusions, identifying events and speaking about the process that might be followed. Emotional congruence between the preacher, the congregation, and the text is vital. The preacher's task is to speak in such a manner that the engagement of all three occurs.

Preachers should be honest with their fears and doubts while also demonstrating trust in the presence and faithfulness of God. Congregations are helped greatly when preachers are honest about these dimensions of their life without these dominating the message. Listeners are encouraged when they know that a preacher does not live in a world which is foreign to theirs, but experiences many of the fears and doubts that they experience framed by hope and trust in the promises of God.

The sermon should be delivered in a hopeful manner. Without being either sentimental or pious, the preacher should allow the text to hold and nurture the congregation following the movement of the text in such a way that the congregation arrives at a destination that is both hopeful and truthful. This will occur differently in different contexts and with different texts.

Some laments simply do not resolve in praise.[36] They are more nuanced than that, but at the heart of lament lies hope. The various forms of lament demonstrate a rich and complex pattern. There is no simple movement from

35. Ibid., 75–79.
36. Powery, *Spirit Speech*, loc. 2431.

lament to celebration, but rather a complex pattern that calls on God for intervention, places deep trust in his promises and lives in anticipation of that intervention. As Harper points out, these psalms are responses of faith, determined to cling on in the belief that God is faithful and dependable.[37] It is an approach to faith that is far richer and more sustaining than the consumeristic theology so in vogue in the contemporary church. The ultimate goal of hope is profound trust in the character and promises of God.

Conclusion

The time is right for a recovery of lament in the preaching of the Western church. There has been a homiletical convergence in recent years that promises to bear fruit in the life of the church as preachers recover this overlooked genre. As the world becomes increasingly volatile and presumed sources of security are shown to be lacking, perhaps the church will turn once more to God in her times of need. This will require the recovery of an ancient language and the determination to be honest with God and with each other as we live out our faith.

New invites us to imagine a people who are schooled in the art of lament, "a church that is not embarrassed by praying their grief and that looks with expectancy to the God who can move them to a place of praise."[38] It is a refreshing and timely vision. It is also a biblical vision. It will require us as preachers to let go of our obsession with the upbeat and help us to rediscover the close connection between lament and praise. Perhaps it will also help to close the back doors of our churches and build connections with people who are hungry for a robust and honest faith centered on the faithfulness of God and patterned on the life of Christ.

Bibliography

Barker Kit. "Divine illocutions in Psalm 137: A Critique of Nicholas Wolterstorff's 'Second Hermeneutic.'" *Tyndale Bulletin* 60 (2009) 1–14.
———. "Psalms of the Powerless." In *Stirred by a Noble Theme: The Book of Psalms in the Life of the Church*, edited by Andrew G. Shead, 205–29. Nottingham: Apollos, 2013.
Braxton, Brad. "The African American Lectionary." http://www.theafricanamericanlectionary.org/PopupLectionaryReading.asp?LRID=10.
Cahill, Dennis. *The Shape of Preaching: Theory and Practice in Sermon Design*. Grand Rapids: Baker, 2007.

37. Harper, "Lament and the Sovereignty of God."
38. New, "The Voice," 39.

Davis, Peter J. "Preaching in a New Age of Mission: Christian Proclamation after Christendom." ThD diss., Sydney College of Divinity, 2010.

Hussey, Ian. "The Other Side of the Pulpit: Listener's Experience of Helpful Preaching." *Homiletic* 39 (2014) 1–19.

Jacobsen, David S. "Augustine's Use of Tyconius' *Book of Rules* in *On Christian Doctrine*: Promise and the Unfinished Task of Homiletical Theology." In *The Academy of Homiletics Papers of the Annual Meeting (15–17 November 2012)*, 215–24.

Lose, David. "Whither Hence the New Homiletic." In *The Academy of Homiletics Papers of the Annual Meeting (30 November—2 December 2000)*, 255–66.

McDaniel, Judith. "The Interpreter of Dreams: Preaching to Effect Change." *Hervormde Teologiese Studies* 62 (2006) 1227–37.

Mitchell, Henry H. *Celebration and Experience in Preaching*. Nashville: Abingdon, 1990.

New, Geoff. "The Voice: From Text to Life." *Stimulus* 19 (2012) 38–39.

Powery, Luke A. *Dem Dry Bones: Preaching, Death, and Hope*. Minneapolis: Fortress, 2012.

———. *Spirit Speech: Lament and Celebration in Preaching*. Nashville: Abingdon, 2009.

Ricoeur, Paul. "Lamentation as Prayer." In *Thinking Biblically: Exegetical and Hermeneutical Studies*, edited by André LaCocque and Paul Ricoeur, 211–32. Chicago: University of Chicago Press, 1998.

Rose, Lucy A. *Sharing the Word: Preaching in the Roundtable Church*. Louisville: Westminster John Knox, 1997.

Troeger, Thomas H. "A House of Prayer in the Heart: How Homiletics Nurtures the Church's Spirituality." *Hervormde Teologiese Studies* 62 (2006) 1239–49.

Villanueva, Federico G. "Preaching Lament." In *"He Began With Moses . . .": Preaching the Old Testament Today*, edited by Grenville J. R. Kent et al, 64–84. Nottingham: IVP, 2010.

15

Singing Lament

ROBERT S. SMITH

THE CONTEMPORARY CHURCH IS neither adept nor comfortable with singing lament.[1] The most obvious reason for this is that many churches have long ago stopped singing the Psalms.[2] This, in turn, has led not simply to a lack of acquaintance with sung lament but to a loss of appetite for it. As Dietrich Bonhoeffer once observed, when "read only occasionally, these prayers are too overwhelming in design and power and tend to turn us back to more palatable fare."[3] Added to this, there are very few contemporary congregational songs of lament. This is in contrast to the balance of the Psalter, where sixty-seven of the one hundred and fifty psalms may be categorized as laments—if not in whole, at least in part. Finally, widespread neglect (and therefore ignorance) of many traditional "lament hymns" (e.g., "Be Still My Soul") has meant that the congregational resources for sung lament are negligible indeed.

In light of this situation, my aim in this essay is to argue for a recovery of the practice of *singing* lament. By this I don't just mean reviving the practice of singing the Psalter (although this would certainly help). I also mean finding (or writing) more hymns and songs that do what the biblical

---

1. Bradbury, *Sowing in Tears*, 11.

2. Even in those that have continued the practice, "the ancient tradition of systematically reciting the whole psalter in a regular cycle is now very rare" (Shead and Cameron, "Singing with the Messiah," 164).

3. Bonhoeffer, *Psalms*, 25.

laments do: help believers to sing their griefs before the throne of grace as we wait for the coming of Christ and the consummation of his kingdom. I will make my case in two steps: firstly, by exploring the value of singing even when singing seems impossible and, secondly, by investigating what can be known of the God-given powers of music and song.

Singing When Singing Seems Impossible

The Value of Sung Lament

The Psalter contains a considerable amount of information about how many of the psalms were (or were intended to be) used in Israel's temple worship. This information is found in a plethora of musical designations and liturgical directions, including specific instructions regarding the use of musical instruments or the employment of particular tunes.[4] In regard to the lament psalms, a strong case can be made for concluding that as many as forty-three were sung in the Temple.[5] Like the praise and thanksgiving psalms, then, the laments were sung communally.[6]

This should not surprise us. As the Psalter unveils God's redemptive purposes through the historical progression of Israelite kingship, one of its chief aims is to teach God's people about the trials and triumphs of the life of faith, and how to respond appropriately as they journey with the Messiah from suffering to glory, from lament to praise.[7] Indeed, because the psalms cover the whole gamut of human emotions, while at the same time giving us divinely inspired words with which to praise and pray, John Calvin had good reason to write:

> I have been accustomed to call this book, I think not inappropriately, "An Anatomy of all the Parts of the Soul"; for there

---

4. For example, Psalms 4; 5; 6; 8; 9; 11; 12; 22; 45; 46; 50; 53; 54; 55; 56; 60; 61; 62; 67; 76; 81; 84; 88, etc.

5. Smith, "Which Psalms?" 173. By way of contrast, post-Christian Jewish liturgies favor the more "positive" psalms. Consequently, the laments do not play a dominant role in contemporary synagogue worship. See Holladay, *Psalms through Three Thousand Years*, 140.

6. That lament was sung communally is also confirmed by the Mishnah. m. *Mo'ed Qat.* 3:9 says: "What is meant by 'Sing lamentations'? When one recites and all of the others respond after her, as it is said, 'Teach your daughters wailing and a woman her fellow a lamentation' (Jeremiah 9:19)."

7. For helpful discussions of the purpose and shape of the Psalter and the structural significance of the kingship theme see Hill and Walton, *Survey*, 346–51; Futato, *Interpreting the Psalms*, 57–116; Hely Hutchinson, "Psalter as a Book," 23–45.

is not an emotion of which any one can be conscious that is not here represented as in a mirror. Or rather, the Holy Spirit has here drawn to the life all the griefs, sorrows, fears, doubts, hopes, cares, perplexities, in short, all the distracting emotions with which the minds of men are wont to be agitated.[8]

Calvin's list of "distracting emotions" clearly indicates that the lament psalms were uppermost in his mind. For these psalms, in particular, reveal the manifold reasons why God's children can feel agitated or aggrieved or become (to use Walter Brueggemann's evocative terms) "dislocated" and "disoriented."[9] What's more, at such times singing praise can be (or at least feel) either impossible or inappropriate.

Psalm 137 As a Test Case

Psalm 137 provides a particularly confronting example of this phenomenon. Its historical point of reference is clear: Israel's experience of exile in Babylon. However, whether it was written in exile or after having returned from exile is a matter of some debate. For our purposes, the question does not need to be settled. Either way, the psalm reveals the strong and painful emotions that were felt at the time of the exile. Indeed, as Derek Kidner writes, "Every line of it is alive with pain, whose intensity grows with each strophe to the appalling climax."[10]

The cause of this pain is twofold. Firstly, there is the memory of Zion (v. 1)—i.e., the horrors of what had been done to it on "the day Jerusalem fell" (vv. 7–8).[11] The consequence of this is that Zion is no longer "a source of strength, as in Psalm 48, but a cause for tears."[12] Secondly, there is the mocking demand of Israel's captors for "songs," "songs of joy," "one of the songs of Zion" (v. 3)![13] This immediately raises the question of v. 4: "How can we sing the songs of the Lord while in a foreign land?" The implied answer is "we can't!"[14] The reason is that "the songs of Zion are pornographic when they

8. See the Author's Preface in Calvin, *Commentary on the Psalms*.
9. Brueggemann, *Praying the Psalms*, 1–11.
10. Kidner, *Psalms 73–150*, 459.
11. All Scripture citations are taken from the NIV.
12. Savran, "How Can We Sing," 45.
13. It's obviously impossible to know what, if any particular, songs were in the minds of the "tormentors." In fact, the request is indefinite ("one of the songs of Zion"). But in the minds of the author and those tormented the most likely candidates are the so-called "Zion songs"—i.e., Psalms 48; 74; 87; 125; 126.
14. Savran, "How Can We Sing," 49.

are sung among those who do not hope in Zion."[15] Thus the lyres remain hung upon the willows (v. 2).

But that is not the end of the matter as far as the writer of Psalm 137 is concerned. Indeed, George Savran argues that v. 4 should be read not as a blanket refusal, but "as a preface to the response of vv. 5f (and vv. 7–9), saying essentially, 'This is how we shall sing.'"[16] Even if this interpretation is questionable, vv. 5-6 clearly function as an oath of self-imprecation in the form of a personal "pledge song."[17] What's more, the psalmist's determination not to forget Jerusalem includes not forgetting to sing of Jerusalem.[18] This is underscored by the references to "right hand" (v. 5) and "tongue" (v. 6)—the musician/singer's tools of the trade. So sing of Zion he must!

But how can this be done? The person who sings under such adverse circumstances can only do so in hope; hope that Jerusalem's day will come again and the songs of Zion will once more be heard. In fact, it is the certainty of this hope that leads the psalmist to reconsider the possibility of singing.[19] That is, because of his confidence in God and his purposes, he is able to sing what Leslie Allen calls "a modified version of a song of Zion."[20]

What, then, is this modified "song of Zion"? It is none other than Psalm 137: a song about the inappropriateness of singing the songs of Zion in Babylon, but a song of Zion nonetheless. Moreover, it contains both a "pledge song"—to sing of Jerusalem in hope of its restoration—and a "vengeance song" (vv. 8-9)—anticipating the just judgment that will come upon Israel's enemies.[21]

Paradoxically, this hope is expressed in the form of a grief-stricken song of lament. And yet lament is actually vital to the nurturing of such hope, for "[h]ope that cannot lament denies the awful reality and the continuing

---

15. Brueggemann, *Message of the Psalms*, 75.

16. Savran, "How Can We Sing," 49.

17. This is suggested by their chiastic structure and the fact that this is the one section of the psalm that is voiced in the singular.

18. His focus upon Jerusalem has little to do with either nationalistic zeal or natural homesickness, but is almost entirely to do with "its sacramental role in God's revealed purposes as reflection of the divine." Loyalty to Jerusalem is thus a measure of his loyalty to Yahweh, and praise of Jerusalem represents praise of Yahweh. See Allen, *Psalms 101–150*, 242–43.

19. Savran, "How Can We Sing," 50.

20. Allen, *Psalms 101–150*, 241.

21. Indeed, it is possible that the "highest joy" of which the psalmist speaks in v. 6 refers to the just retribution articulated in the "song" of vv. 7–9. See Lenowitz, "Mock-śimchâ," 155–56.

power of death and sin."[22] The practice of singing lament, then, is designed to awaken and inspire hope as God's people persevere through yet-to-be-resolved pain. True lament, thus, nurtures faith: faith that our sovereign and gracious God will deliver us from evil and restore us to unhindered praise.

The God-Given Powers of Music and Song

As we noted earlier, a large number of psalms of all "types" "were intended to be *musical* worship responses."[23] Why? What does music add? And what, in particular, is the advantage of *singing* lament rather than simply *speaking* it? Scripture answers these questions in several complementary ways, and both historic Christian reflection and the human sciences provide further supporting insights. We will explore these answers and insights by looking at the powers of music and song for proclaiming, recalling, consoling, and uniting.[24]

Power for Proclaiming

Firstly, a number of Old Testament texts reveal a connection between liturgical music and the declaratory activity of prophecy (e.g., 1 Sam 10:5–6; 2 Kgs 3:11–19). In addition to this, David's appointment of "some of the sons of Asaph, Heman and Jeduthun" is specifically said to be "for the ministry of prophesying, accompanied by harps, lyres and cymbals" (1 Chron 25:1). The nature of their ministry is amplified in v. 3 where we are told that they "prophesied, using the harp in thanking and praising the Lord." Part of the reason for this designation is that the concept of prophecy, in both Old and New Testaments, includes not only foretelling (prediction) but also forthtelling (proclamation).[25] Prophecy, then, is an entirely appropriate rubric under which to gather all divinely inspired words, including praise and lament.

---

22. Verhey, *Christian Art of Dying*, 269.

23. Hustad, "Psalms as Worship Expressions," 407.

24. In speaking of music's "powers" it needs to be said that these are neither independent nor absolute. It is the word of God (special revelation) that directly and explicitly accomplishes God's saving and sanctifying work. Music (as part of general revelation) can participate in this work only indirectly and implicitly. However, when music fulfills its true created function it acts as a parabolic witness to this word. See Watson, "Theology and Music," 462–63.

25. Kaiser and Silva, *Biblical Hermeneutics*, 139.

Although Scripture provides no detailed analysis of the specific psychological or educational benefits of singing the word of God, empirical studies would suggest that these are bound up with music's capacity to aid cognition and to express and evoke emotion. In terms of cognition, educationalists and therapists of various kinds have long been aware that "songs enhance cognitive processing by involving the brain in sequencing of information, short-term as well as long term memory storage, and motor learning as individuals respond to auditory cues."[26] In terms of emotional expression and evocation, both *intrinsic* factors (i.e., structural or melodic features of the music itself) and *extrinsic* factors (i.e., emotionally significant associations triggered by the music) combine to make music "one of the most emotionally potent media we know."[27]

What is of especial interest at this point, however, is the way the singing of meaningful words connects both the cognitive and affective dimensions of both singers and listeners. Key to this connection is the fact that the words of a song not only enable the communication and reception of the *cognitive content* of the song, but the singing of them facilitates the expression and evocation of the *emotional reality* they describe.[28] This combination enables the words of the song to "circulate through our system" in a way that they might not otherwise.[29] Reflecting on this phenomenon, Martin Luther concluded:

> Thus it was not without reason that the fathers and prophets wanted nothing else to be associated as closely with the Word of God as music. Therefore, we have so many hymns and Psalms where message and music join to move the listener's soul . . . After all, the gift of language combined with the gift of song was only given to man to let him know that he should praise God with both word and music, namely, by proclaiming [God's word] through music and by providing sweet melodies with words.[30]

The making of music and song, then, is one divinely appointed way of proclaiming the word of God, even if that word is being addressed directly to God and irrespective of whether it takes the form of adoration or praise, petition or lament. The flipside of this power to proclaim truth is the power

---

26. Taylor, *Biomedical Foundations*, 41.

27. Begbie, *Resounding Truth*, 294. See also Juslin and Sloboda, "Psychological Perspectives," 91–96.

28. Smith, "Music, Singing and the Emotions," 469.

29. Bell, *The Singing Thing*, 57.

30. Luther, "Preface," 321, 323–24.

to impart understanding and so to generate faith[31]—vital keys to survival in times of deep distress.

Power for Recalling

Secondly, music and song also enable God's word to be recalled. Consequently, such recollection is not only a feature of the praise and thanksgiving psalms (e.g., Pss 105:5; 143:5), but also of the laments (e.g., 42:6; 137:6). That music has the capacity to evoke memories is well recognized.[32] In fact, both personal and corporate memories are embedded in music, so that often when the past is unrecoverable by other means, a sense of identity and hope can be regained through familiar music. Furthermore, when the human voice is brought into the picture and truthful and meaningful words are articulated in song, the effect is even more powerful. The musical accompaniment, however, remains integral. As Don Saliers writes: "The remembrance of the words is carried and prompted by the melody and sometimes the harmonic and rhythmic elements."[33]

This is one of the reasons why music and song played an important role in Israel's life of faith, particularly in times of distress. For singing of God's mercies in days past was a way of putting the present into perspective and awakening hope for the future. The Israelites, thus, not only understood the connection between recollection and lament, but also the power of song to articulate grief in a way that ameliorates it. Consequently, "Israel enacted and trusted liturgical practices that made the transformation of pain vivid, powerful, and credible. It did its singing and praying and praising in ways that shaped pain into hope, and grief into possibility."[34]

Psalm 77 illustrates this. Its title—"For the director of music. For Jeduthun. Of Asaph. A psalm"—tells us plainly that it is a song. It is also a song with a focus on remembering. This is clear from the repeated use of a series of related verbs—"remember" (זכר, *zkr* [x 4]), "meditate" (שיח, *śyḥ* [x 3]), "ponder" (הגה, *hgh* [x 1]), "consider" (חשב, *ḥšb* [x 1]) and "seek" (דרש,

---

31. Such a view of the educational and emotional benefits of proclaiming the word of God in song is not confined to the Old Testament. Paul's instruction in Colossians 3:16 reveals the same understanding.

32. Consequently, an increasing number of psychological and neurological studies are seeking to better understand the connection. See, for example, Bergland, "Why Do the Songs," and Janata, "Neural Architecture."

33. Saliers, *Worship as Theology*, 161.

34. Brueggemann, *Israel's Praise*, 136.

drš [x 1]), all of which "indicate the energy the speaker is turning inward."³⁵ However, it is the structure or journey of the song that is of greatest interest. The first nine verses contain the lament of one who is in such distress that he can neither sleep nor speak (v. 4). His memories only provoke his lamentation (v. 3), and recalling his "songs in the night" (v. 6)³⁶ forces him to articulate a series of troubling doubts and painful questions (vv. 7-9).

But in v. 10 the psalm takes a dramatic turn. The psalmist decides to think back to "the years when the Most High stretched out his right hand" (v. 10); that is, to the Lord's deliverance of Israel at the time of the exodus. So he vows:

> ¹¹ I will remember (זכר, *zkr*) the deeds of the Lord;
> yes, I will remember (זכר, *zkr*) your miracles of long ago.
> ¹² I will consider (הגה, *hgh*) all your works
> and meditate (שׂיח, *śyḥ*) on all your mighty deeds.

The effect of this is that "the psalm engages in concrete remembering which takes the mind off the hopelessness of self. The memory of hurt resolved contextualizes present hurt, as yet unresolved."³⁷ However, Marvin Tate questions whether the process of transformation is quite so complete. He suggests that the psalm leaves both speaker and the reader waiting "for a new revealing of the unperceived steps of God through the great waters."³⁸ He has a point. The psalm certainly ends with only a historic reference to the Lord's leadership of Israel (v. 20); no contemporary act of deliverance appears to have yet taken place. So, Tate concludes, the psalmist's recollection "does not bring an immediate end to doubt and waiting."³⁹

This is both right and wrong. Certainly, "God moves on his own schedule and often the faithful must endure the anguish of waiting."⁴⁰ But the psalmist's remembering effectively resolves his doubt. In fact, by the end of the psalm, as Kidner notes, "the pervasive 'I' has disappeared, and the objective facts of the faith have captured all his attention and all of ours."⁴¹ Thus, the psalm does "what praise and confession are meant to do—represent the God of revelation as the reality and subject of truth in the face of

---

35. Tate, *Psalms 51-100*, 274.

36. This, presumably, refers to happier days when he could sing the praises of Yahweh freely. See Kidner, *Psalms 73-150*, 278, and Delitzsch, *Psalms*, 351-52.

37. Brueggemann, *Israel's Praise*, 138.

38. Tate, *Psalms 51-100*, 276.

39. Ibid.

40. Ibid.

41. Kidner, *Psalms 73-150*, 277.

all circumstances and contrary experience."[42] In other words, despite his present affliction, the psalmist's recollection of God's redeeming grace in the past grants him a new perspective on the present and so awakens his hope for the future. This is the gift he offers to all who will sing his psalm and embrace its message. As Elmer Leslie writes:

> The psalmist's purpose is clear. Through this brilliant ending to his psalm he will say to worshiping Israel in its hour of deep dejection that the God of Israel's ancient and glorious past is still leading His people through waters that threaten to engulf them and will still provide "shepherds" like unto Moses and Aaron.[43]

In short, the practice of singing lament has proved effective—not because it has removed the source of the psalmist's distress, but because it has renewed his trust in the Lord in the midst of continuing trial.[44] Furthermore, the musical form of the psalm is far from incidental in achieving this outcome.[45] Not only are human memories and human emotions profoundly intertwined, but music simultaneously taps both the emotional and memory centers of the brain.[46] When divinely inspired truth (or "credo")[47] is added to the mix and articulated in song, the combination is a potent one. Consequently, "the ones who sing and recite can remember when it was not like it is now, and can hope for when it will again not be like it is now."[48]

The practice of singing lament is, thus, one divinely appointed way of recalling the grace of God in times past and so renewing trust in times present. Not surprisingly, this power to recall enables both the renewing of faith and the strengthening of hope.

---

42. Mays, *Psalms*, 253.

43. Leslie, *The Psalms*, 240.

44. So Harrichand, "Language of Lament," 107, writes: "it is within the prayer of lament that Israel recalls its covenant relationship with God, which then gives rise to Israel's hope."

45. In fact, once recent neuropsychological study on those who have sustained brain injuries found that music was "more efficient at evoking autobiographical memories than verbal prompts" (Baird and Samson, "Music Evoked," 125).

46. Pereiral et al., "Music and Emotions."

47. See Wright, *God Who Acts*.

48. Brueggemann, *Israel's Praise*, 149.

Power for Consoling

Thirdly, music and song also have a remarkable ability to console.[49] Research from a wide range of disciplines has demonstrated music's many therapeutic benefits in the areas of psychological, physiological, social, emotional, and cognitive functioning.[50] Given our focus on lament, what is particularly noteworthy is the way music provides not only an outlet for expressing grief but also a means of processing and resolving it.[51] This provision is seen most powerfully in the practice of singing therapy, where singing is used to assist trauma victims to release suppressed emotions in order to "process the truth and reality behind their inner pain."[52] Aware of this power, Luther was unrestrained in his praise of music:

> Next to the Word of God, music deserves the highest praise. She is a mistress and governess of those human emotions . . . which control men or more often overwhelm them . . . Whether you wish to comfort the sad, to subdue frivolity, to encourage the despairing, to humble the proud, to calm the passionate or to appease those full of hate . . . what more effective means than music could you find.[53]

Perhaps the earliest biblical instance of the consoling power of music is found in 1 Samuel 16. After the Lord afflicts Saul with an evil spirit (v. 15), his servants suggest he finds someone who is able to play the lyre.[54] David is found and, as they anticipated (v. 16), whenever the "spirit" came upon Saul, David played his lyre and not only would "relief . . . come to Saul," but "the evil spirit would leave him" (v. 23).

Not surprisingly, some have seen here "an early acknowledgment of the possibility of music therapy."[55] But not just any music. As Francis Wat-

---

49. See Diamond, "Therapeutic Power," 517–37.

50. Boso et al. ("Neurophysiology," 190) write: "the musical experience—by reducing stress, and improving social relationships and wellbeing—is not only an important part of our own life, but could also play a role in the rehabilitation of a number of different neurological and psychiatric diseases."

51. See Bright, "Music Therapy."

52. Smith, "Music, Singing and the Emotions," 469. This has repeatedly been shown to be the case with traumatized war veterans (see St John, "Iraqi War") and traumatized refugees (see Orth, "Music Therapy").

53. Luther, "Preface," 323.

54. Saul's affliction here appears to be a periodic depressive disturbance or inconsolable mood or, what Gordon calls, "bouts of Kierkegaardian melancholia." See Gordon, *1 & 2 Samuel*, 152.

55. Hustad, "Psalms as Worship Expressions," 408.

son notes, "purely celebratory music would jar with the king's initial mood; it would not console, it would mock."[56] The only music that could have the desired therapeutic impact would be "a music that acknowledges and encompasses the negatives of existence but nevertheless transforms them through the power of musical form and artistry, so that negativity gives way to consolation."[57] This, in God's kindness, is what happened to Saul. For as much as the Lord was the cause of Saul's affliction, his gifts (of both music and David's skill) were also the source of Saul's consolation.

Music's power to console, however, deserves further probing. As we've already noted, "music connects with our emotions, expresses and evokes them, and makes them humanly livable."[58] It does this not only by facilitating expressions of joy but also by aiding the expression of both difficult feelings and inchoate responses. In fact, this ability "to give structure to emotionally charged experiences is what makes music such a powerful aid to the process of mourning."[59] Jeremy Begbie refers to this as "representative concentration,"[60] explaining that, "in music, emotionally significant bodily movements are embodied in a concentrated (musical) form, in such a way that the music can represent us and concentrate us emotionally as we are drawn into its life."[61] In this way, music can "enable *a more concentrated emotional engagement with the object or objects with which we are dealing.*"[62]

Sung lament is more powerful still. For sung lament, being both instrumental and vocal, draws on the therapeutic powers of both music and singing, combining both "languages" (the affective and the cognitive) into one. While the dominant power is in the words that proclaim (particularly if God's word is being sung), the "music is by no means a superfluous addition to the words that might equally well convey consolation simply by being read. On the contrary, the music enacts the consolation of which the text speaks."[63] Nor is it being "placed at the disposal of some purpose that is alien to its own nature: it exercises its power to console by purely musical

---

56. Watson, "Theology and Music," 449.
57. Ibid.
58. Ramshaw, "Singing at Funerals," 206.
59. Ibid.
60. Begbie, "Faithful Feelings," 349.
61. Ibid., 352.
62. Ibid., 350 (emphasis original).
63. Watson, "Theology and Music," 451. Watson's insights are offered in the context of a discussion regarding Handel's *Messiah*. However, they are equally true, if not more so, in regard to the singing of the Psalter or any other part of Scripture.

means, although in conjunction with the text."⁶⁴ What we are dealing with here, theologically speaking, is the bringing together of the twin voices of the *opera Dei* (the works of God) and the *oracula Dei* (the words of God), or the natural harmony between general and special revelation.

Although the original tunes to which the biblical laments were sung are now lost to us, the fact that they were written to be sung is instructive.⁶⁵ This is not to suggest that singing is some kind of "silver bullet" for transforming pleading into praising. But it does underscore its ability to assist in the honest articulation of sorrow, the effective processing of pain, and the awakening of hope. As Logan Jones writes, "the psalms of lament do not dismiss or deny or seek to avoid sorrow. On the contrary, they allow a grieving person to move more fully into the valley of the shadow; knowing on different levels, that no matter what, God is indeed present in the sorrow."⁶⁶ In fact, it is precisely because lament "can be a movement toward God, it became a component part of worship. This assumes that the experience of profound suffering can bring one to God, provided the experience is verbally articulated in the lament."⁶⁷ But, to be clear, the power lies less in the act of articulation and more in the fact of an emotionally honest turning *to God*. It is for this reason that, while the primary focus of lament "is on *process* rather than *result*," it "must be recognized that there is a patent expectation, on the part of the psalmist, of some kind of resolution."⁶⁸ Consolation and hope cannot, thus, be separated. Not surprisingly, "an ineradicable strain of hope and expectancy surrounds the lament."⁶⁹

The making and singing of songs of lamentation, then, is one divinely appointed way of consolation. Not surprisingly, this power to console generates both the power to hope and the power to heal.

Power for Uniting

Finally, music and song have a remarkable power to unite. Singing, in particular, creates a sense of solidarity and belonging. As Elaine Ramshaw writes, "group singing bonds the community. Singing together is a physical as well as emotional and spiritual experience of unity: We enter into a

---

64. Ibid.
65. Stenhouse, "Psalms of Lament," 194–95.
66. Jones, "Psalms of Lament," 47.
67. Westermann, *Praise and Lament*, 273, n. 16.
68. Cohen, *Why O Lord?* 78 (emphasis his).
69. Murphy and Carm, "The Faith of the Psalmist," 235.

common rhythm and we make one sound."[70] Although this experience is not as widespread in Western society as it is in less individualistic cultures, most westerners have known it at various points—perhaps as sports fans rally behind their team by singing the club song or as demonstrators express their unified opposition to some form of oppression in a rousing protest song. In this latter scenario, the sense of unity can be palpable, for in "the defiance that prompts the singing, there is the understanding that one is not alone."[71]

All corporate singing, to some degree, has this effect. In fact, a number of recent neurochemical studies have found that group singing increases participants' oxytocin levels, indicating an experience of intense social bonding.[72] It should not surprise us, then, that almost a quarter of the lament psalms are communal in form (i.e., written in the first-person plural).[73] Nor should we be misled by the predominance of individual laments. Far from being an indication that these should not be sung corporately, they are actually presented as "a model for how the community can express and resolve its doubt."[74] More than that, the "I" of the individual psalms often has a representative function (i.e., it is a "Collective 'I'");[75] for it is, ultimately, none other than the "I" of the king, the Messiah.

This insight highlights a point of major interpretative importance. For while the book of Psalms is, first and foremost, a book about the historic progression of Davidic kingship in light of the promise made to the Lord's anointed (Ps 2:7; see also 2 Sam 7),[76] God's Messiah is never to be thought about independently of those "who take refuge in him" (Ps 2:12). The king may be in the foreground, but his subjects are always in the background. The Psalter, then, also tracks the journey of the Messiah's people. For this reason, the Messiah invites his followers "to join in his words of trust in God, his words of longing for deliverance, his prayers for the overthrow of the enemies of the Lord and of his Christ, his joy in God's salvation."[77] Indeed, in the communal laments, the people step into the foreground and

---

70. Ramshaw, "Singing at Funerals," 207.
71. Hawn, "The Truth Shall Set You Free," 410.
72. See, for example, Keeler et al., "Neurochemistry."
73. For example, Pss 12, 44, 58, 60, 74, 49, 80, 83, 85, 89, 90, 94, 123, 126, and 129.
74. See Stevenson, "Communal Imagery," 227.
75. Mowinckel, *Psalms in Israel's Worship*, 42–46.
76. See Hely Hutchinson, "Psalter as a Book," 25–43.
77. Woodhouse, "Psalms as Christian Scripture," 57.

the Messiah sometimes seems to disappear from view! Yet even here we are able "to see in the pattern of Israel's national life a Christ-shaped echo."[78]

Psalm 44 provides an example of this. The opening words make very clear that this is a "lament by the people and for the people."[79] Furthermore, it is a *maśkîl* of "the sons of Korah" addressed to "the director of music," and therefore a lament intended to be sung. What is unique about Psalm 44, however, is its clear profession of innocence (vv. 17–22). As Franz Delitzsch comments, "In this psalm, Israel stands in exactly the same relation to God as Job and 'the servant of Jahve' in Isaiah."[80] Thus we hear the "Christ-shaped echo."

But we also hear a church-shaped echo. This is why, in Romans 8:36, Paul can cite v. 22 ("Yet for your sake we face death all the day long; we are considered as sheep to be slaughtered") and apply it to Christians. Indeed, for Paul, "Christians are called to share in their Lord's sufferings, sufferings foreshadowed in those of the righteous sufferer in the psalms, whose voice is heard in so many of the lament psalms, such as Psalm 44."[81] This, then, is a lament that is sung by the Christ through his persecuted people so that they might sing it back to him in their hour of need.[82]

Our chief interest, however, lies in the *communal* nature of this lament and the consequent importance of singing our prayers *together*. For singing "'transports' us not only to God, but connects us to the people with whom we are worshiping. Singing builds and strengthens the assembly."[83] Indeed, the cultivation of collegiality is one of the great gifts of the Psalter. As Bonhoeffer explains:

> The psalms teach us to pray as a fellowship. The Body of Christ is praying, and as an individual one acknowledges that his prayer is only a minute fragment of the whole prayer of the Church. He learns to pray the prayer of the Body of Christ. And that lifts him above his personal concerns and allows him to pray selflessly.[84]

For this reason, the activity of singing "is both an enactment and an exposition of the church's unity. Singing, we might say, is a sounding image of the

---

78. Shead and Cameron, "Singing with the Messiah," 168.
79. Ibid., 174.
80. Delitzsch, *Psalms*, 66-67.
81. Wenham, *Psalms as Torah*, 193.
82. Longman III, *How to Read the Psalms*, 71.
83. Werner Hoenen, "How Can I Keep from Singing?"
84. Bonhoeffer, *Life Together*, 38-39.

unified church."[85] Moreover, the reality of the unity fostered by communal singing has further implications. It lifts us above ourselves and helps us to pray larger prayers, prayers more reflective of the needs of others, prayers more in line with the will of God.[86]

The practice of singing lament, then, is one divinely appointed way of uniting God's people in seasons of sorrow "so that with one mind and one voice [we] may glorify the God and Father of our Lord Jesus Christ" (Rom 15:6).

Conclusion

If there is truth in the dictum, "Tell me how you lament, and I will tell you how you are," then many contemporary churches are in poor shape. Of course, it's always possible that, like Paul and Silas in the Philippian jail (Acts 16:25), the determination to sing praise in the midst of trial is a laudable manifestation of a resilient faith. But more often than not "a church that goes on singing 'happy songs' in the face of raw reality is doing something very different from what the Bible itself does."[87] In fact, the inability to lament typically reveals "a frightened, numb-denial and deception that does not want to acknowledge or experience the disorientation of life."[88]

The only way to remedy such a tendency is through a humble acknowledgment of the problem, a genuine turning to God, and a thoroughgoing change of practice. This will inevitably involve the reemployment of older laments (principally the Psalter)[89] as well as the discovery (if not the writing) of fresh songs of lament.[90] The alternative is to inhabit unreality and, worse, to deprive the people of God of a full knowledge of God. For

---

85. Guthrie, "The Wisdom of Song," 385.

86. As Bonhoeffer puts it: "It does not depend, therefore, on whether the Psalms express adequately that which we feel at a given moment in our heart. If we are to pray aright, perhaps it is quite necessary that we pray contrary to our own heart. Not what we want to pray is important, but what God wants us to pray." Bonhoeffer, *Psalms*, 14–15.

87. Brueggemann, *The Message of the Psalms*, 52.

88. Ibid., 51.

89. The Psalter is key here. As Endres ("Psalms and Spirituality," 154) writes: "The Psalms tutor us in the language of prayer; they teach us new ways of praying and more expressive ways of articulating our hopes and fear, our joys and sorrows."

90. For a start in this direction, see Freestone, "You Are the God Who Saves Me" (chapter 21 in this volume). See also the lists and links compiled by Shumann, "Lenting and Lamenting," Kauflin, "Songs for Hard Times" (parts 1–3), as well as my own, "I will trust you in the darkness" (CCLI Song Select, Song Number: 3400238).

as Michael Jinkins cautions, "We cannot expect a people's understanding of God to reach much higher than their hymnbooks."[91]

Our singing, therefore, needs to reflect the fact that God is not only sovereign over our sufferings but also present with us in them. It also needs to express the christological reality (reflected in the shape of the Psalter) that just as suffering is the road to glory, so the path to praise passes through lament. Given the manifold powers of music and song to aid us on the journey of discipleship, we would do well to harness them faithfully and make use of them for the sake of our souls, the health of the church and, above all, the glory of the triune God.

Bibliography

Allen, Leslie C. *Psalms 101–150*. Word Biblical Commentary 21. Waco: Word, 1983.
Baird, Amee, and Séverine Samson. "Music Evoked Autobiographical Memory after Severe Acquired Brain Injury: Preliminary Findings from a Case Series." *Neuropsychological Rehabilitation: An International Journal* 24 (2014) 125–43.
Begbie, Jeremy S. "Faithful Feelings." In *Resonant Witness: Conversations between Music and Theology*, edited by Jeremy S. Begbie and Steven R. Guthrie, 323–54. Grand Rapids: Eerdmans, 2011.
———. *Resounding Truth: Christian Wisdom in the World of Music*. London: SPCK, 2007.
Bell, John L. *The Singing Thing: A Case for Congregational Song*. Chicago: GIA Publications, 2000.
Bergland, Christopher. "Why Do the Songs from Your Past Evoke Such Vivid Memories?" https://www.psychologytoday.com/blog/the-athletes-way/201312/why-do-the-songs-your-past-evoke-such-vivid-memories.
Bonhoeffer, Dietrich. *Psalms: The Prayerbook of the Bible*. Minneapolis: Augsburg, 1970.
———. *Life Together*. New York: Harper & Row, 1954.
Boso, Marianna, et al. "Neurophysiology and Neurobiology of the Musical Experience." *Functional Neurology* 21 (2006) 187–91.
Bradbury, Paul. *Sowing in Tears: How to Lament in a Church of Praise*. Cambridge: Grove, 2007.
Bright, Ruth. "Music Therapy in Grief Resolution." *Bulletin of the Menninger Clinic* 63 (1999) 481–98.
Brueggemann, Walter. *Israel's Praise: Doxology against Idolatry and Ideology*. Philadelphia: Fortress, 1988.
———. *The Message of the Psalms: A Theological Commentary*. Minneapolis: Augsburg, 1984.
———. *Praying the Psalms: Engaging Scripture and the Life of the Spirit*. Eugene, OR: Wipf & Stock, 2007.
Calvin, John. *A Commentary on the Book of Psalms*. Translated by James Anderson. Volume One. Christian Classics Ethereal Library. http://www.ccel.org/ccel/calvin/calcom08.vi.html.

---

91. Jinkins, *In the House of the Lord*, 34.

Cohen, David J. *Why O Lord? Praying Our Sorrows*. Milton Keynes: Paternoster, 2013.

Delitzsch, Franz. *Psalms*. Translated by Francis Bolton. Commentary on the Old Testament. 10 vols. Reprint ed. Grand Rapids: Eerdmans, 1982.

Diamond, John. "The Therapeutic Power of Music." In *Handbook of Complementary and Alternative Therapies in Mental Health*, edited by Scott Shannon, 517–37. San Diego: Academic Press, 2002.

Endres, John C. "Psalms and Spirituality in the 21st Century." *Interpretation* 56 (2002) 143–54.

Futato, Mark D. *Interpreting the Psalms: An Exegetical Handbook*. Grand Rapids: Kregel, 2007.

Gordon, Robert P. *1 & 2 Samuel: A Commentary*. Exeter: Paternoster, 1986.

Guthrie, Steven R. "The Wisdom of Song." In *Resonant Witness: Conversations between Music and Theology*, edited by Jeremy S. Begbie and Steven R. Guthrie, 382–407. Grand Rapids: Eerdmans, 2011.

Harrichand, James J. S. "Recovering the Language of Lament for the Western Evangelical Church: A Survey of the Psalms of Lament and Their Appropriation within Pastoral Theology." *McMaster Journal of Theology and Ministry* 16 (2014–2015) 101–30.

Hawn, C. Michael. "The Truth Shall Set You Free: Song, Struggle and Solidarity in South Africa." In *Resonant Witness: Conversations between Music and Theology*, edited by Jeremy S. Begbie and Steven R. Guthrie, 408–33. Grand Rapids: Eerdmans, 2011.

Hely Hutchinson, James. "The Psalter as a Book." In *Stirred by a Noble Theme: The Book of Psalms in the Life of the Church*, edited by Andrew G. Shead, 23–45. Nottingham: Apollos, 2013.

Hill Andrew E. and John H. Walton. *A Survey of the Old Testament*. Grand Rapids: Zondervan, 2000.

Holladay, William L. *The Psalms through Three Thousand Years: Prayerbook of a Cloud of Witnesses*. Minneapolis: Fortress, 1993.

Hustad, Donald P. "The Psalms as Worship Expressions: Personal and Congregational." *Review & Expositor* 81 (1984) 407–24.

Janata, Petr. "The Neural Architecture of Music-Evoked Autobiographical Memories." *Cerebral Cortex* 19 (2009) 2579–94.

Jinkins, Michael. *In the House of the Lord: Inhabiting the Psalms of Lament*. Collegeville: Liturgical Press, 1989.

Jones, Logan C. "The Psalms of Lament and the Transformation of Sorrow." *The Journal of Pastoral Care & Counseling* 61 (2007) 47–58.

Juslin, Patrik N., and John A. Sloboda. "Psychological Perspectives on Music and Emotion." In *Music and Emotion: Theory and Research*, edited by Patrik N. Juslin and John A. Sloboda, 71–104. Oxford: Oxford University Press, 2001.

Kaiser Jr, Walter C., and Moisés Silva. *An Introduction to Biblical Hermeneutics: The Search for Meaning*. Grand Rapids: Zondervan, 2007.

Kauflin, Bob. "Songs for Hard Times, Pt. 1." http://www.worshipmatters.com/2005/11/15/songs-for-the-hard-times-pt-1.

———. "Songs for Hard Times, Pt. 2." http://www.worshipmatters.com/2005/11/16/songs-for-the-hard-times-part-2.

———. "Songs for Hard Times, Pt. 3." http://www.worshipmatters.com/2005/11/17/songs-for-the-hard-times-part-3.

Keeler, Jason R., et al. "The Neurochemistry and Social Flow of Singing: Bonding and Oxytocin." *Frontiers in Human Neuroscience* (23 September 2015). http://dx.doi.org/10.3389/fnhum.2015.00518.

Kidner, Derek. *Psalms 73-150*. Tyndale Old Testament Commentary. Leicester: IVP, 1975.

Lenowitz, Harris. "The Mock-śimchâ in Psalm 137." In *Directions in Biblical Hebrew Poetry*, edited by E. R. Follis, 149-59. JSOTSup 40. Sheffield: JSOT, 1987.

Leslie, Elmer A. *The Psalms: Translated and Interpreted in the Light of Hebrew Life and Worship*. New York: Abingdon-Cokesbury, 1949.

Longman III, Tremper. *How to Read the Psalms*. Downers Grove: IVP, 1988.

Luther, Martin. "Preface to Georg Rhau's Symphonoiae iucundae." In *Luther's Works*, edited by J. Pelikan and H. T. Lehmann, translated by C. M. Jacobs and E. W. Gritsch, 53:321-24. Saint Louis: Concordia, 1955-1986 [orig. 1538].

Mays, James L. *Psalms*. Louisville: John Knox, 1994.

Mowinckel, Sigmund. *The Psalms in Israel's Worship*. Grand Rapids: Eerdmans, 2004.

Murphy, Roland E., and O. Carm. "The Faith of the Psalmist." *Interpretation* 34 (1980) 229-39.

Orth, J. "Music Therapy with Traumatized Refugees in a Clinical Setting." *Voices: A World Forum for Music Therapy* 5 (2005). https://voices.no/index.php/voices/article/view/227/171.

Pereiral, Carlos S., et al. "Music and Emotions in the Brain: Familiarity Matters." *PLoS ONE* 6 (November, 2011). http://www.ncbi.nlm.nih.gov/pmc/articles/PMC3217963.

Ramshaw, Elaine J. "Singing at Funerals and Memorial Services." *Currents in Theology and Mission* 35 (2008): 206-15.

Saliers, Don E. *Worship as Theology: Foretaste of Glory Divine*. Nashville: Abingdon, 1994.

Savran, George. "How Can We Sing a Song of the Lord: The Strategy of Lament in Psalm 137." *Zeitschrift für die alttestamentliche Wissenschaft* 112 (2000) 43-58.

Shead, Andrew G., and Andrew J. Cameron. "Singing with the Messiah in a Foreign Land." In *Stirred by a Noble Theme: The Book of Psalms in the Life of the Church*, edited by Andrew G. Shead, 158-80. Apollos: Nottingham, 2013.

Shumann, Luke. "Lenting and Lamenting, Part II: Hurting with God." *Jucuthin: Justice, Theology & Culture* (February 26, 2016). https://jucuthin.wordpress.com/2016/02/26/lenting-and-lamenting-part-ii-hurting-with-god.

Smith, J. A. "Which Psalms Were Sung in the Temple?" *Music & Letters* 71 (1990) 167-86.

Smith, Robert S. "Music, Singing and Emotions: Exploring the Connections." *Themelios* 37 (2012) 465-79.

St John, Alison. "Iraq War Veteran Finds Healing in Singing." *KPBS* (January, 2010). http://www.kpbs.org/news/2010/jan/05/iraq-war-veteran-finds-singing-healing.

Stenhouse, Tara J. "The Psalms of Lament in the Experience of Suffering Christians." In *Stirred by a Noble Theme: The Book of Psalms in the Life of the Church*, edited by Andrew G. Shead, 181-204. Apollos: Nottingham, 2013.

Stevenson, Gregory M. "Communal Imagery and the Individual Lament: Exodus Typology in Psalm 77." *Restoration Quarterly* 39 (1997) 215-29.

Tate, Marvin E. *Psalms 51-100*. Word Biblical Commentary 20. Waco: Word, 1990.

Taylor, Dale B. *Biomedical Foundations for Music as Therapy.* Saint Louis: MMB Music, 1997.

Verhey, Allen. *The Christian Art of Dying: Learning from Jesus.* Grand Rapids: Eerdmans, 2011.

Watson, Francis. "Theology and Music." *Scottish Journal of Theology* 51 (1998) 435–63.

Wenham, Gordon J. *Psalms as Torah: Reading Biblical Song Ethically.* Grand Rapids: Baker, 2012.

Werner Hoenen, Allison. "How Can I Keep from Singing? An Appeal to Christians to Sing the Faith." *Journal of Lutheran Ethics* 10 (2010). http://www.elca.org/JLE/Articles/254#_edn20.

Westermann, Claus. *Praise and Lament in the Psalms.* Translated by Keith R. Crim and Richard N. Soulen. Atlanta: John Knox, 1981.

Woodhouse, John W. "The Psalms as Christian Scripture." In *Stirred by a Noble Theme: The Book of Psalms in the Life of the Church*, edited by Andrew G. Shead, 46–73. Apollos: Nottingham, 2013.

Wright, G. Ernest. *God Who Acts: Biblical Theology as Recital.* London: SCM, 1952.

16

Praying Lament

Malcolm J. Gill

Prayer, for many believers, is considered to be the most difficult of all Christian disciplines to master. While all would acknowledge that followers of Jesus *ought* to pray, for a sizeable number prayer is an aspirational habit that is seldom practiced. The struggle around praying can relate to personal challenges such as the busyness of life and time restraints, but more often than not, the absence of prayer has more to do with the believer's uncertainty as to its value and effectiveness, coupled with a lack of familiarity regarding *how* to pray.

When we consider the absence of general prayer in the life of many within the Christian community then it should come as no surprise to discover that particular prayers, such as those of lament, are even less common. If it is hard to know how to pray during regular seasons of life, it is even harder when enduring grief, confusion, and loss. Lamenting in prayer feels counterintuitive, difficult, and even ungodly. When we think about lament, questions naturally arise. How do we speak with God during seasons of hardship and pain? What is the appropriate language of prayer to use when we converse with the Almighty, particularly when words themselves feel inadequate? How does individual lament fit within the corporate dynamic of a praying community? What role should the practice of lament play in the prayer life of the follower of Christ? While it is not possible to address all of these questions, the following will seek to explore a few ways in which the lament psalms can be used to facilitate the practice of prayer for the individual or group navigating hardship.

The Relational Nature of Praying Lament

Out of all the books of the Bible, the Psalter is one of the most embraced at a popular level. Its poetic beauty, variety, and personal earthiness richly express the deep longings of our human emotions. In the Psalms we find inspiration, solace, and confidence. Along with songs of deliverance and joy, the Psalter also provides a wonderful gift when it grants us songs of lament. As one author rightly observes, "Lament psalms can be numbered among the most disturbing passages of the Bible, until one actually encounters crisis, and then they can become the most comforting and helpful."[1] The lament psalms, when understood properly, lead us to a God who knows our needs and deeply longs to care for us in our moments of common frailty.

Christianity, unlike many other religious faiths, is built upon the presupposition that God is relational and *can* be known. The Bible doesn't present God as disinterested and detached from his creation; rather, it presents him as one who speaks and is intimately involved in the affairs of this world. The clearest demonstration of his engagement with the world can be seen in his sending of Jesus Christ who "made his dwelling among us" (John 1:14).[2] The author of Hebrews writes, "In the past God spoke to our ancestors through the prophets at many times and in various ways, but in these last days *he has spoken* to us by his Son" (Heb 11:1; emphasis mine). God is not silent and indifferent; rather, he speaks into our world and reveals himself with clarity in his son Jesus. God, through Christ, has reached out to us in order that we might know him intimately.

While God has made himself known to us through the written word that speaks of his Son Jesus, the living Word, God also, incredibly, invites us to commune with him through the practice of prayer. In prayer we have the opportunity to come to him in all seasons of life and to engage with him. Prayer is commonly understood to be the process of asking God for things, yet prayer is far more than that. Prayer is relational. It is the practice of individuals and communities personally conversing with their Creator. When we pray, particularly when we lament, there is a spiritual intimacy

---

1. Broyles, "Psalms of Lament," 394.
2. Unless otherwise stated, all translations are taken from the NIV.

that is forged. When we narrowly suppose prayer to simply be a functional practice to "get something" then we fail to understand its purpose or value.

The Relational Nature of Lament in the Psalms

In the Bible, perhaps the best examples of the relational nature of prayer can be seen in the Psalter. In the Psalms we have individuals and groups singing to God and sharing their deepest and most personal thoughts with him. From the first psalm, which speaks of the blessed person, to the last, an anthem of praise, these ancient songs reflect the various seasons of life experienced by the child of God. The psalms provide the paradigm *par excellence* of how the godly should engage with their God. The Psalter includes a variety of songs ranging from delight and thanksgiving, to confession and repentance, from psalms of wisdom to songs of lament. In each of the various song styles there is one common denominator: the psalms present an interactive dynamic between God and his people.

While most within the family of God feel comfortable utilizing the biblical songs of joy and thanksgiving to commune with God, many don't know whether they *can* or *should* speak to God using the language of the lament songs. They identify with the pain and anguish of the lament psalms, yet they fail to pray these psalms because they feel that it is inconsistent with being a joyful follower of Christ. Nothing, however, could be further from the truth.[3] Rather, throughout the lament psalms we discover a God who cares for his people and yearns to hear their voice of dependence. When we ignore the wisdom of the psalms, including the songs of lament, we minimize the full picture of who our God is.

The Relational Nature of Lament in the New Testament

In the contemporary Christian community the role of lament has all but been ignored. Broyles rightly observes:

> The motif that is most foreign to modern Christian prayer is also the longest: the lament itself. Prayers today usually consist primarily of requests or petitions. But the lamenting psalms were no mere "business agenda" or "shopping list" telling God what to do. The laments testify to the value of simply telling one's story to God. God is not portrayed simply as "Mr Fixit"; he

---

3. See also Burge, "Man of Sorrows, What a Name!" (chapter 9 in this volume), for further discussion.

is the supreme listener. The image of God reflected in the psalms is one who is interested not only in healing but also in pain. Remarkably, they testify that God can be moved.[4]

Prayers of lament are erringly dismissed as irrelevant to the follower of Jesus under the false notion that the Christian life should always be one of joy not sorrow. This is simply not the case. It is true that Christ brings a peace that "transcends understanding," but this doesn't minimize the reality that there are serious moments of grief, loss, and hardship in the Christian experience. The early Christian communities were familiar with being "hard pressed on every side" (2 Cor 4:8) as they experienced "momentary troubles" (2 Cor 4:17). Indeed, Jesus warned his disciples that difficulty would be part of their common experience when he said to them, "In this world you will have trouble" (John 16:33). Even a cursory reading of the New Testament discovers the early Christian community's existence was one full of suffering and pain.

Rather than denying the reality of brokenness and hardship, the New Testament contains several examples of the godly crying out to God in moments of distress and anguish. Three will suffice. First, Paul "*pleaded* with the Lord" three times to take away the thorn in his flesh (2 Cor 12:7-8; emphasis mine). While there is debate as to the nature of what the "thorn" was, there is no doubt Paul calls out to God at a time of difficulty. Nowhere in the passage that records his trials is the apostle lambasted for crying to God. Paul, following the lead of lamenters in the Old Testament, is transparent and godly as he wrestles openly with his Father about his trouble.

Second, Jesus in the garden of Gethsemane exemplifies genuine lament in the New Testament era when he pleads with his heavenly Father regarding the overwhelming prospect of the cross. Jesus, fully identifying with humanity, cries out to God when facing "great sorrow to the point of death" (Matt 26:38). Jesus experienced real grief, and spoke of this with his Father when three times he cried, "My Father, if it is possible, may this cup be taken from me. Yet not as I will, but as you will" (Matt 26:39-43). Jesus, like the psalmists, lamented openly to his Father.

Third, the clearest example of lament in the New Testament occurs at the highest point of grief in humanity history. As Jesus dies for humanity in order to bring them to God he cries out, using a lament psalm, "My God, my God, why have you forsaken me?" (Matt 27:46). In this most astonishing and significant event, Jesus publicly laments to his Father. In quoting Psalm 22:1, Jesus not only validates the process of lament, but he also demonstrates his solidarity with *our* broken humanity.

---

4. Broyles, "Psalms of Lament," 394.

Rather than shying away from lament, the Christian believer, following the model of the godly through the ages, should incorporate it as a genuine part of the Christian discipline of prayer. Indeed, more than the Old Testament writers, the New Testament people of God have the Spirit living within them and moving them to great intimacy with God. It is this Holy Spirit who in our grief leads us to our God when "by him we cry, '*Abba*, Father'" (Rom 8:15). In contrast to those who might discourage lament, we find in the New Testament that it is the Holy Spirit who facilitates our grieving process. Paul writes, "the Spirit helps us in our weakness. We do not know what we ought to pray for, but the Spirit himself intercedes for us through wordless groans" (Rom 8:26).

Just as a child naturally cries out to his or her parents in times of distress, so the Christian believer should be encouraged to call out to God during pain and loss. Prayerful discourse should not be reserved simply for seasons of thanksgiving and delight, but also and *especially* for those dark valleys of grief and loss.

In the Lord Jesus Christ the people of God have their strongest assurance that their lament will be heard. The author of Hebrews explains, "Therefore, since we have a great high priest who has ascended into heaven, Jesus the Son of God, let us hold firmly to the faith we profess. For we do not have a high priest who is unable to empathize with our weaknesses, but we have one who has been tempted in every way, just as we are—yet he did not sin" (Heb 4:14-15). Jesus experienced the emotionally and physically taxing aspects of our broken world. He did this in order that we might, in the coming kingdom, live with him. Through his lament and sorrow comes solace that our God understands our predicament and knows our weakness. It is because of this relationally caring God that we can and should come to him at all times with our own grieving and hardships. Thus we should encourage those within the church of God with the exhortation the author of Hebrews gives: "Let us then approach God's throne of grace with confidence, so that we may receive mercy and find grace to help us in our time of need" (Heb 4:16). Prayers of lament are an invitation from a caring God to sinners who desperately need grace.

In summary, because of the personal nature of God and his willingness and desire to listen to the cries of his children, Christians should feel liberated to speak freely with God—not only during moments of felicity, but also and especially during dark nights of the soul. Disciples of Christ should be exhorted to process their grief through honest and transparent discourse with their heavenly Father.

Praying Lament in Personal Hardship

Given the relational nature of lament, its practice will tend to be more organic than structured. Just as a young boy's conversation and personal engagement with his father can be unpredictable and unplanned, so there is a natural element of fluidity between the children of God and their heavenly Father. In real life, people often appreciate what children say because they frequently express themselves without too many filters. When the relational nature of the believer to God the Father is understood and emphasized there is a certain validation provided, which frees the believer to engage with God in a way that expresses that same transparent and familial dynamic. But how does one do this?

Praying with or from a Lament Psalm

We often struggle to find words to communicate our feelings when traversing difficulties in life. There are seasons when we simply groan, along with creation, desiring for all things to be made right. In our yearning, however, we are not alone in that throughout our common history others have known and navigated hardship. The Psalter, of course, records the inspired lamentations of God's people. The psalms provide us with an excellent resource that enables us to voice our struggles. By reading, reflecting, or even singing the psalms, we can pray *with* the psalmist.

Given the poetic style of the psalms, the individual songs contained in the Psalter provide a wide range of common experiences with which we can identify. With this in mind it can be immensely helpful for anyone wrestling with God to use the lament psalms as the voice for one's prayer. While we might not know the circumstances surrounding the psalmists' despair, their heart's cry verbalized in each song can become our own. As Howard Wallace observes, "If the psalm with which we pray is appropriate for a situation, then the fact that we pray in the words of the one 'who has been there' can give a freshness and honesty to the words we pray, which we might not have achieved in the course of composing our own prayer."[5]

Praying *with* the psalmist in moments of despair and angst can facilitate honest expressions when words seem difficult to find. There are, however, other times when, rather than praying *with* the psalmist, we pray *from* the psalms. We may, for example, use a portion of a lament psalm as a starting point to vocalize our own unique situation. That is to say, we may reflect on a few verses of an individual lament psalm and then interject

---

5. Wallace, *Words to God, Words from God*, 117.

specifics to God that relate to our own hurts. Rather than simply reciting the poetic language of the psalmist, we could use the vehicle of poetry to then launch into particular features relating to our distress. In this way we both keep a shape to our prayer and allow for the spontaneity of our relational discourse.

Using the Laments of Others

As the need to lament is common to the lives of all Christians, we can also find solace in using the laments of others, even outside of the Bible. Over the course of history, the people of God have often recorded prayers that others have found useful in their own prayer lives. For example, the musician Steven Curtis Chapman, who tragically lost a daughter in a family accident, recorded an album to verbalize his pain and loss. In this album, *Beauty Will Rise*, the song "Questions" expresses the feelings of many of us.[6] While the circumstances surrounding Chapman's songs won't be familiar to many, the searing pain found in the lyrics resonates with the despairing soul. Listening, praying, and singing through the laments of others, like Chapman's, can help facilitate dialogue with God during our moments of need.

Not only are the lament psalms helpful for individuals processing grief and loss, but, as we will now see, they are also exceedingly beneficial for the collective people of God.

Praying Lament in the Context of Community

Someone once said that there are many things in life you can do by yourself, but being a Christian is *not* one of them. The relational nature of the Triune God and our creation in God's image points to the intentionality of living in relationship with others. Loving God means, by necessity, loving our neighbor. When pressed on the greatest commandment, Jesus said, "'Love the Lord your God with all your heart and with all your soul and with all your mind.' This is the first and greatest commandment. And the second is like it: 'Love your neighbor as yourself'" (Matt 22:38–40). Clearly within the sovereign purposes of God is the ideal of living in union with others.

Harmony among the people of God is easy enough when things are going smoothly. When tragedy strikes, however, there is a great temptation to shrink away from people into isolation. This is particularly true in most Western cultures where rampant individualism has led many to the false

---

6. For lyrics, see http://stevencurtischapman.com/music/.

notion that grief and loss is not something to share, but something to process individually.[7] In the earliest Christian communities, however, this was not the case. In Galatians 6:2, for example, the Christians were exhorted to "carry each other's burdens." These believers were to share the load and stand in solidarity with others, even during difficult times. In this way they are said to "fulfill the law of Christ" (Gal 6:2).[8]

The unity of the people of God was to extend to all seasons of life. Writing to the early Christian community in Rome, Paul urged, "Rejoice with those who rejoice; mourn with those who mourn" (Rom 12:15). While we tend to find it fairly straightforward to "rejoice with those who rejoice," many struggle with knowing how to "mourn with those who mourn."[9] The complexity and challenges of the broken world in which we live means that there is a significant amount of mourning that occurs, even within the Christian community. Among God's people there is often heartbreak. Cancer, the death of a child, injustice, poverty, natural disasters, infertility, persecution, and loss—these leave us all yearning for a better world. In the midst of these difficulties, however, the Christian community has the responsibility to carry each other's burdens. Indeed, for the church to effectively grow and mature it must realize the indispensable nature of lamenting together. In observing the communal nature of prayer in the psalms, author Eugene Peterson writes:

> The praying people, whose prayers are in the Psalms, prayed as a worshipping community. All the psalms are prayers in community: people assembled, attentive before God, participating in a common posture, movement and speech, offering themselves and each other to their Lord. Prayer is not a private exercise, but a family convocation.[10]

Prayer, particularly lamenting prayer, should not be viewed as the reserved practice of a few select *individuals*; rather, it should be understood as the

---

7. For an exploration of some of the factors that contributed to this state of affairs, see Ciano, "Lament Psalms in the Church" (chapter 1 in this volume).

8. In the Old Testament there are numerous examples of those who lamented corporately. In Genesis 50:3, for example, we read that after the death of Jacob, "the *Egyptians* mourned for him seventy days" (emphasis mine). Similarly, we read that after the death of their leader, "The *Israelites* grieved for Moses in the plains of Moab thirty days, until the time of weeping and mourning was over" (Deut 34:8; emphasis mine).

9. In the Old Testament, of course, this idea was not completely foreign. Intercessory prayers were often made as individuals prayed for and on behalf of other people. For an example of intercessory prayer, see Psalm 72.

10. Peterson, *Answering God*, 18.

necessary and important practice of the *combined* people of God. So how do we facilitate this? Let me make a few suggestions.

Provide a Safe Context to Be Transparent in Lament

Many people find the psalms a source of comfort because they address our common human experience. As observed previously, however, while most feel comfortable about sharing seasons of joy and thanksgiving, lament is often hidden away from public viewing. The soul that is discouraged often perceives, falsely, that lament is impious and a signal of spiritual defeat. What is needed to alleviate this is to provide an atmosphere where a person's experience can be shared, whether a high or a low.

In order for people to feel safe in a given context to share about their own grief and loss, it is imperative that they sense an ethos of love and compassion. Generally, people will not share their struggles if they feel they will be judged or patronized by clichéd answers. When a community, whether the local church meeting, a Bible study, or a small group, provides love, support, and a context of mutual vulnerability, then practicing lament becomes viable.

For small groups meeting in homes, corporate lament might look like community times where people are vulnerable with each other, sharing specifics about how they are struggling in order that the group might carry each other's burdens. These times are not to spiral into chat rooms of despair, but to promote awareness of genuine hardship and to provide a safe haven where people will feel heard. Whatever the practice, for genuine lament to occur in the context of community the people of God must be willing to share each other's lives and burdens.

Sometimes there may be *specific* groups that can find great solace from lamenting together. Groups can often bond around similar areas of hardship. There are groups for those navigating cancer, marital breakdowns, sexual abuse, physical disability, and mental health problems. Each of these groups provides a forum for both lament and the process of healing.

David and Nancy Guthrie run one such group called *Respite*. This specific ministry is for those who have gone through, or are going through, the grief of losing a young child. Helping families to grieve, they provide open channels and opportunities where parents can talk, lament, pray, and share tears as they process their varying levels of heartbreak. *Respite* describes its retreats as follows:

> Respite is for couples with strong marriages, and for those whose marriages are struggling under the load of grief. It's for those whose faith has grown through this loss, and for those who have lingering questions. It's for those who want to talk about their experience and their child, and for those who are tired of talking. It's for couples whose loss is fresh, and for those who've been walking down this road for a while.[11]

The ministry of *Respite*, and groups like it, provides an avenue whereby genuine lament and the carrying of each other's burdens can take place. Creating space for mutual vulnerability and a place to be genuinely heard is desperately needed among God's people.

Incorporate Lament into the Life of the Church

The most obvious, and yet absent, context of lament is the gathered church. Great numbers of people are lamenting in the midst of church, yet there seems to be little reflection of this in the typical Sunday service. In spite of this, there are several healthy practices that churches sometimes use to facilitate lament. Some churches, for example, include open times of prayer in their service where people can stand up and publicly share with the congregation an issue in their life, whether a high or low, and then have the church pray on their behalf. By verbalizing their challenges, or asking for prayer on behalf of others, the individual brings to the minds of those in attendance the common difficulties of life, and this reminds the whole body of Christ of its need of God's grace.

Some church traditions include within their services various forms of liturgy that lend themselves to the practice of lament. Written prayers that the congregation recite together, such as those found in the *Book of Common Prayer* or *Prayers on the Psalms from the Scottish Psalter*, provide not just excellent prayers, but also a wide range of prayers, including laments.[12] Many of these prayers and Bible readings provide the solid theological foundation upon which the worshiper can base their engagement with God. To have a lament psalm read in church, even without comment, provides voice to those silently sinking under the weight of grief. To collectively re-

---

11. http://www.nancyguthrie.com/respite-retreat.

12. For another valuable resource for public prayer see Bennett, *The Valley of Vision*.

cite a prayer of sorrow encourages the downcast that they are not the only ones bearing the burden of grief. Though quite rare, a musical lament via a traditional hymn or contemporary song can also verbalize the depths of pain when normal words can't be found.

Another way to aid lament is to have a whole service that focuses on the process of lament. Just as a lament psalm has common movements as it makes a way from orientation, to disorientation, to reorientation, so also a service could follow the same structure. It could look similar to the example listed below.

> Prelude
> Pastoral Introduction (Orientation)
> Congregational Song (one emphasizing lament)
> Lamenting Our Grief (Disorientation)
> > Psalm 13:1–2
> > Psalm 61:1–2
> > Psalm 71:1–4
> Quiet reflection: An opportunity to silently pray
> Pastoral prayer (possibly from a liturgy)
> Praying Our Grief
> > Psalm 13:3–4
> > Psalm 56:1–9
> > Psalm 71:5–13
> > Quiet reflection: An opportunity to silently pray
> > Pastoral prayer (possibly from a liturgy)
> Congregational Song (possibly one of trust)
> Sermon (on a select lament psalm)
> Response
> Trusting During Grief (Re-Orientation)
> > Psalm 13:5–6
> > Psalm 57:5–11
> > Psalm 71:12–24
> Quiet reflection: an opportunity to silently pray
> > Pastoral prayer (possibly from a liturgy)
> Closing Song (one of trust)
> Benediction

In order for the service to have a strong corporate sense, it would be helpful to use a variety of people in the service. The perception is often that the "professional" pastors are unaware of the reality of everyday hardship and grief. Though this is generally not true, a significant representation of people reading the Scriptures and leading in lament and prayer has a powerful impact and speaks highly of the reality that struggle is not just limited to a few. To highlight the common struggle of lament, it may be helpful to have the Bible readings recited by someone standing *in the midst* of the congregation rather than from the front of the church.

The Benefits of Lamenting for the People of God

There is a great spiritual dividend for those who are taught to lament. At least three benefits arise when we teach people to pray the lament psalms.

Lamenting Liberates Our Prayer Life

As observed earlier, there is reluctance among many people to pray the lament psalms because they assume them to be impious or only appropriate for certain people (e.g., King David). As people read the laments there is often the underlying thought, "That is exactly how I feel, but I could never say that to God." This faulty notion is prevalent throughout the Christian community and sadly hinders many from having genuine transparency before God. Solid teaching on the psalms, particularly the lament psalms, is helpful in that it liberates people to see that they can be honest with God. The emotions they have need not be suppressed but may be directed toward their heavenly Father who cares deeply for them. Helping them to see that they are not alone in their feelings provides great solace.

Praying Lament Fosters Unity and Strength

One of the great tragedies of silent grief is that consistent introspection can often lead to feelings of isolation and inadequacy. When we harbor difficulty alone it usually leaves us feeling emotionally exhausted. The value of corporate lament is that it allows the strong to help carry the burdens of those feeling weak. In the sovereign plan of God, he has purposed for us to live in relationship with others. One of the benefits of this is that we not only celebrate high points in life with others, but intimacy and harmony is promoted when we share in walking with others through dark valleys. Proverbs 17:17 reminds us that "A friend loves at all times, and a brother is born for a time of adversity." Loving our neighbor is often best demonstrated when that neighbor is most in need. Mourning with those who mourn promotes unity and fosters mutual concern.

Lamenting Teaches Us to Pray

There is a great deal of emotional relief when we share our feelings, no matter how raw, with God. In the same way, when public prayer contains transparent lament it can be an effective vehicle in leading others to similar honesty with God. Due to the broad absence of lament in Christian contexts, many people don't know how to approach God during dark valleys. When, however, they see it modeled publicly it teaches them *how* to lament. The value of corporate lament is that it often provides immediate spiritual blessings as well as long-term spiritual insight. Peterson picks up on this when he writes:

> The Psalms train us to pray with others who have prayed, and are praying: put our knees on the level with other bent knees; lift our hands in concert with other lifted hands; join our voices in lament and praise with other voices who weep and laugh. The primary use of prayer is not for expressing ourselves, but in becoming ourselves, and we cannot do that alone. The "only child" is not God's. It follows that this primary condition in the making of the Psalms, praying "in step" with others, is also a condition for praying them and learning to pray.[13]

Conclusion

Our world is ravaged by injustice, heartbreak, and broken people who are struggling to navigate the deep waters of despair. The follower of Jesus is not exempt from the hardships of the world and must face them head on. But how should the godly negotiate such seasons of anguish? One of the chief ways, as has been argued in this chapter and throughout this volume, is through the practice of prayerful lament. Because of the relational nature of prayer, the Christian should, indeed *must*, speak openly with God both in seasons of joy and especially in seasons of sorrow. Lament, both individual and corporate, is liberating for the people of God as it reaffirms our common need for God's mercy and intervention in our lives as broken people in a damaged world. Lament frees us to be ourselves before a heavenly Father who not only loves us, but also bends his ear to hear our cries. May the church rediscover the healing balm of God's grace as expressed in the gift of lament.

---

13. Peterson, *Answering God*, 19.

Bibliography

Bennett, Arthur, ed. *The Valley of Vision: A Collection of Puritan Prayers and Devotions.* Edinburgh: Banner of Truth, 1975.

Broyles, Craig C. "Psalms of Lament." In *Dictionary of the Old Testament: Wisdom, Poetry, and Writings,* edited by Tremper Longman III, and Peter Enns, 384–99. Downers Grove: IVP, 2008.

Brueggemann, Walter. *The Message of the Psalms: A Theological Commentary.* Minneapolis: Augsburg, 1985.

Peterson, Eugene. *Answering God: The Psalms as Tools for Prayer.* San Francisco: Harper Collins, 1991.

Wallace, Howard N. *Words to God, Word from God: The Psalms in the Prayer and Preaching of the Church.* Aldershot: Ashgate, 2005.

17

Lament and Pastoral Care

Kirk R. Patston

> The task of the practice of lament is to produce a form of character that can live with unanswered questions, not through repression or denial, but by expression and active acceptance of the reality of evil and suffering and the love of God in the midst of it. By learning the practice of lament, we become the type of people who take seriously the pain and sadness of the world but refuse to be crushed by it.[1]

AFTER A STRESSFUL DAY we like nothing better than to find a soft chair, a movie and, perhaps, some chocolate and wine. After a harrowing week, we book a massage or switch off the alarm clock and hope that our neck muscles will soften again. When life keeps bringing difficulties to us we find ourselves drawn to holiday brochures with the thought that some quiet, unhurried days surrounded by clear horizons will restore our souls. And amid all this, Christians might also go to church or call on a pastor to see them. Whether in a corporate or individual setting, Christians rightly seek pastoral care to face life's challenges. Is the hope that prayer, preaching, singing, and companionship will soothe and soften the troubled body and mind? Will faith be another way of escaping?

Lament may eventually soothe us—but to lament is not to escape. Lament is not another self-care technique but something more demanding

---

1. Swinton, *Raging with Compassion*, 113.

and courageous. It is a willingness to live in harmony with what is real.[2] As such, it is part of the practice of biblical wisdom and is, from a biblical viewpoint, an expected element of the dynamic between the human person and God.

The Necessity of Lament in Pastoral Care

The church can unfortunately create the impression that it brings nothing unique to the problem of human pain. In contemporary church practice, Sunday services mimic the forms of professional conferences and music concerts, perhaps embodying the notion that people need, or at least seek, entertainment. In traditional churches, Sunday services can give the message that people are looking for an experience that is predictable and orderly. Through the week, one-to-one conversations with a pastor come close to being therapeutic encounters where the most important thing is one's self esteem and sense of wellness. The Psalms, and the Bible as a whole, offer much more.

Throughout this volume, various chapters have exposed the disarming honesty of the psalms in naming and describing experiences of injustice, loss, and loneliness. The psalms are not the only biblical texts that do this. In this regard, the Psalter resonates with the so-called wisdom literature. In the book of Job, the main character would rather have an encounter with the living God than settle for either a technique that will restore his wealth or for instruction that insists that the ways of God make sense to the human mind. And, while he may overreach at times, he is finally commended, and even comforted, by the magnificently dangerous vision of creation his God gives him. The writer of Ecclesiastes wisely beckons us to see that joy only comes with the willingness to see our life as God's creatures for what it is: fleeting and impossible to control. This will hurt, "For in much wisdom is much vexation, and those who increase knowledge increase sorrow" (Eccl 1:18).[3] Proverbs balances this out by insisting that wisdom is still a delightful gift of God and that wise living will frequently bring prosperity. The book, however, will not deny the troubling episodes that will be told, even in the story of a wise and just person: "The field of the poor may yield much food, but it is swept away through injustice" (Prov 13:23). "Even in laughter the heart is sad, and the end of joy is grief" (Prov 14:13).

---

2. Wisdom has a comprehensiveness that is attentive to the day-to-day elements of human experience, including times of darkness of soul. See, for example, Bartholomew and O'Dowd, *Old Testament Wisdom Literature*, 286–87, 316–26.

3. All Scripture quotations in this chapter are taken from the NRSV.

Consistent with the wisdom literature, other sections of the Old Testament do not project a life in God's service that is unambiguously positive. Often the anguished personal realities of Israel's history find voice in the book of Psalms. For Moses it involved the frustration of trying to lead a people with stubborn wills (Ps 95) and a dreadful sense of human life lived fearfully before a God of uncompromising holiness (Ps 90). For David it meant confronting the depth of his own sinfulness (Ps 51) and the treachery of his political foes (Pss 3, 13). Jeremiah knew isolation, misunderstanding, and physical abuse, and penned laments that would easily fit in the Psalter (Jer 12:1-4; 20:7-18). Ezekiel had to endure the loss of his wife as part of his enacted ministry of the word, and we can only imagine the pain he carried in silence (Ezek 24:15-18).

Walter Brueggemann's way of approaching Old Testament theology is instructive here.[4] He takes seriously the variety of perspectives about God on view in the pages of the Old Testament and proposes an unresolvable tension between *core testimony* and *countertestimony*. Core testimony is the usual stuff of our theologizing, preaching, praying, and singing. Core testimony claims that God creates, makes promises, delivers, commands, and leads. He is constant in his governance and sustenance. Countertestimony, however, notices that often in human experience God is hidden and his people cry out and lament with feelings that he is unreliable, contradictory, and maybe even abusive. Importantly, Brueggemann maintains that "Israel's countertestimony is not an act of unfaith. It is rather a characteristic way in which faith is practiced."[5]

A corollary of this approach to ways of talking about God in the Old Testament is that one needs a comprehensive approach to the task of being human in relationship with this God. With great insight, Brueggemann surveys what he sees as the disciplines of humanness.[6] Some are correlates of the core testimony: since God is good and faithful humans listen and obey, exercise wisdom and discernment, and live with a primal trust. Some are correlates of the countertestimony: when God is absent humans complain, petition and, finally, give thanks. More broadly, Brueggemann suggests that humans praise and hope. In this survey of being human, it is easy to see how the psalms of lament have had impact on Brueggemann's thought.

The scope of this model is of great value in pastoral work. It articulates a vision of humanity broad enough to cope both with the seasons of prosperity and certainty as well as the darker days of pain and loss. The

---

4. Brueggemann, *Theology of the Old Testament*, 317-18.
5. Ibid., 318.
6. Ibid., 460-85.

dynamic of constant exchange between core testimony and countertestimony validates lived experience where our own emotions and ideas often remain unsettled. The model allows the pastor to sit non-anxiously with all kinds of utterances about God's disappointing ways, without feeling a need to correct or admonish what may simply be an expression of a person of genuine faith who is courageous enough to name what is really happening.

There is, of course, an important difference between lament and grumbling that involves the direction and substance of one's speech. Lament is directed to God because it has a foundational trust that the events of one's life come, in some way or other, from the hand of God. Grumbling is more likely to be a third-person account, speaking about God as though he has left the room. The substance of lament is outrage and despair arising from an energized, even desperate, attempt to insist that God *is* reliable and good in spite of current evidence. Grumbling is more resigned and reveals a suspicion that God never was as trustworthy as he claimed. Lament is faith seeking understanding—and comfort and hope. Grumbling is unbelief content to seek *human* empathy or validation.

Sometimes in pastoral conversations there is a pressing urgency for people to understand and explain their suffering. This is not unexpected when we live in a culture familiar with scientific thinking and the investigation of causality. Much of the way we manage pain is through medicine and psychological techniques, and this brings with it a necessary search for causes so that treatments can have the most effect. This model, however, makes for a poor guide in matters to do with God's mysterious providence. Causal thinking about our suffering starts us on the road to theodical thinking—attempting to justify the ways of God. The practice always ends up on the horns of a dilemma: either God lacks the will to prevent or remove suffering and so does not really love me, or God lacks the power to do anything and so is not really sovereign.

John Swinton has made the telling observation that once we let our thinking unfold in this way, our explanation of evil is almost itself evil. It causes harm by denying truths about God that the Bible affirms.[7] Theodicy is a sophisticated form of unbelief in God's love or God's power and arises from a false assumption that human conceptions of justice are a valid reference point for assessing the character of God. Lament, of course, provides another way to process this problem.[8] The lament psalms allow us to voice

---

7. Swinton, *Raging with Compassion*, 27–29.

8. It is no mistake that the book of Job offers both a sustained critique of human reason as a reference point for assessing God's ways and a protagonist who spends much time in lament.

confusion and hurt without arriving at a rational, cohesive explanation of what God is doing and why. Put another way, lament does not arise from the assumption that suffering is a philosophical problem to solve. Rather, lament is one of the modes of being in the world that God has given his people to help them resist and transform experiences of evil and "enable Christians to live faithfully in the midst of unanswered questions as they await God's redemption of the whole of creation."[9]

Lament, however, can feel unfamiliar. Swinton suggests that a wise pastoral practice is to help people craft their own prayers of lament, using the lament psalms as a template. Following a proposal from Bill Gaventa, he suggests a six-element structure: address to God, complaint, expression of trust, appeal or petition, expression of certainty, vow of praise.[10] In my experience of doing this I have been forced to think hard about what it is that is causing me to feel uneasy and to think what it is that I know about God that is relevant to this situation. For example, if it is an issue of family relationships that is concerning me, I can find myself praying to the God who "sets the lonely in families" (Ps 66:6), the one "from whom every family in heaven and on earth derives its name" (Eph 3:15). As I become increasingly familiar with the psalms of lament, I find that the complaints and expressions of trust I want to say sound like the things that others have said, centuries before me. The act of uttering a certain expectation and a promise to praise makes hope particular and real. In short, going to the trouble to construct a lament is an act of prayer that in the very praying brings clarity and solidarity—even before God has acted to answer.

There may well be a feeling of incompleteness when the task is finished, but this is exactly the point. The mystery of providence and the tangled depths of suffering are both given genuine recognition in the uttering of a lament. What follows are matters of character and the heart: patience, humility, perseverance, and the longing for grace.

One of the benefits of such practice is that it guards us from triumphalism. This is sorely needed in today's religious marketplace. I was recently in a large Christian bookstore and I scanned the books that were featured in the shop's displays. The titles clustered around claims of victory, transformation, growth, and experiences unconstrained by limits. Yet the Christian shoppers looked ordinary enough. I found myself longing for titles about faithfulness in the midst of funerals, disappointing family life, unemployment, and chronic pain.

---

9. Swinton, *Raging with Compassion*, 4.
10. Ibid., 128.

In a judicious discussion of American church life, one commentator has noted the correlation between evangelical Christianity, population growth in white, middle-class suburbs, and a desire to maintain the status quo.[11] Within this cultural setting, one lives with expectations that one lives in a settled world where life will succeed and, with the right amount of ingenuity, enterprises will profit and problems will be solved. Christianity is enlisted as simply another way of telling the story. Pastors of growing churches end up writing books and giving speeches much as successful entrepreneurs in the business world end up with corporate speaking engagements and popular websites. Australian political and economic narratives about resourcefulness, innovation, and individualism easily resonate with the American scene. Such cultures gravitate toward singing and praying that celebrates God's blessing and does not long for things to change.

In churches that use prayer books, there may be a regular practice of reading psalms aloud. But a survey of the prayer books of several denominations has revealed a tendency to omit psalms of lament. A similar phenomenon happens in hymnbooks. While some 40 percent of psalms involve lament, in Churches of Christ, Presbyterian, and Baptist hymnals lament appears in well below 20 percent of the hymns. In the top one hundred of the songs sung in contemporary churches, statistics from Christian Copyright Licensing International point to only five songs that "would even remotely qualify as a lament."[12] Modern churches love to praise and sing "How Great is Our God," "Glorious Day," and "Victory in Jesus."[13]

Is this triumphalism in need of critique or is it an accurate reflection of a genuine difference between Old Testament and New Testament expressions of the life of faith?[14] It is possible to argue that the coming of Jesus marks an end of the need to lament. The lamenting characters of the New Testament are those who call out for healing and, in the person and work of Jesus, they find an answer. Some readers of the Bible notice that the New Testament does not provide us with new laments. When Jesus told the women of Jerusalem to weep for themselves and not for him, it was a unique moment in salvation history appropriate for the horror of what was happening and the fall of Jerusalem to come (Luke 23:28). The command to rich land owners to weep and wail functions as a warning that should stir

---

11. Rah, "The Necessity of Lament," 55–60.

12. Ibid., 61.

13. These titles are taken from the list of the top five songs. See ibid., 61.

14. For further discussion, see West, "The Shape and Function of New Testament Lament," and Burge, "Man of Sorrows, What a Name!" (chapters 8 and 9 in this volume).

repentance rather than an endorsement of lament as a normative practice (Jas 5:1).

If the New Testament does not explicitly teach us to lament it may be because its writers assume continuity with the practices of the psalmists, rather than evidence that lament is left behind. Jesus, our model human being, is a man who laments. Jesus experienced the frustration of misunderstanding and misrepresentation, the sting of betrayal, and the lash of a whip. He, too, turned to lament on the cross (Ps 22). Even beyond his resurrection and ascension, he identified with the pain of his persecuted followers (Acts 9:4). The epistles reveal the hearts of apostles who also found that life with God involved physical harm, relational wounds, and emotional pain. The martyred believers of the early church are presented in the book of Revelation as those who easily take up the psalms on their lips. The heartfelt question "How long?" features in Psalms 4, 6, 13, 35, 62, 74, 79, 80, 82, 89, 90, and 94. These psalms are given a timeless relevance as the souls of those who had been slain for witnessing to the death, resurrection, and lordship of Jesus ask, "How long, Sovereign Lord, holy and true, until you judge the inhabitants of the earth and avenge our blood?" (Rev 6:10).

Challenges to the Practice of Lament in Pastoral Care

Pastors who want to include lament in their practice face two challenges that require the application of wisdom. The first is to find the balance between individual and corporate experiences of disorientation. In pastoral conversation with individuals in distress, the use of lament is a natural thing to suggest. When a congregation gathers, however, it is hard to come up with language that would be true for everyone present. Even at a funeral, there will be some for whom the experience of loss is cataclysmic, while some will gather out of obligation or duty with little sense of pain. The sensitive pastor can acknowledge this but need not abandon the lament as a public exercise. After all, we all know we plan services with elements such as children's talks and with songs that will form different levels of connection for different people. Public lament may not resonate with all who gather, but it will teach all who gather something of the contours of the life of faith. Even if a member of a gathering merely observes the congregation reading a lament together, they will know that there is a way of naming and processing pain that, one day, may be exactly what they need to do.

The second challenge is to find a way to balance despair and hope. As a preacher, I want people to leave church encouraged to keep on going as disciples of Jesus. In counseling sessions, people tend not to come back if all the news is bad. The common shape of the lament psalms deals with this by making a statement about the way God has been experienced in the past and by ending with a hope of praising God again.

When using lament psalms with people experiencing depression, the wise pastor will recognize the tendency for depressed people to get stuck in ruminations that attend only to what is going wrong. Randall Christensen warns against sustained meditation on psalms of lament when people are experiencing depression.[15] Handled with care, though, the lament psalms may help the person realize that God understands their emotional world and that others have moved through despair to hope. Importantly, the form of lament psalms invites people in pain to articulate more than just complaint. Rumination draws attention to situations that are unfair, painful, and seemingly beyond hope. Lament psalms give these real concerns a place, but hold them alongside words that name God, rehearse belief in his faithfulness, and express a desire to remain faithful to him. This has potential to make the intrusive and negative thoughts of depression less powerful. The mood-lowering ideations become only one element in the prayers of the downcast.

Specific Practices

Individual Laments

When the experience of disorientation arises in pastoral conversations, it would be good to ask people whether they have shaped their feelings into a lament. We could encourage people to write prayers during their private times with God. We could sit with people and coach them through the process.

I have recently been feeling a sense of hopelessness around the amount of support my son needs as he lives with intellectual disability and autism in the years after school has finished. I can easily ruminate on this and can begin to feel exhaustion and despair. I have found something valuable in writing and praying the following:

---

15. Christensen, "Depression and Lament," 304.

Address	God who knits us together in the womb Father of our Lord Jesus who with a word and a touch could make the lame walk and the blind see
Complaint	I feel overwhelmed at the constant and seemingly endless need my son has for support It feels that we as a family and we as a nation can't afford to provide the level of care he needs The hours we spend trying to develop his skills seem hidden away and fruitless I worry for the way our whole family is exhausted
Expression of trust	But you are the God who numbers the hairs on our heads and notices the sparrow who falls to the ground I want to trust in your attentiveness, your real presence, your practical, creative kindness
Appeal or petition	So, work to provide for my son by renewing my strength by making the community of your people aware and active by superintending government programs that are wisely conceived and implemented with justice and compassion by building a future beyond what I can imagine
Expression of certainty	I know that you work all things for good and that you do not want to break me
Vow of praise	I want to find in my experiences with my son reasons to offer you praise and I would love it if his life and words could also bring glory to you

Table 17.1 An individual lament

Corporate Laments

Beyond work with individuals, pastors who want to value lament will think about the regular and extraordinary elements that may be included in a Sunday church gathering. It would be good to expand the types of prayers we routinely offer. I tend to rely on the old adoration-confession-thanksgiving-supplication pattern. It would be good to add lament. There is also a good case to be made to return to practices that were common in earlier centuries: the corporate reading and singing of psalms. In previous generations a prayer book would have furnished every congregational member with the words of the psalms, set out for easy reading. Perhaps the new generation of graphic designers and film makers need to give us thoughtful, resonant videos that give us words to say and imagery to ponder. In previous generations a hymnbook would have meant that every congregational member held a copy of all the psalms set in memorable, metrical form. In the spirit of the Sons of Korah,[16] we need musicians to make a disciplined effort to recapture the psalms for us in the musical idioms of our times.[17]

As pastors it is worth being courageous about naming the reasons to lament that our communities will face. On any given Sunday, there will be individuals dealing with enemies and conflict, loss, and a sense of anxiety around a lack of control. Beyond the life of individuals, perhaps the community is low in number due to illness or there are factional tensions in the life of the congregation that are keeping people away. Sometimes a leader will fall and cause disillusionment. In the seasons of the year, certain weeks will be heavy with memories of bushfires and earthquakes or of battles and wars. These should not just be the topics of conversation at morning tea but need to be turned into prayer to the God who is particularly and passionately involved in every situation.

I live in the Blue Mountains of Western Sydney and can still recall the weeks of living on edge in October 2013. With bushfires raging and schools closed, friends who could not access their home came to live with us, and everyone seemed to have a friend who had lost everything. My memory of church in the midst of this is that we gave time to let people tell their stories. We assumed that our life with God included the tiring and distressing drama we were all living through. The churches came up with creative ways of offering care. I do not recall that we prayed a deliberate prayer of lament. Perhaps we might have offered something like this:

---

16. The Sons of Korah, a modern band, compose, record, and perform the psalms. On their website they describe themselves as "an Australian based band devoted to giving a fresh voice to the biblical psalms." See www.sonsofkorah.com.

17. For one example of what this might look (and sound) like, see Freestone, "You Are the God Who Saves Me" (chapter 21 in this volume).

Address	God of all creation, strange creator of trees and possums, oxygen and combustion, water and rain
Complaint	We are feeling scared and out of control We are feeling our own powerlessness over the whims of the weather, the comings and goings of the wind and rain We are feeling scared and out of control because the way and the path of a fire is so hard to predict and manage We have been frightened for the lives of those in our community We are scared for the exhausted fire fighters We are worried that dangerous, destructive fires like this will hit us every summer
Expression of trust	But we trust in your grace, even when it's not our first inclination We trust in your wisdom, even when it's hidden from us We trust that it was a special expression of your mercy that no lives were lost in this fire
Appeal or petition	We want you to provide for people who have nowhere to live We want insurance companies to come through with cash fairly and efficiently We want local, state, and federal government responses to be wise, relevant, and generous We want you to refresh and encourage the fire crews who have served us We want guidance and strength in order to be your people and to express the reality of Jesus even in this situation
Expression of certainty	We know that most of our Australian lives are filled with your blessing and protection whether we recognize it or not And we know that your heart is generous
Vow of praise	We want to look back on this time in years to come and to be able to tell stories of your goodness, faithfulness, and presence And we want our neighbors who rarely think about you to join us in that praise.

Table 17.2 A corporate lament

Conclusion

The Bible does not shy away from the complex glory and pain of being human. We are increasingly surrounded by descriptions of the human life that are thin and even false. It is unsustainable and unkind to offer a form of Christianity that attends only to experiences of success and growth. Pastoral carers need courage to stand against the mythology of triumph and the cult of technique. The pastor who helps form lament in the lives of individual Christians and the gathered people of God will be enabling an ancient, biblical practice that brings to words a perspective on reality that cannot be ignored. Wise pastors will dare to cry, appeal, and hope, trusting that such prayers can be instruments of life.

Bibliography

Brueggemann, Walter. *Theology of the Old Testament: Testimony, Dispute, Advocacy.* Minneapolis: Fortress, 1997.
Bartholomew, Craig G., and Ryan P. O'Dowd, *Old Testament Wisdom Literature: A Theological Introduction.* Downers Grove: IVP, 2011.
Christensen, Randall M. "Parallels between Depression and Lament." *The Journal of Pastoral Care and Counseling* 61 (2007) 299–308.
Rah, Soong-Chan. "The Necessity of Lament for Ministry in an Urban Context." *Ex Auditu* 29 (2013) 54–69.
Swinton, John. *Raging with Compassion: Pastoral Responses to the Problem of Evil.* Grand Rapids: Eerdmans, 2007.

Part V

The Demonstration of Lament

18

"A Strengthening Song for the Sad Soul"
A Sermon on Psalm 13

Malcolm J. Gill

This sermon was delivered at a large church—Stonebriar Community Church—in Frisco, Texas, on October 4, 2009. As a visiting speaker I was given freedom to preach on whatever I desired. I chose Psalm 13 for two reasons. First, as a guest speaker the psalm lent itself to a one-off message—there is no significant contextual background needed for the song. Second, I chose to deliver a message on a song of lament as these psalms are often neglected or misunderstood. Given that the church numbered in the thousands, it was highly likely that within the congregation there would be many dealing with a wide variety of difficult issues and sorrows in their day-to-day experiences. Preaching a lament psalm would give them an opportunity to hear the voice of the godly psalmist and how he navigated a difficult season of life. I chose the metaphor of a "rogue wave" with the purpose of finding a memorable image to carry the outline of the message. After the service, many indicated how liberating it was to discover they could pray the laments of the Scripture. For many, this was the first time they had heard a sermon from a lament psalm.

Introduction

Deep-sea fishing is something that I've only done a handful of times in my life. To be perfectly honest with you, I'm no fisherman. I don't like the smell of fish on my hands, I don't like getting cold or wet, and I don't like waiting for the fish to come and nibble at my bait. While everyone else seems to catch something, all I seem to catch is a cold while the proverbial "big ones" get away.

In spite of my inability as a fisherman, I have in recent times been able to live out my desire to catch fish another way. You see, a few years ago I discovered a television show entitled *The World's Deadliest Catch*. This reality-based program follows the lives of deep-sea fishermen who scour dangerous oceans in search of the mighty Alaskan snow crab.

While participating in this fishing experience, albeit via the big screen, I've learned much about the ocean. The sea is a deep, dark, and scarily powerful place. In my deep-sea fishing education, I've discovered that one of the most feared aspects of the ocean is a phenomenon called the "rogue wave," sometimes referred to as the "freak wave." This rare event is a natural occurrence where a wave of unusual size appears out of nowhere, creating a devastating path of destruction.

Whereas a normal large swell may be ten to fifteen feet in the ocean, a rogue wave can be as high as a five-story building swelling at upwards of one hundred feet. A rogue wave is almost always unexpected and completely unwanted. More than once, vessels have been destroyed, cargo decimated, and lives tragically lost due to the effects of the rogue wave. When a rogue wave crashes over a ship, it leaves very little, apart from despondent fishermen who are left to pick up the pieces.

While I'll never experience the dangers of the open ocean in such a horrific form, I feel that in my own Christian experience, there are times when I feel like my soul has been washed over by something like a rogue wave. Situations arise periodically that leave me floundering in despair. When they occur they are usually unforeseen and have left me reeling.

For my wife and I, a major rogue wave stuck us three years ago. As we sat in a doctor's office we listened to our physician explain to us that I had serious cancer. I had a tumor in my sinus that would require serious chemotherapy and radiation over the course of nine months. As he explained the difficulties before us, it was as if a rogue wave of despair flooded over us. Why me? Why now? This was unexpected and unwanted news. The wave of despair overwhelmed us.

Have you ever had a rogue wave smash over your soul? Rogue waves of despair come in many shapes. A rogue wave of despair may come in the form of a job loss. You thought you would be the last person the company would seek to let go, and yet they have no further need of your services. The rogue wave of despair comes to the faithful husband or wife who, in spite of years of loving commitment, is served papers of divorce. The rogue wave of despair comes over the souls of the married couple seeking to have children, yet who are told they are not able to. The rogue wave of despair comes slowly to the single person who, despite years of purity, finds himself or herself lonely on a Friday night. Rogue waves of despair come to us as we are told by a doctor that we or a loved one has an inoperable disease. These rogue waves of despair come—and they are almost always unexpected and completely unwanted.

The question for you and me this morning is, *What do you do when the rogue wave of despair crashes over your life?* To answer this, we look to the Scriptures, and in particular, to Psalm 13. In this inspired passage of God's word we will discover a man with a despairing soul. As he records for us his song, we listen in, and will receive insight into how we can respond when waves of despair crash over our lives.

Context

By way of background, Psalm 13 is considered by scholars to be an "individual lament psalm"; that is, this psalm poetically expresses the existential cry of an individual going through a time of trial and despair. Just as in our own day different songs represent different emotions in our lives, so also in the recorded songs of the Bible, commonly referred to as psalms. In them we find not only songs of joy and delight, but also songs of hardship and pain.

The song of lament, which we have in front of us, is actually the most common type of song in Israel's hymnbook that we refer to as the Psalms or the Psalter.

You'll notice in your Bibles the title of the psalm; it reads, "For the choir director. A Psalm of David."[1] Here we can observe two things. First, the psalm's origin is connected to David, Israel's king. Second, it is connected to "the choir director," revealing that it is a song composed to be sung by others. The significance of this is simple: while it is a song born out of the struggles of David, the message transcends his context and can be sung by anyone going through hardship. While there are strong indications that the issue is despair and personal turmoil in the psalm, there are no *specific* life events from David's life connected to this song. This is intentional. Like all good poetry, the psalmist invites readers to identify the words

---

1. Unless otherwise stated, all translations are taken from the NIV.

with their own situations. The purposeful ambiguity of the song's historical circumstances lends itself to listeners who are able to identify with the lyrics of a hurting soul.

From a birds-eye view, Psalm 13 falls into three clear and helpful movements that will teach us how the godly should orient themselves when overcome by the rogue wave of despair. First, in vv. 1–2 there is a lamenting cry. Second, in vv. 3–4 requests are made to God. Finally, in vv. 5–6 we see the psalmist's hope restored.

Body

First, the psalm itself begins with a series of questions that reveal a state of crisis and despair. What the cause of this despair is, is not certain. What is certain, however, is that the songwriter is emotionally and spiritually hurting. Notice the four-fold repetition of the question, "How Long" (vv. 1a, 1b, 2a, 2b). The writer of the song does not hide behind a superficial piety in regard to his despair. He breaks down and asks the question that many of us ask when the wave of despair he crashes over us: "How Long?" The realness and raw transparency of the psalmist is remarkable and leads us to our first observation. That is: waves of despair often lead to times of questioning.

Waves of Despair Often Lead to Times of Questioning (13:1–2)

Unlike many modern-day self-help tools, the Bible is realistic in its presentation of the struggle and despair that overwhelms us. It does not shy away from the reality of despair, and here it shows that godly King David, who has committed no sin, cries to God when a wave of despair crashes over his soul.

The psalmist admits to God his feeling of abandonment in no uncertain terms. First, he asks, "How long, O Lord? Will you forget me forever?" (13:1a). Notice the temporal nature of his opening cry. He feels like God's abandonment is "forever." There is no penitence or confession here. The psalmist is not writing to God in despair because of an apparent sin; rather, he is crying to God because he feels overwhelmed and alone in his pain. He is in an emotional wrestle and feels the time of this is stretching out in an almost eternal manner.

David has been hit by a rogue wave, and his helplessness seems to linger on and on and on. He continues his lament, "How long will you hide your face from me?" (13:1b). Here we have a poetic figure of speech. David is not saying that God has a large physical face; rather, he is using a human image to convey a truth about God. The imagery of God looking upon you with his face is rich. The connotation is that when God "looks upon" someone there is blessing and joy. That is why Moses prayed the famous blessing in Numbers 6:24–25, "The Lord bless you and keep you; the Lord make *his face* shine upon you and be gracious to you; the Lord turn *his face* toward you and give you peace" (NIV [emphasis added]).

The "face" represents God's looking upon you and the idea is that his beauty, grace, peace, and favor rests upon those he looks upon. While it is wonderful to feel that God is extending his blessing on your life, David feels just the opposite is occurring in his circumstances. "How long will you hide your face from me?" he cries.

For David, he feels that in light of his crisis God must have removed his blessing. God, as it were, is looking elsewhere, and in doing so his goodness and peace have all but disappeared. David feels that God is removed, distant, uninterested in his activity, and he cries, "How long?"

He continues in v. 2. "How long must I wrestle with my thoughts and day after day have sorrow in my heart?" The phrase "I wrestle" is a curious one and is translated helpfully in the *New Living Translation* that says, "How long must *I struggle* with anguish in my soul?" (NLT [emphasis added]). The psalmist is again reiterating that his heart, his soul, his very being, is plagued with despair. And this despair feels like it is there "all day." This is no fleeting moment, this is an extended period of despair, and he asks God, "How long?"

His final "How long?" comes at the end of v. 2 when he says, "How long will my enemy be exalted over me?" Here an "enemy" is highlighted. This enemy is referred to again in vv. 3 and 4, and most have assumed the issue is David's wrestle with sickness and death. We will look at that in a few moments.

Whether the enemy here is death or not, the psalmist is crying to God because he feels that evil and brokenness will soon rejoice over his demise. So he cries, "How long?" In fact, this is now the fourth time he has asked that same question.

Friends, what are we to make of this opening refrain? No doubt, if you are like me, upon hearing these cries of despair you probably feel a little bothered, uneasy, or possibly even embarrassed. Upon first reading we might say, "What is David doing here? Shouldn't he be godlier in his speech? Can he really question God? Isn't he being disobedient by accusing God of abandonment? Shouldn't he quietly submit and keep his problems to himself?"

It might surprise you, but here in Psalm 13, God gives us an authorized and legitimate expression of how his children may come to him. In fact, in ancient Judaism, this psalm, along with the other lament psalms, was viewed as the correct and godly way for people to despair. The Scriptures present to us here a real way of dealing with hardship. David does not downplay or ignore his emotions and feelings. He does not stoically ignore the issues of his life or suppress them as if they don't exist. Rather, in the context of a personal relationship, he cries out to a Father who loves him. He expresses to God his feelings of despondency.

Expressing your feelings to God is not forbidden in Scripture. In fact sharing your thoughts, even if they are despairing thoughts, is legitimized in the example given to us here. One scholar writes concerning the lament prayers, "The laments testify to the value of simply telling one's story to God. God is not portrayed simply as 'Mr Fixit'; he is the supreme listener. The image of God reflected in the psalms is one who is interested not only in the healing but also in the pain."[2]

God does not despise his children who cry out to him in times of need. Indeed, in the most despairing cry of history, God's only Son, the beloved Lord Jesus, demonstrates his association with our common human pain when he cries out in lament, quoting another lament psalm, saying, "My God, my God, why have you forsaken me?"[3] His Father heard his cry, as he also hears ours.

Friends, I want to encourage you today that if a rogue wave has crashed over your soul, there is an appropriateness in God's economy for you to ask the difficult questions. When the unwanted diagnosis comes to you or a loved one, be real with God. When you feel belittled because you can't earn money to support your family, share your disappointments with God. When you discover you're unable to have children, when your promotion never occurs, when you wrestle with mental illness, go to God with all of your hardships. God is not afraid for you to ask a "Why me" question, or a "How long?" question, or a "What is going on?" question. Don't feel ashamed or embarrassed by your heavy heart. Share your thoughts openly and honestly with God. As 1 Peter 5:7 exhorts us, "Cast all your anxiety on him because he cares for you."

The cry of the godly psalmist in vv. 1–2 reminds us that waves of despair often leads to times of questioning. But let's look at the second movement of the song in vv. 3–4. Here we discover that waves of despair should move us to pray.

---

2. Broyles, "Psalms of Lament," 394.

3. Jesus is recorded as quoting Psalm 22:1 in Matthew 27:46.

Waves of Despair Should Move Us to Pray (13:3–4)

It should not surprise us, but the psalmist does not remain in lament. Though still having major concerns and despair in his life, the songwriter demonstrates that cries of lament and pain should move us to petitions of prayer.

You will notice in vv. 3–4 that there are three imperatives of request made. First, "Look on me" (13:3a) or more literally "See me." Here again the picture is of God giving his look of blessing on someone's life. The psalmist, rather than questioning God's care, simply asks to receive God's favor.

Second, "Answer me" (13:3b). Here the psalmist requests through prayer an answer to his situation. He brings his despair to God and wants God to respond. You will notice that there is a voice of trust in his statement, "O Lord, my God." Here he is reminding God that there is a personal relationship involved. He wants that personal God involved. God is not just a God who is out there; he is a God who answers because he is "My God."

Third, he prays that God would "Give light to my eyes." Here the image is perhaps both literal and metaphoric. Perhaps suffering illness and facing the "enemy" of death, the psalmist cries out for life and health. In a metaphoric sense the cry is to have vibrancy in his "eyes" or life once again. He has lost the sparkle, the joy of life, and he beseeches his Father to help him gain it.

These three cries represent a movement from despair toward hope. While the waves have not disappeared, there is a growing sense of hope in the life of the songwriter.

Friends, while waves of despair often lead us to times of questioning, that should not be the final outcome. Waves of despair should move us to pray. But there's a third observation that we can make in this passage and that comes in vv. 5–6. Here we discover that waves of despair can be calmed.

Waves of Despair Can Be Calmed (13:5–6)

There is considerable progress in this psalm as the psalmist moves from lament to confident trust. In just six short verses, David moves from overwhelming waves of despair to calm waters of hope. The literary marker that shows the movement of the psalm to a place of calm is the simple word "but" (13:5). In spite of the apparently unstoppable, unannounced, and even unwanted despair, there is a "but." There is a contrasting component to despair; it is "trust."

In this final stanza the psalmist finds his hope and confidence in God as he writes, "but I trust in your unfailing love" (13:5). The term "unfailing love" is a significant word that is closely connected with God's loyal covenant-keeping love. By using the term "unfailing love," the author is looking at promises kept in the past, which in turn gives rise to confidence for his future.

Here the psalmist does not delight in the action of his current circumstances; rather, he resolutely reflects on the uncompromising promise-keeping love of God. David reflects on God's previous faithfulness in his life, and concludes that God can be trusted in his current circumstances. Thus, in these final verses, David is expressing trust, yet his lament continues as he appeals to God's character, reminding God that his "unfailing love" should not fail now.

Conclusion

David, in this short psalm, moves us from waves of despair to a calm sea of peace. He has transitioned from questioning, to prayer, to resolute trust. His rogue wave has subsided and a calm repose now surrounds him. We've observed:

1. Waves of despair often lead to times of questioning (13:1–2)
2. Waves of despair should move us to pray (13:3–4)
3. Waves of despair can be calmed (13:5–6)

Well that sounds great in David's life, but coming back to our original question: *What do we do when the rogue wave of despair crashes over our life?*

I think the application is quite clear. When facing rogue waves of despair, *trust in the promise-keeping God*. Trust in the promise-keeping God when you don't understand why it is you who has been diagnosed with a mental illness or a degenerative disease. Trust in the promise-keeping God when you don't get the promotion and the dishonest guy does. Trust in the promise-keeping God when you are following Christ as a single person even though the world invites you to compromise. Trust in the promise-keeping God when you unexpectedly lose a loved one.

You and I may feel blindsided when the waves of despair crash over our lives, but the Scriptures remind us of our God's character and promises. Just as he kept you tightly in his hands in the past, so also in the future when the waves crash over your soul, he will hold you tightly. Our God is trustworthy. Trust in the promise-keeping God to watch over your soul.

There are at least three ways you can practice this. First, *remember God's promises*. Friends, dwell on the sure promises found in God's Word. When the waves crash over your soul, appeal to God's loving-kindness. Remember, God says, "I will never leave you nor forsake you" (Heb 13:5). Remember the promise, "The Lord is with me; I will not be afraid" (Ps 118:6). Remember that "[nothing] can separate us from the love of God that is in Christ Jesus our Lord" (Rom 8:39).

There's a second way we can trust the promise-keeping God, and that is to *remember the cross*. The basis of our hope in the midst of suffering is the finished work of Christ. Our greatest enemy—sin and death—has been conquered through the work of the Lord Jesus Christ. In looking at the cross, we see God in the flesh truly identifying with our pain. The Lord Jesus, while dying on the cross, fully identified with our humanity and brokenness when he cried, "My God, my God, why have you forsaken me?" (Matt 27:46). We have a God who is familiar with our pain and suffering.

Yet, our Lord Jesus does not end his life with lament; even while on the cross he moves to a prayer of trust in the promise-keeping God when he cries, quoting another lament psalm (Ps 30:5), "Father, into your hands, I commit my spirit" (Luke 23:46). Our Lord Jesus Christ conquered the rogue wave of sin and death, on our behalf, as he rose triumphantly from the grave. Brothers and sisters, he has calmed the greatest storm, therefore trust him with your rogue waves. What do you do when the rogue wave of despair crashes over your life? *Trust in the promise-keeping God*.

This brings us to a final point of application. Remembering God's promises and remembering the cross should lead us to another act of trust ... lament. Like most of the psalms, our appropriate response to Psalm 13 is to pray like this when the "rogue wave" crashes. Crying out to God who knows our pain and has promised to save demonstrates our faith in him when our faith is deeply tested. Remember his promises, remember the cross, and take up a cry of lament.

Bibliography

Broyles, Craig C. "Psalms of Lament." In *Dictionary of the Old Testament: Wisdom, Poetry, and Writings*, edited by Tremper Longman III, and Peter Enns, 384–99. Downers Grove: IVP, 2008.

19

"My Only Friend—Darkness"
A Sermon on Psalm 88

G. GEOFFREY HARPER

THIS SERMON (SLIGHTLY REVISED) was originally preached at Petersham Baptist Church, Sydney, on 26 April 2015, as part of a short series on the Psalms. I chose this particular psalm to preach from for a number of reasons.

First, I wanted to preach on a lament psalm as a means of helping people in the church to engage with an unfamiliar part of Scripture and (hopefully), by doing so, to begin to help them appreciate the importance and value of lament for the life of faith. Thus, the sermon ventures beyond the purview of Psalm 88 to think about the place of lament in the lives of believers more broadly.

Second, I chose Psalm 88 because of its lack of movement and unremitting determination to remain in the "darkness." I felt this was important, because without any prospect of retreating to a "happy ending," the role of this psalm in the canon comes more sharply into view (aiding a wider understanding of the role of lament). Lament is not so much focused on the *result* of reaching a (happy) ending; it is more interested in providing a means for God's people to remain faithful as they negotiate the *process* of grief and loss.

Third, I chose to preach on this psalm because a number of individuals and families in the church had recently experienced times of great distress and sadness—palpable "darkness." The sermon was thus offered as a means of helping those in such circumstances and as a way of giving everyone else a window into their experience.

The response was (I think) generally favorable; certainly, the sermon sparked a number of ongoing conversations about the role of lament in the life of the church.

Introduction

At college on Thursday, I was teaching a class on Deuteronomy. Afterwards, one of the women in the class came up to talk to me. During class, we had looked briefly at Deuteronomy 28—a passage that outlines the potential blessing or cursing that Israel could expect, dependent upon her obedience. Along the way I had pointed out some of the horrific images you find there—especially in the section that describes the effects of siege on a city. That is what Rebecca[1] wanted to talk to me about.

Rebecca had been reading through the book of Kings in preparation for her essay, making notes on the themes she found along the way—God's goodness and mercy; his great power; his ability to speak through the prophets—until, that is, she came to the description of the siege of Samaria (2 Kgs 6:26–29). There we read that the famine in the city had been so severe that two women made an agreement to eat their own children. She said to me, "I don't know what to do with that. If I was reading a novel and it turned really violent and graphic and dark—I'd stop reading it. But this is the Bible. Why is this stuff in here?"

It's a great question isn't it? Why is this stuff in here? Rebecca asked that question about what she was reading in Kings. You might have found yourself asking something similar when this psalm was read for us. Why is this in here? There might even have been a time when you were flicking through the psalms—looking for words of comfort; looking for something to remind you of God's faithfulness; something to cheer your heart. Or maybe you were looking for something suitable to read out at the start of church. Your page opens at Psalm 88, and you begin to read, and then recoil—"No. That's not what I'm looking for at all"—and you quickly keep flicking.

Why is this psalm here? This dark, brooding poem that offers no glimmer of hope. At least other lament psalms have some sort of movement in them. The psalmists might be in trouble, they might cry out to God, things might look dicey for a moment, but then finally, God steps in and the psalm moves to praise. But Psalm 88 has no movement; there is no relief. There

---

1. Name changed to preserve anonymity.

is only unremitting lament—a bitter cry from start to finish which ends in Hebrew with the word "darkness." Surely we don't need to read this kind of thing. How could it possibly do us any good? Surely we can just keep on flicking and get back to "The Lord is My Shepherd"—or even better, back to the Gospels.

But maybe Psalm 88 is exactly what you need. I said to Rebecca on Thursday that one of the things these uncomfortable bits of the Old Testament do is force us to think differently—because they challenge our sheltered theologies and expose our shallow view of God as they force us outside of our comfort zones. While that can be hard, while it can be deeply confronting, while it can raise all sorts of questions for us—in the end it can lead us to a deeper understanding of God and his ways that is good for us.

That's exactly what Psalm 88 has to offer this morning: a challenge to your sheltered theology. While it might be confronting, in the end this psalm may prove to be the very thing your soul needs.

Life Sucks and We All Know It

Anyway, as bleak as Psalm 88 is, we can identify with it, can't we? The psalm definitely gets one thing right: there are times when life sucks and we all know it. Now you may be thinking, "Here we go again—glass half empty as always." But it's true, isn't it? Of course it's not like that all the time. Of course there are moments of joy and lots of laughter (especially when you live with kids like ours). There are good friends, good cups of coffee, and good memories. But haven't there also been times when you have felt what the psalmist describes in v. 3—which literally reads, "My soul has had its fill of miseries."[2] Times when you were so overwhelmed by circumstances that you couldn't even get out of bed; when your heart and your emotions were at breaking point for weeks; when you wept bitter tears, day after day, and still the grief remained; when all there was, was the cold, lonely, darkness. "My soul has had its fill of miseries" (v. 3).

That is where the writer of this psalm is:

> Lord, you are the God who saves me; day and night I cry out to you. May my prayer come before you; turn your ear to my cry. I am overwhelmed with troubles and my life draws near to death. I am counted among those who go down to the pit; I am like one without strength. I am set apart with the dead, like the slain who lie in the grave, whom you remember no more, who are cut off from your care. (vv. 1–5 NIV)

2. Translations of Psalm 88 are my own unless otherwise noted.

This is a prayer that comes from the edge of life. Whether the issue is physical or emotional or spiritual, the result is the same. Things are so serious that the writer even says in v. 3, "My life has touched *Sheol*." It's a powerful image. He feels so close to death it's as if he can reach out his hand and touch *Sheol*, the land of the dead. That feeling of being close to death crops up again in vv. 10–12. "Do you show your wonders to the dead? Do their spirits rise up and praise you? Is your love declared in the grave, your faithfulness in Destruction? Are your wonders known in the place of darkness, or your righteous deeds in the land of oblivion?" (vv. 10–12 NIV).

Before all the alarm bells go off in your head, we need to remember that Old Testament believers had far less information about what happens when you die. God has given a lot more revelation since then. But you can hear what he's saying, can't you? These are words from a person on the verge of death; from someone about to enter the realm of the dead—called here by four different names: "the grave," "Destruction," "the place of darkness," and "the land of oblivion." When that happens, it will be too late. Too late then for God to work his wonders. Too late for love and faithfulness.

Life Sucks, but God Can Save

But, like we do, the psalmist has a good option to pursue: he can call out to God to deliver him. Life sucks, but God can save. Three times, this psalm is punctuated by cries made to God: "Lord, you are the God who saves me; day and night I cry out to you. May my prayer come before you; turn your ear to my cry . . . my eyes are dim with grief. I call to you, Lord, every day; I spread out my hands to you . . . But I cry to you for help, Lord; in the morning my prayer comes before you" (vv. 1–2, 9, 13 NIV).

There are a couple of things to note here. First, there is an acknowledgment that Yahweh is the God who saves. Literally in v. 1 he says, "Yahweh— God of my salvation." The psalmist knows God can save, just like we know it. His theology is good.

Second, note that the situation is so desperate that it has resulted in a continual crying out to God to do exactly what he is able to do: to save. "Day and night I cry to you" (v. 1); "I call to you O Lord every day" (v. 9); "I cry to you for help, O Lord; in the morning my prayer comes before you" (v. 13). The issues press in so much that as soon as he awakens it all comes rolling in again. But even then, first thing in the morning, he prays for help. Day and night, every day, the psalmist cries out to God—to the God who can save him.

But, third, note the desperation. The word "turn" in v. 2 is an imperative—it's a command directed to God: "*Turn* your ear to my cry." In other words, "Hey! Listen to me. Respond to my prayers." This is where we expect the turnaround. This is the moment when the music should start to swell to build anticipation for what is about to unfold, to signal the coming deliverance that will usher in a happy ending. But it doesn't come. In fact, it gets worse.

Life Sucks and It's Your Fault God

The psalmist is suffering. He feels as if he is touching death. Three times we hear a desperate cry to the "God who can save me." But there is no deliverence. In fact, we read: "But I cry to you for help, Lord; in the morning my prayer comes before you. Why, Lord, do you reject me and hide your face from me?" (vv. 13–14 NIV). But there's more:

> *You* have put me in the lowest pit, in the darkest depths. *Your* wrath lies heavily on me; *you* have overwhelmed me with all *your* waves. *You* have taken from me my closest friends and have made me repulsive to them. I am confined and cannot escape; . . . Why, Lord, do *you* reject me and hide *your* face from me? From my youth I have suffered and been close to death; I have borne *your* terrors and am in despair. *Your* wrath has swept over me; *your* terrors have destroyed me. All day long they surround me like a flood; they have completely engulfed me. *You* have taken from me friend and neighbor—darkness is my closest friend. (vv. 6–8, 14–18 NIV [emphasis added])

This is where an uncomfortable psalm becomes unbearable. If only the psalmist had blamed his circumstances; if only he had pointed his finger at society, or at the health system, or at his doctors. Even if he had blamed his family and friends, that would be better than this. Because instead, he looks God in the eye, as it were, and says: "You have put me in this pit. You are the God who can save me. I cry out to you day and night. Why do you hide your face from me and leave me afflicted and close to death?" The real problem for the psalmist is not illness, or turmoil. It's God. What causes him the greatest anguish is God's silence. That is why his cry is so bitter. Desperate circumstances, met with desperate prayer, met with absolute silence. "My only friend—darkness."

Life Sucks and So Does This Psalm (Or Does It?)

Why is all of this here? (Maybe you're thinking: "I was depressed before I came to church.") Life might suck, but so does this psalm. Well, I suggested at the start that Psalm 88 might present a challenge to our sheltered theology; that it might be confronting; but that in the end it might be the very thing that our souls need. As it turns out, Psalm 88 has much to teach us.

Relief in Our Sorrow

Perhaps the most immediate thing Psalm 88 might do is bring you relief. Relief that you are not the only one to have felt the way you are feeling. To know that as you cry in the night and weep lonely tears, that you are not alone. That when God seems distant and silent, when you know he can save but doesn't, that others have also asked: "Why O Lord do you reject me?" "Why do you hide your face from me?"

The brokenness of the world we live in, the brokennes of our own lives, means that these questions are *our* questions. You're not the only one.

A Reality Check: Life Sucks

Secondly, Psalm 88 is proof (if you needed it) that life doesn't always turn out the way you want it to. That sometimes, life really does suck. That's why we have lament psalms. If life were always rosy, then all the psalms would be praise psalms, but they're not. More than half of them are laments.

The presence of so much lament creates a real tension in the book. Because the psalm that introduces the collection, Psalm 1, states clearly that the "one who meditates on torah will be blessed." In other words, the one who sides with God, who takes a stand on his word, will be blessed. But life isn't that simple. So often, there's a disconnect between promise and reality. It's the falling short of expectation that causes the psalmists to cry out to God to save, to deliver, to rescue. And frequently God *does* save and deliver and rescue. But Psalm 88 reminds us that sometimes there is no happy ending. Some days start, and end, in the place of darkness.

A Voice for the Darkness

But importantly, Psalm 88 gives us a voice to use in the darkness. Like all the other psalms, this one demonstrates for us what a righteous response looks like and it invites us to make it our response in similar circumstances. Psalm 88 invites you to make its words your words; to let it express what you feel inside, but can't vocalize; to let it provide you with something to say when grief and loss are so overwhelming that you've got nothing.

This is an area where we need help, because when it comes to grief and sadness and loss and death, we excel at distancing ourselves from it—we're like Unikitti in *The LEGO Movie*. We drown out negative emotion with TV, music, work, alcohol. Doing anything we can to avoid the reality.

You see that at funerals here in Australia. I have yet to go to one where the coffin has been in the room. You see it in the trend in recent years to stop calling Christian funerals "funerals," but to call them "celebrations" instead. Of course there is an element of truth to that, but there's also an element of denial. We need help, because we have forgotten how to lament.

You can even see that here in PBC,[3] can't you? When was the last time we sang a lament together? Prayed a lament? (Have we ever sung a lament together?) But haven't sad things happened among us that have broken our hearts? Haven't there been great tradegies in our city? Isn't oppression and violence running rampant around the world? Why are we not lamenting?

We need help to lament. The psalms can help us. Psalms like this one present us with a righteous way of responding and invite us to copy them. Did you hear that? Lamenting is a righteous response. Understanding that is a helpful corrective for many Christians who view the expressing of lament, or the voicing of grief and sadness, as an *unspiritual* response—even as an *ungodly* response. That unless you can at any moment in life say "praise God" then you are somehow deficient in your faith. But the result is churches full of people who are silently suffering, yet who feel they can never talk about it. People who feel compelled to put on a brave face, to maintain a stiff upper lip and say, "I'm fine," when "fine" is the last thing they are. But the psalms declare that attitude to be profoundly unbiblical. Instead, psalms like Psalm 88 are presented to us as models for expressing lament, because expressing lament is what the righteous do when the going gets tough.

These Are Words You Must Say

But I think Psalm 88 goes further still. Yes, the psalm comes as an invitation to us to make its response our response, but the model it presents is not just one possible option among many—some advice we can take or leave. The role of the psalms in Scripture is more definite than that. With Psalm 88 God is not only inviting us to respond like this, he is saying this is how you

---

3. That is, Petersham Baptist Church.

must respond. A respose that must include those pointed words that make us feel so uncomfortable: "You have put me in the lowest pit, in the darkest depths. Your wrath lies heavily on me; you have overwhelmed me with all your waves . . . Your wrath has swept over me; your terrors have destroyed me. All day long they surround me like a flood; they have completely engulfed me" (vv. 6–7, 16–17 NIV).

This is the way of speaking God wants you to use as you cry out to him, because to do anything less, to shy away from using the language of "you," to blame other things or other people, would be a denial of God's sovreignty—to deny that he is fully in control.

That is what makes Psalm 88 different from just an angry rant. Yes, the psalmist is complaining, but he is complaining *to* God. He knows he has no option but to go to the Lord of all the earth. So even though all he can see and feel is darkness, the psalmist does not abandon trust in God, but keeps on crying out to him. Unanswered prayer does not lead to lack of faith, or silence, or resignation—but to more petition, because the believer knows there is nowhere else to turn. The unrighteous response in the face of suffering is to say nothing—to remain silent. The righteous thing to do is to cry out to God in lament.

And as we learn to submit to the psalms, to be conformed by the psalms; as we learn to voice our laments and our griefs, we find strange company. For Jesus also lamented. As he hung on the cross he did not remain silent. He didn't just try to maintain a stiff upper lip, to remain strong for the sake of his disciples. No, he cried out in anguish. Taking up the words of the lament psalms Jesus cried out to God, to the God he knew was in control even though the suffering was intense: Psalm 22, "My God, my God, why have you forsaken me?"; Psalm 31, "Into your hands I commit my spirit."

Suffering is not evidence that God is powerless or has lost control. And when suffering does not end, Psalm 88 says this is how you must respond.

Conclusion

Why is this psalm in here? Simply, because we need it to be. We need it to make us take off our rose-tinted glasses and to acknowledge the brokenness of the world we live in. We need it to give us a voice to lament our suffering. We need it to open our ears to hear the suffering of others. We need it to help us keep talking to God when there does not seem to be a God to talk to.

Why is this psalm in here? Because God, in his grace, has given it to us.[4]

---

4. Following the sermon, a song was played to allow for silent reflection. For the video used, see https://www.youtube.com/watch?v=WsLhN-RtSTE.

20

"How Could We Sing?"

A Sermon on Psalm 137

Kit Barker

While I have preached on Psalm 137, I have not preached this particular sermon. For the volume at hand, I chose to present something less contextually specific and take the opportunity to discuss the nature of imprecation. In our context (and, I imagine, many others), a preacher cannot assume that the audience will accept that these words were appropriate responses to violence, and many will struggle with the suggestion that God continues to commend, even command, such a response today. Consequently, a preacher cannot offer an application of the text without first explaining how it functions as Christian Scripture. Thus, as will become apparent, this sermon functions in part as an apologetic, defending the place of imprecation in Scripture and on the lips of Christ's church. I also wanted to include Psalm 137 as it represents some of the most shocking language in the Psalter and, for that matter, in all of Scripture. These are certainly lost words. Demonstrating the loyalty and righteousness inherent to imprecation unlocks words essential for a righteous response to this world. If hearers are convinced of the possibility and importance of appropriating these words, then a large portion of the Psalms, previously "unavailable" to them, suddenly becomes relevant, powerful, and necessary.

"How Could We Sing?": A Sermon on Psalm 137

> Blessed is he who seizes and smashes your infants on the rock.[1]

What on earth are words like this doing in Scripture? How can this response to violence and oppression continue to be justified when Jesus calls us to love our enemy and pray for those who persecute us? Should we assume that psalms like this reflect ungodly or sub-Christian prayers, or is it the case that somehow these words are still okay, perhaps even righteous, on the lips of God's people? Can we sing this psalm? Can we pray like this?

C. S. Lewis didn't think so. Listen to what he says about this kind of psalm:

> One way of dealing with these terrible or (dare we say?) contemptible Psalms is simply to leave them alone. But unfortunately the bad parts will not "come away clean"; they may, as we have noticed, be intertwined with the most exquisite things. And if we still believe that all Holy Scripture is "written for our learning" or that the age-old use of the Psalms in Christian worship was not entirely contrary to the will of God, and if we remember that Our Lord's mind and language were clearly steeped in the Psalter, we shall prefer, if possible, to make some use of them. What use can be made? . . . I feel sure still, that we must not either try to explain them away or to yield for one moment to the idea that, because it comes in the Bible, all this vindictive hatred must somehow be good and pious. We must face both facts squarely. The hatred is there—festering, gloating, undisguised—and also we should be wicked if we in any way condoned or approved it or (worse still) used it to justify similar passions in ourselves.[2]

Lewis was right that these "bad parts," as he calls them, do not "come away clean." The imprecatory prayers are embedded within great expressions of praise and thanksgiving—"intertwined with the most exquisite things," as he says. However, I believe Lewis was wrong when he said that these psalms are examples of wickedness that must not be condoned or imitated. As we reflect on this most difficult of psalms, I hope we will find that its words, although shocking, are still God's words, and that his words are always "exquisite."

---

1. Psalm 137:9, my translation.
2. Lewis, *Reflections on the Psalms*, 24–25.

Psalm 137 is a desperate cry for God to bring justice. As we consider what God might be saying to us today with these words, we must, first of all, appreciate two qualities of this cry. The first is that *this is a loyal cry*. The psalmist's loyalty to God is clear and is the main point of the opening section of the psalm. Look again at vv. 1–4.

> By the waters of Babylon,
> there we sat down and wept,
> when we remembered Zion.
> On the willows there
> we hung up our lyres.
> For there our captors required of us songs,
> And our tormentors, mirth, saying,
> "Sing us one of the songs of Zion!"
> How shall we sing the Lord's song in a foreign land?[3]

The psalmist is reflecting on his experience of the Babylonian exile. Jerusalem had been destroyed, the temple burned, and the people massacred. The survivors now live out their lives in captivity, grieving the loss of family, friends, culture, and life in God's presence in his promised land. The psalmist, who was probably a former temple singer, remembers how the Babylonians taunted the exiles, demanding that they entertain them by singing one of the famed "Songs of Zion." The psalmist recalls that he refused such a demand. He and his fellow musicians hung up their harps and lyres and would not sing such a song. How could they when they were on foreign ground? They could not. This refusal to sing was an act of loyalty.

In far less profound circumstances, it's like being beaten 50–nil in a rugby match (or in a game of American football) before being forced to stand before the victors and sing your team song. It is humiliating—and for the Israelites in exile, what's at stake is far greater than personal humiliation. Their God is being mocked. They're in exile. Was their God not strong enough to save them?

The Babylonians were clearly familiar with the Israelite psalms, which praised Yahweh for his supreme power and his sovereignty over all nations—and indeed, all the earth. Now, sitting on the banks of a river in Babylon, at the mercy of their captors, the Israelites are told to sing one of those songs: "Go on, sing one of your songs of Zion. Praise your God for being more powerful than all the other gods, more powerful than our god." Because the psalmist and his fellow singers believed what the songs of Zion proclaimed, they wouldn't sing them in a context where those words would be mocked. They refused because of their loyalty to God.

---

3. All Scripture quotations are taken from the ESV unless otherwise noted.

They refused to sing a song of Zion, a song praising God for his supremacy and victory, yet it's possible they did sing something for their captors. The psalm shifts in vv. 5–9 to a song, a prayer to God that declares the psalmist's loyalty and asks God to judge those who have oppressed his people. So perhaps the Israelites did sing their captors a song. Perhaps they said, "You want a Zion song? Here's a new one. We've written it just for the occasion." And then, in a language unknown to their captors, they sang the following words in Hebrew:[4]

> If I forget you, O Jerusalem,
> let my right hand forget its skill!
> Let my tongue stick to the roof of my mouth,
> If I do not remember you,
> If I do not set Jerusalem above my highest joy!
> Remember, O Lord, against the Edomites, the day of Jerusalem,
> how they said, "Lay it bare, lay it bare, down to its foundations!"
> O daughter of Babylon, doomed to be destroyed,
> Blessed shall he be who repays you with what you have done to us!
> Blessed shall he be who takes your little ones and dashes them against the rock! (Ps 137:5–9)

It's unclear whether vv. 5–9 formed such an immediate response to their captors' attempt to mock God. It could be that the psalmist wrote Psalm 137 upon his return from exile when the pain and injustice was still acute. We don't know for sure. What we do know is that the psalmist and his companions remained loyal to God. Their refusal to comply with Babylonian attempts to mock God is reflected in their prayer of self-cursing in vv. 5–6. Here the psalmist evokes a curse upon himself if he does not prove faithful. If he forgets Jerusalem, if he acquiesces to the demands of his captors and participates in mocking God's power and sovereignty, then he prays that God would stop him, that God would strip him of his ability to play and to sing: "May my right hand forget . . . may my tongue stick to the roof of my mouth."

This is a loyal cry, a cry made in response to loss, enslavement, and derision. In the midst of this suffering, the psalmist's chief concern is the glory of God: that Jerusalem, the symbol of God's kingdom, be exalted above all else. I said there were two qualities of this cry that we needed to appreciate. The first is that *this is a loyal cry*; the second is that *this is a righteous cry*.

Psalm 137 is not alone in this regard. While this and other psalms contain language that is shocking, making it hard to imagine that these words

---

4. See Alter, *The Book of Psalms*, 475.

could be righteous, God offers all the psalms as righteous responses to similar circumstances. There is no indication that some psalms are models to follow while other psalms are counterexamples to be avoided. As Lewis said, the difficult language doesn't come away clean. We can't just rip it out of the Bible because it's uncomfortable or because we don't think it fits. In fact, the language of Psalm 137 fits the psalms and the Bible perfectly well—both Old and New Testaments, as I will demonstrate in a moment.

Each section of Psalm 137 presents itself as a righteous cry. We have already noted that the rhetorical question of v. 4, "How shall we sing the Lord's song in a foreign land?" demands a particular answer: "We shall not. We must not. Not when it would mean being disloyal. Not when it would mock our God." The righteous response is to remain loyal—the very thing that Psalm 137 enacts. The righteousness of the response is further demonstrated in the following section where the psalmist declares that Jerusalem is his highest joy, that God's kingdom and his glory are his highest priorities. Finally, the concluding verses, which call for God to judge the Edomites and Babylonians, are also presented as a righteous response. The psalmist appeals for God's justice to be commensurate with the sin of the nations. The Edomites had rejoiced at the destruction of Jerusalem, calling for it to be "laid bare" or "stripped." The chilling last line of the psalm that calls for Babylonian infants to be "seized and smashed upon the rock" seems at first glance to be cruel, brutal, and unwarranted. However, even this cry is portrayed as righteous. Verse 8 highlights the desire that the Babylonians receive a punishment "exactly as" that which they inflicted upon Israel. The dashing against rocks is probably a memory of the siege of Jerusalem where those inside were murdered on the rocky slopes of the city. Furthermore, the declaration that the one who brings about this justice upon Babylon is blessed demonstrates that the act and the request for it to happen are both righteous. Blessing is a quality of the righteous, as readers are reminded at the opening of the psalms. Psalm 1 declares that the righteous are blessed and the wicked are destroyed. Finally, this particular judgment is the very thing that God promised to enact upon Babylon. In the book of Isaiah, God reveals that Babylon is not going to get away with all of its cruelty and oppression. In Isaiah 13:16, God declares, "Their infants will be dashed in pieces before their eyes; their houses will be plundered and their wives ravished," describing their imminent defeat by the Medes. So the psalmist is crying out for God to do exactly what God himself had promised to do— deliver his people and judge those who oppressed them.

God offered this psalm to his people as a righteous response to cruelty, oppression, and injustice. *It is a loyal cry* and *it is a righteous cry*. The question for us today is whether God is still offering these words to his people. Is this still a righteous cry? I believe so.

There are a number of reasons I believe this psalm and psalms like it continue to function as righteous responses. Firstly, the New Testament records similar prayers that are concerned with God being glorified through the judgment of the wicked. In his letter to the Galatians, Paul hopes that those teaching circumcision as a basis for salvation would "slip with the knife" and castrate themselves. He also opens his letter by wishing that those who are teaching a false gospel would be "anathema" or condemned to hell. Paul's primary concern is that God's glory in the gospel be protected and maintained. And Paul is not alone. The book of Revelation records the souls of martyred saints using the words of Psalm 79 to cry out for justice, that their "blood be avenged" through the destruction of their oppressors. These saints recognize that it is God's kingdom and it is up to him to make right every wrong.

Perhaps most poignant is the content of the Lord's Prayer where Jesus commends a paradigm of prayer to his people, demonstrating a righteous response to any and every circumstance. The opening lines of the prayer request, "Your kingdom come, your will be done, on earth as it is in heaven." I'm not sure that we realize the fullness of what we're asking when we faithfully pray these words. Fundamentally, we're asking that Christ would return and that the kingdom of God would be fully realized, that all wrongs be made right, and that all people would know that Jesus is Lord. With this prayer, God offers us words to convey our desire for his rule to be complete and for all opposition to his rule to be removed. It is a prayer for God to be glorified. It is a prayer for justice to be done. It is a prayer for judgment to come.

So, the first reason I believe Psalm 137 remains a righteous cry is that we have patterns of prayer in the New Testament that mirror the imprecatory psalms in their call for God to exercise his rule and judge the wicked.

The second reason I believe this psalm is a righteous cry is that the New Testament reminds us that Babylon remains. Though the ancient nation was defeated two and half millennia ago, Babylon will be among us until Christ returns in glory. The consummate destruction of Babylon is cause for great celebration in the New Testament. In Revelation 19, upon hearing of the final destruction of Babylon, heaven erupts with the cries of God's faithful servants:

> Hallelujah!
> For the Lord our God the Almighty reigns.
> Let us rejoice and exult

And give him the glory. (Rev 19:6b–7a)

There is much more that could be said, but let me explain one last reason for why I believe Psalm 137 is a righteous cry. In the face of violence and oppression, Psalm 137 allows God to be the judge. It models a response that acknowledges his rightful rule and allows "vengeance to be his." It does not meet violence with violence, but with prayer, handing judgment over to the one who can justly judge and vindicate his people.

God continues to speak to his people in the cry of Psalm 137. He commends these words to us as a righteous response to violence and oppression, as a declaration of loyalty to him, and as an expression of our desire that his kingdom and his justice will come. *This remains a loyal cry and it remains a righteous cry.*

God *commends* these words to us and at the same time he questions our own response to violence and oppression. Fundamentally, God speaks to us today in the words of Psalm 137 and asks of us, "For what do you cry?"

I recently enjoyed a weekend away with my extended family to celebrate our parents' combined birthdays. My siblings have children, and our children love spending time with their cousins. In fact, driving home from the weekend together, my wife and I noticed our youngest quietly crying in the back seat. He didn't want the time to end. He already missed his cousins and the freedom they had had to roam around the country property. For a seven-year-old, it was heaven. Yet, his time away hadn't been perfect at every turn. As the youngest, he's developed a particular superpower—a hyper-awareness of his surroundings and, in particular, whether his siblings are enjoying something without him: screen-time privileges, desserts, or, as on this occasion, soft drink. He's had soft drink ("pop" for our American friends) before, but we've (mostly) avoided giving him caffeinated beverages. His older cousins, however, are allowed this indulgence, and my wife and I decided that we'd allow our eldest to indulge this time as well. As you can imagine, my youngest son's superpowers didn't fail him and his tears flowed because the soda didn't. It didn't matter that his older brother had never enjoyed such privileges at his age. The injustice of it was too much to bear. For a seven-year-old this was worthy of tears.

What's worthy of your tears? *For what do you cry?* How do you respond to injustice? How do you respond to the violence and injustice that remains every day? Have you cried out to God for it to stop and for justice to be done? Perhaps you aren't exposed to violence and oppression at the hands of the wicked. Perhaps you live in relative comfort, largely sheltered from such cares. Many do not. Many suffer daily at the hands of the wicked. There are seven-year-olds who have never known the freedom to run safely through the countryside, never known a life outside of war, outside of slavery, outside of exploitation. Psalm 137 may not reflect our personal situation from day to day; but for many it does. Psalm 137 reminds us that violence and oppression at the hands of the wicked is a daily reality for many and that this must not continue. Psalm 137 confronts us with its shocking language but, more importantly, it confronts our apathy and ambivalence. God speaks to us in this psalm and asks, "For what do you cry?"

There have been a number of occasions where, in my reflection on Psalm 137, I have been led to prayer. There have been other occasions where my reflections on Psalm 137 have come to mind when confronted with disturbing news. I recall one particular time when a friend informed me of his concern for children in his extended family. The family situation was difficult, and these children were in very real danger from a particular individual from whom they had little hope of escape. The authorities were aware of the situation but there was little they would do at this point and nothing that my friend and I could do other than pray. So we prayed. We prayed for the safety of the children and we prayed against this individual. We prayed that God would stop him by whatever means necessary. We prayed for justice. We prayed for judgment.

Violence and oppression are never far away. Like my seven-year-old, we need to be continually aware of the world around us: the suffering of the innocent from war and terror; the slavery and exploitation of human trafficking; the detention of refugees in horrific conditions; the persecution of God's people by extremists; the oft-hidden yet ubiquitous domestic violence, and the abuse of children by sexual predators. Psalm 137 is part of the cure for our ignorance—or worse, our apathy. It reminds us that Babylon is still here and that God is still sovereign. It reminds us of continued suffering at the hands of the wicked. It reminds us that *our cries against evil are loyal cries and righteous cries.* Such cries demonstrate a desire for Christ to return, for his kingdom to come, for his justice to reign, and for his salvation of the downtrodden and oppressed to be complete. The absence of such a cry suggests ignorance or, worse still, a callousness and ambivalence to the suffering of those around us. God's people cannot and must not remain silent in a world where violence and injustice remain. With Psalm 137, God confronts us and asks, "For what do you cry?"

Bibliography

Alter, R. *The Book of Psalms: A Translation and Commentary,* New York: W. W. Norton, 2007.
Lewis, C. S. *Reflections on the Psalms,* London: Harper Collins, 1967.

21

"You Are the God Who Saves Me"
Singing Psalm 88

Nick Freestone
(with reflections from Kit Barker and G. Geoffrey Harper)

Can you remember singing a lament with your congregation in church? Your answer is probably no. In fact, there are few examples of lament available for congregational singing. There are some lines in hymns, verses here and there in some modern worship songs, but they tend only to dip into lament before making a quick jump to praise. Very few contemporary songs dive into the pool of sustained lament. Consequently, the church lacks songs that allow us to faithfully and corporately present our pain, grief, doubt, and confusion before God.

Creating, Engaging, and Singing Lament

It is in light of the above deficiency that I set out to write a song based on a lament psalm. I chose Psalm 88 because I wanted to cover the "ground" of this particular psalm and ask the hard questions it contains. The melody was crafted in an attempt to capture the determination of a community to evoke God's nearness and salvation.

Creating Lament

To start the process of creating a lament song, I first sought a landing point for the chorus. Based on v. 1, I settled on "You are the God who saves me." This became the conclusion, not just of the chorus, but also for the song as a whole. Wherever the lament journeys, it always find its way back to the statement of faith in v. 1—its truth and its challenge. I then decided to bookend the chorus with the strong ending of Psalm 88, which is a challenge regarding intimacy with God. The chorus therefore begins, "Where is your voice in this darkness?" This is close to a summary of the song, and it is the heart-cry that remains unanswered.

With the chorus set as a repeated point of focus, I pooled Psalm 88's themes into three verses. Verse one pictures our cry for help in our awful state. Verse two identifies that it is God who is actively sovereign over our plight. Verse three questions why God would allow all this to happen. After grouping these verses, and with rough chorus lyrics in mind, I sought out a set of minor scale steps for the melody, somewhat darker than would normally be used in church songs. I was particularly concerned with the major/minor seventh on the very first note of the chorus and the instrumental melody. The result is a clash that is familiar to us, but is at the same time unusual and jarring. To counteract the darker harmonic minor-scale steps in the chorus, I added a major for minor chord substitution halfway through each verse. That exchange adds to the feeling of freedom of expression and honesty in the verse melody. Once the song started to feel like it was "together," I attempted to sing it a few times and commit it to memory. Not until I really let my heart connect with the song did I feel the shock and struggle of it.

Engaging Lament

As I rehearsed the song I felt a strong urge to "play it safe" and to soften some of the lines. They almost felt wrong as I imagined my church singing them. We are not used to putting frustration, faith, anger, and yearning together in our songs to God. As I hammered out chord, melody, and word changes and the song was finalized, I *felt* the difference that articulating lament meant for me.

While I am yet to share this song with my church, I have already experienced its benefits. I now have a chorus that pounds in my head in dark moments, and a melody that fills my heart amid doubt. To come to the God who saves me and ask him why darkness seems closer than his voice is *good for me.* It seems healthy to do so, and I had no way to do that in song before. I look forward to the amplification of these benefits when the song is sung together in a Sunday gathering.

Sharing Lament

Creating this lament song was certainly a challenge, but a bigger challenge remains: how, practically, do we introduce the practice of singing lament in our churches? I think the first step is acknowledging our need to bring a new level of authenticity and honesty to singing in church. Lament contains the most affronting lyrical content. The goal is to engage with, learn from, and take hold of lament in our services. This will require a careful and wise re-introduction of these words within our congregations. We will need to become convinced of both the validity and necessity of corporate lament in song. Lament contributes an essential voice to a "gospel-shaped" repertoire of songs, one that reveals its truth, gravity, beauty, and effectiveness. Lament has a place in our corporate worship. It is our faithful response as the people of God to the brokenness of this world and the hope of the present and coming kingdom.

A Lament Song: Lyrics

You Are the God Who Saves Me[1]

Verse 1:
All day and night I cry for You
Allow my prayer before You
Incline Your ear to hear my plight
Lord turn Your gaze to me
See my weary hands like shadows
Touching death itself
I breathe the dust of misery
My soul has had its fill

Refrain:
Where is Your voice in this darkness?

---

1. Nick Freestone, "You Are the God Who Saves Me." © 2016 Nick Freestone Music. CCLI 7071501. Used with permission.

Lord are You faithful to me?
Where is Your love that You promise?
You are the God who saves me

Verse 2:
You send me out, abandon me
To deep despair, forgotten
You drown my screams with ceaseless waves
And pin me down with wrath
Blind and chained with griefs and sorrows
Near my grave from youth
Oblivion I call my home
With shame to soothe my fears

Verse 3:
Will Your assaults and horrors heal?
Your praise swell while You slay me?
Shall I proclaim Your righteousness
If all I love are lost?
Lord, why turn Your back and shun me?
Where are You my God?
Your terrors strike and flood with doubt
And darkness is my friend

You Are the God Who Saves Me: Lead Sheet[2]

You are The God who saves me

Based on Psalm 88

Nick Freestone

Verse 2:
You send me out, abandon me
To deep despair, forgotten
You drown my screams with ceaseless waves
And pin me down with wrath
Blind and chained with griefs and sorrows
Near my grave from youth
Oblivion I call my home
With shame to sooth my fears

Verse 3:
Will Your assaults and horrors heal?
Your praise swell while You slay me?
Shall I proclaim Your righteousness
If all I love are lost?
Lord, why turn Your back and shun me?
Where are You my God?
Your terrors strike and flood with doubt
And darkness is my friend

Reflections

This song by Nick Freestone is an excellent (and perhaps unique) example of the application of lament to contemporary worship. I (Kit) was recently invited to speak to the creative ministries team at an influential church in Sydney. To open the evening, I asked the group of several dozen leaders to give an example of a contemporary lament song designed for congregational

---

2. To hear the song performed, visit nickfreestonemusic.bandcamp.com.

participation. The silence was broken by the tentatively offered suggestion, "Blessed Be Your Name?" I regularly ask this same question in my Psalter classes and the result is the same: "Blessed Be Your Name"[3] and "Desert Song."[4] However, neither of these is a lament and, in fact, both present something at odds with the practice. In both melody and lyrics, each song affirms that, while the situation may be difficult, the proper response is one of *praise*, as articulated in the refrains. Unfortunately, these songs represent some of our closest attempts at corporate lament (at least in an Australian context), yet when given the opportunity, each avoids the practice. I'm not suggesting that these songs are inherently problematic. However, a problem exists if these are our best (and only!) musical responses to suffering, for rather than moving us to lament, they in the end require us to praise. Consequently, the opportunity to lament is subverted and the practice is implicitly rejected. So from church services to funerals, our collective response to suffering lacks commensurate words. We are told to celebrate, to be thankful, and to praise, when at times the right response is to be honest, to question, and to cry out in pain.

One of the interesting things to emerge as we have discussed the topic of this book in various classes, churches, and morning tea conversations is that *singing* lament seems to be particularly problematic for people. The idea of preaching on a lament psalm doesn't raise an eyebrow; that people might pray the words of a lament (especially in private) or read them with someone who is suffering is generally acceptable. But to stand and sing a lament, corporately, in church, raises all sorts of questions. Is it right to do that? What if everyone is not in the "place of lament"? Can we sing *these* words as Christian people? While questions such as these raise important issues that need to be carefully thought through, they also point to a much more fundamental issue: we have truly lost the notion of corporate solidarity when it comes to situations of distress, along with the words to express our identification with those who are in the darkness.

In light of this, our hope is that Nick's song might represent a step towards recovering a lost practice in corporate worship. The melody and lyrics he has composed are true to the content and mood of Psalm 88.[5]

---

3. Matt Redmond and Beth Redmond, "Blessed Be Your Name." © 2002 Thankyou Music. CCLI 3798438.

4. Brooke Ligertwood, "Desert Song." © 2008 Sony/ATV Music Publishing Australia. CCLI 5060793.

5. Such correspondence is not necessary for contemporary appropriation. Nick's song represents just one example of lament, where the explicit intent was to follow closely the language of the psalm. There is also a place for contemporary congregational laments that are inspired by the psalms but do not follow the wording so closely.

While many biblical laments contain a shift to confidence and an expectation of future praise, Psalm 88 does not. It is not without hope, but it does not move to praise. Nick's song is similarly relentless. Its minor key and lack of a "change up" leave participants in the darkness of the psalm: sad, confused, and exhausted by the relentless waves of suffering. The final verse concludes with the closing words of the psalm, "And darkness is my friend"; yet Nick returns to the start of the psalm by finishing with the refrain. Here unanswered questions resound, and the first line of psalm is placed before the throne of God—as much a challenge as a declaration of faith: "You are the God who saves me." This move represents the very heart of lament. It reminds the congregation that the right response to suffering is to place it before God: to confront him with our questions, with our confusion at the dissonance between faith and experience, and with our corporate cry for it to stop. As I (Geoff) discussed in my earlier chapter, Psalm 88 reflects a profound faith, even though the psalmist has experienced a life "full of evils" with no deliverance from his situation. In the midst of suffering, hope is found in the persistent cry of the psalmist and in the word of God that extends an invitation to his people: "When the pain is unbearable, pray and sing like this. I'm here in the darkness."

While this beautifully crafted song is an excellent representation of Psalm 88, some might argue that it could be improved (a different mood, different lyrics, a quicker tempo, no refrain), and perhaps it could. However, it must be remembered that this is a single example of how we could appropriate a psalm of lament in Christian, congregational worship. It is one song, on one psalm, at one time, in one culture. Much more remains to be done. We need more songs like this, songs that reflect the variety of situation and response found in the Psalter. The reason we asked Nick to compose a lament for this volume was not to present the definitive example, but rather to provide a model and catalyst for the writing of others.

22

If Jesus Wept, You Can Too

Sharon Wood

I STOOD TREMBLING AT the bus stop. I'd just waved off a woman whom I'd met that afternoon in connection with my pastoral ministry role among women in a local church. I sat with her as she told me her devastating news. I'd prepared myself for meeting up with her to see how she was coping after life-changing surgery. I'd prepared for that. However, neither I, nor she, was prepared for the news she had received at a follow-up appointment just an hour before we met. The doctors had made a mistake. The surgery had not been necessary and it could certainly not be undone or rectified. It was devastating news. We sat on a park bench. She wept quietly as she choked back sobs. Tears echoed in my eyes and an ache grew in my throat. This tragedy was cause for great lament. There was ample space right there on that park bench for gaping questions—questions to ask of her doctors and, more devastatingly, questions to ask of her God and mine. Instead, she said, "Sorry for being so upset. I know I should trust God in this. I should be stronger."

Later that same week, I spent time with a woman who was facing the reality of a sudden injury, which would take at least six months to heal. It was a big shock to her, with injuries to both her body and her independence. As I asked how she was coping, she expressed sorrow and frustration. Then she said, "Sorry, I'm not being a very good Christian. If I was, I wouldn't be this upset."

Why did these women feel that being a faithful Christian precluded lamenting their tragic circumstances before the God they followed? Why did they feel they had to apologize to me for feeling sorrow and grief? Was it something in my ministry, or the ministry of the church, or their understanding of God, that gave these women cause to feel that their confusion, sorrow, anger, and grief was wrong—that expressing those feelings was to be stifled, retracted, or apologized for?

I came part way in answering these two women who wept. I reminded them that Jesus wept in the garden of Gethsemane. His weeping was bloody. His soul was overwhelmed and deeply troubled. I reminded them that Jesus did not passively accept the inevitable, raising his arms to heaven saying, "Bring it on. Whatever will be, will be!" Before Jesus asked that his Father's will be done, he cried out to his Father asking that the cup might be taken from him. He asked this not just once, but three times. I wanted these women to know it was okay to cry out to God with anguished tears, to say to God that they were not okay with their suffering! I wanted them to be okay with saying that.

There was some understanding and relief for them at the time, as we sat and talked and then prayed. But I wondered if that relief carried on, deep in their hearts, beyond our meeting. I also wondered later, years later, why when I had prayed for them, I had not offered strong words of lament on their behalf. In my words to them, I had given permission to echo Jesus's lament, but in my words to God, I had gone straight to asking God to give them strength to trust his will in their suffering.

As time has passed and I've listened to prayers, sermons, and words of comfort given to those who suffer, I've become more convinced that, as Christian friends, carers, and pastors, we are moving people too quickly to utter "your will be done," while not even briefly expressing or acknowledging the desire to have the cup of suffering taken from them. When sitting opposite a woman who has just been diagnosed with a devastating illness, I want to cry out to the Lord, "Take this from her!" Yet, years of modeled prayer and my own lack of confidence to utter those words before God have me settling for "If it's your will." I know well enough that God will heal her, or not, according to his will. But why am I so reluctant, so frightened, to first ask him to take it away? Jesus did. Why can't I?

At other times, the devastation is final and cannot be taken away, as was the case with a woman at a weekend at which I was speaking. She had received news that her family and friends in her home village in Africa had just been slaughtered for their faith in Christ. The news came to her in a phone message during the morning tea break. The break was between my two talks on Romans 8. As the woman sat in the corridor and wept with a friend, I was asked by the conference organizers if I would pray for her at the start of my next talk. Would I? Could I? Would I be able to form the words with my mouth, or would my efforts be thwarted as shared sorrow caught hold of my facial muscles and strangled the words on their way out of my mouth?

In the end, I was required to share her grief and lead others in sharing that grief, and to do it in a mere five minutes' time—while those not yet aware of the tragedy chatted to me over a cup of Nescafé. With a minute to spare, I scanned my talk, my eyes taking in the phrases "first world problems" and "sheep to be slaughtered." The woman was still out in the corridor—I could see her in my peripheral vision—so I could probably manage this if I kept looking straight ahead. As I took a deep breath, ready to start praying, she walked into the room and sat in the front row, right in front of the lectern. She looked up through wet, red-stained eyes and waited. I can't remember if I used words of lament as I prayed. I remember I was trying to hold it together, to measure my words so I wouldn't end up saying the wrong thing, and so I wouldn't end up crying. Whatever I did or didn't end up praying, God's word soon said it for me as we read from Romans 8.

Women have often expressed surprise when, in Bible talks, I've drawn their attention to all the "groaning" in the first half of Romans 8. They know that "all things work together for good" and that "nothing can separate us from the love of God in Christ Jesus."[1] But they haven't always noticed the groaning before these promises. The "good" that God works (v. 28) is heavily bracketed by groaning, on the one side, and the realities of death and slaughter, on the other. God's love and good work is assured, but the groaning, slaughter, and death are likewise present realities. They are the painful context of all God's promises to us. Furthermore, the groaning is not just the experience of the melancholic minority. We are confronted in those verses with the reality that we all groan—along with creation, and along with the Holy Spirit who groans on our behalf with groans that are beyond our words.

Perhaps there were no other words I could have expressed. Perhaps I should have remained silent. But God's word was not silent that morning. The Lord gave that devastated woman permission to groan and to grieve before him, in deep trust that he heard her cries and that his Spirit was crying out with her.

We've all heard sermons on suffering that focus on the growth it brings in our faith, and the glory God receives through it. I've preached and offered words of pastoral counsel like that myself. While it is right to encourage one another in these responses to suffering, isn't it also right to encourage godly groaning in the face of suffering, or at least to permit it?

---

1. All biblical quotations are taken from NIV unless otherwise stated.

I once sat with a woman who shared how hard it had been for her to sit and listen to a sermon on suffering that focused only on the believer's growth in faith and God's glory in our trials. I have experienced similar struggles myself at times. This woman had been suffering physically and emotionally for some years and was feeling like she'd come to the end of comfort. She struggled with the preacher's examples of faithful followers who, while suffering great pain, were still experiencing God's gift of joy in those trials. These were the only examples given.

Both she and I would have benefited from hearing also of faithful followers of Christ who did not feel that same joy. What about those who felt alone in a garden of darkness and unceasing anguish? Were anguish and sorrow legitimate responses to one's suffering? Was it possible that a believer could grow, and God could be glorified, in anguish as in joy? The experience of Jesus's suffering in Gethsemane, the psalms of lament composed hundreds of years before, and the present day experience of believers clinging to God in their sorrow without the relief of felt joy, all tell me that it is possible.

It's all very well for me to critique a sermon on suffering, but how am I doing in my own use of lament? To be honest, though I'm firmly convinced of the need, I have a long way to go in my personal practice. It's often easier for us to lead others in lament than it is to mouth the words ourselves, in our own pain and confusion.

Many of us have found or will find ourselves experiencing a sleepless night tossing and turning, our tumultuous thoughts leading us down darker and darker paths. In the valley of deep disappointment and pain, we can find ourselves feeling a deep disappointment with God. We know that our heavenly Father is in control of all things and that he is good. Yet sometimes it seems we've stretched out our hand in fragile trust to ask for bread, only to receive something that turns to stone in our mouth. We've asked him for a fish, only to feel a scorpion's sting. Then we might ask him for help to keep trusting his goodness, even though we can't see it, and it feels like he's not hearing us. No joy or answers come, and we can start to wonder if God is there at all. These can be terrifying thoughts for those who have been faithfully following the Lord. We can feel that we've gone too far! We struggle to get our thoughts back onto a more "acceptable" path.

I have often found great help and comfort in the pastoral writings of Dale Ralph Davis as he reflects on different parts of the Scriptures. Two of his books recognize the many words of lament and confusion recorded for us in the psalms. At a time when I personally needed encouragement to bring my words of lament before the Lord, I found in Davis's comments on Psalm 13 both an encouragement to speak and a rebuke for thinking it was not okay to speak. The Psalmist had asked:

> How much longer, Yahweh, will you go on forgetting me?
> Forever?
> How much longer will you go on hiding your face from me?
> How much longer must I lay plans within me
> —agony in my heart by day? (Ps 13:1–2a)[2]

In the shadow of the cross, Jesus "offered up prayers and supplications, with loud cries and tears, to him who was able to save him from death, and he was heard for his godly fear" (Heb 5:7). Could I not also cry out to the Lord in sorrow, in confusion? Perhaps if the psalmist and Jesus could, so could I. Davis gave a timely answer to my fearful wonderings:

> You may still be unsure whether you ought to pray prayers like this . . . don't be ashamed to pray these prayers. Jesus wasn't— He was right down here in the darkness, praying "working-class" prayers like this. How dare you say that you are somehow above these cries![3]

I still don't find it easy to utter personal words of lament to the Lord. It still feels wrong somehow. Perhaps I'm not meant to try lamenting on my own. Perhaps I'm meant to lament alongside the people of God. I know I find greater comfort and help when I do. I suspect that's the way forward. Dare I say it *is* the way forward? God's people groaning together with the words he has given us, in the company of Jesus our Savior and brother, with the help of the Spirit who intercedes with groans that words cannot express when our own words fail us. We cry and cry out, knowing Jesus did too. In the company of God's Spirit and his people, we do not groan alone.

Bibliography

Davis, Dale Ralph. *Slogging Along in the Paths of Righteousness: Psalms 13–24*. Fearn: Christian Focus, 2014.

---

2. Davis's own translation (*Slogging Along*, 11).
3. Davis, *Slogging Along*, 23.

www.ingramcontent.com/pod-product-compliance
Lightning Source LLC
Chambersburg PA
CBHW071234230426
43668CB00011B/1431